the strumpet muse

the strumpet muse

Art and Morals in Chaucer's Poetry

ALFRED DAVID

INDIANA
UNIVERSITY PRESS
Bloomington & London

For Linda

Published in Canada by Fitzhenry & Whiteside Limited, Don Mills,
Ontario

Manufactured in the United States of America

Library of Congress Cataloging in Publication Data
David, Alfred, 1929–
The strumpet muse.
Includes bibliographical references and index.
1. Chaucer, Geoffrey, d. 1400—Criticism and interpretation.
I. Title.
PR1924.D3   1976   821'.1   76–11939
ISBN 0–253–35517–6   1 2 3 4 5 81 80 79 78 77

Contents

Acknowledgments

I am grateful to the Indiana University Foundation, the Guggenheim Foundation, and the Fulbright Commission for grants without the aid of which this book would never have been completed. I wish to thank the Master and Fellows of Corpus Christi College, Cambridge, the British Library, and the Bodleian Library for permission to reproduce the illustrations from manuscripts in their collections, and the editors of *Publications of the Modern Language Association, Annuale Mediaevale,* and *College English* for permission to use parts of essays originally appearing in these journals. All my quotations from Chaucer are taken from the second edition of F. N. Robinson (Boston: Houghton Mifflin, 1957). My debt to the cooperative enterprise of Chaucer scholarship is greater than I can acknowledge; I have tried to indicate my most direct obligations in the notes. However, I owe a special debt to E. T. Donaldson whose criticism of Chaucer and personal encouragement have had a great deal to do with the shaping of this book. I am also grateful to him for reading the manuscript. John Ganim and Daniel Rubey have also read the manuscript and provided me with extremely helpful advice. The readers for the Indiana University Press made many valuable suggestions. Much of this book was first written for my students at Indiana University, and they in turn have responded with many an idea that has been incorporated in these pages. My wife Linda has been the best critic of this book, but that is only a part of her share in it. In giving it to her, I am returning, "as I kan best," what she has given to me.

the strumpet muse

Left: Boethius tended by the Muses
Right: Fortune before Philosophy
(Bodleian Library, MS Douce 298)

INTRODUCTION

And whan she [Philosophy] saugh thise poetical Muses
aprochen aboute my bed and enditynge wordes to my
wepynges, sche was a litil amoeved, and glowede with cruel
eighen. "Who," quod sche, "hath suffred aprochen to this
sike man thise comune strompettis of swich a place that men
clepen the theatre; the whiche not oonly ne asswagen noght
his sorwes with none remedies, but thei wolden fedyn and
noryssen hym with sweete venym."

Boece

THE IMAGE of stern-eyed Philosophy driving the Muses from
Boethius's bedside may bring a smile to the modern reader—especially in Chaucer's translation where the "scenicas meretriculas"
become "thise comune strompettis." The image itself is theatrical
enough; nor does Philosophy reject poetry altogether, affirming
divine providence in some of the most beautiful Latin meters of
the Middle Ages. Nevertheless, her condemnation of the Muses
expresses a prevalent authoritative view of poetic fiction that poses
a question for any serious medieval poet. Is he a dispenser of
"sweet venom" or of the wholesome remedies by which Philosophy
seeks to restore Boethius to spiritual health?

Such a question did not arise for the generation of great Chau-
cerians who established the poet's texts and sources and once again
made his works available to a popular audience. For them poetic
fiction was sufficient justification unto itself as long as it followed
"Nature." The quality the older scholars valued in Chaucer was
the one they most enjoyed in the literature of their own day, that is
his mimetic power, his gift of faithfully mirroring human life and
character. Dryden first formulated an attitude toward Chaucer's
characters that remained unchanged through the first half of this
century:

We have our forefathers and great-grandames all before us,
as they were in Chaucer's days: their general characters are
still remaining in mankind, and even in England, tho' they
are called by other names than those of Monks, and Friars,
and Canons, and Lady Abbesses; and Nuns; for mankind is
ever the same, and nothing lost out of Nature, tho' everything is altered.

Kittredge still writes as the inheritor of the neoclassic view when he
describes *Troilus and Criseyde* as "the first novel, in the modern
sense, that ever was written in the world" and the *Canterbury Tales*
as "a Human Comedy." Kittredge and his contemporaries showed
little sympathy and only a limited understanding for the more
conventional and medieval characteristics of Chaucer's poetry, for
example his observance of the artificial code of "courtly love," his
adherence to the rules of the rhetoric books (except when these
were parodied), and, most important, the moralism found especially in the Parson's Tale and the Tale of Melibee but also, in
varying degrees, in nearly all of his works.

Much of the criticism written during the last quarter-century
represents a reaction against the comfortable assumption that
Chaucer, in spite of the distance that separates his time from ours,
is in all essentials "one of us." The strength of this criticism has
been its insistence that Chaucer's moralism cannot be dismissed as
a concession to the conventions, tastes, and biases of a former age.
Such criticism has been genuinely "historical" in treating history
not as something dead that needs to be explained to the modern
reader but as something alive to Chaucer and his audience. It will
never again be possible to ascribe Chaucer's religious or didactic
passages to the limitations of his age or to patronize them as dull
and conventional. This more recent approach does confront the
question raised by Philosophy's condemnation of the Muses; however, in practice it tends to circumvent the problem by assuming
that all of Chaucer's fictions contain a veiled core of orthodox doctrine. Thus the "general characters" Dryden so much admired become mere types of vices and virtues. The unity of Chaucer's
artistic purpose is asserted, but often at the price of subverting
the plain sense of the text and denying its human content. An

insistence upon Chaucer's "medievalism" seems as reductive in its way as the former view that finds the poet's great achievement in a supposed naturalism.

The choice criticism offers between a "modern" or a "medieval" Chaucer, a "naturalistic" or an "allegorical" Chaucer hardly exhausts the possibilities. These opposite views are, indeed, alike in assuming that a poet's aesthetic goals remain constant; but great poets have a way of changing the direction of their art, and changing it more than once. A poet like Chaucer may hold the fundamental beliefs of his age and nevertheless create an image of man that exists beyond all faiths and all times. The poet's vision may proclaim an independence that the poet himself is not prepared to ratify. Chaucer began by imitating the dream visions of other poets; he gradually came to create a vision that has the energy and vitality of life itself; he finally disavowed that vision.

Like most poets, Chaucer felt the pressures of orthodoxy in his art as well as in his life. It is a poet's lot to confront patrons, or critics, or well-intentioned friends eager to dictate what he should write and the manner in which he should write it. The orthodoxies to which Chaucer was subject may be broadly classified as being of two kinds: social and moral. He was a court poet writing for an audience consisting in large measure of his social superiors who expected that the poetry read to them would be aristocratic. At the court of Richard II this meant that the poet had to concern himself with the theme of "fin amour," the ideal love celebrated in lyric, romance, and dream vision by French poets from the troubadors to Chaucer's immediate predecessors, Guillaume de Machaut and Jean Froissart. Both poet and audience, however, were responsive to an even more pervasive pressure, the requirement that all poetry to earn its right to exist must be moral, that the poet has an obligation to educate and uplift his audience, and that the audience, for its part, must look for instruction and edification and not only for entertainment.

The practice of poetry involved Chaucer in a constant effort to reconcile his obligations as a medieval author with his own artistic vision. I shall be arguing that for Chaucer such a reconciliation was difficult and finally impossible because it involves a fundamental contradiction. The aim of the medieval poet is to make us aware of the superficial and illusory character of the life we perceive through the senses, which is no more than a reflection seen in a glass darkly, and to awaken our minds and our hearts to the spiritual reality beneath our sense impressions. This seems to me the common intention behind both an explicitly religious poem like the *Divine Comedy* and a courtly allegory like the *Roman de la Rose*. Yet the poet, of necessity, must communicate by means of images, and the more powerfully he evokes those images, the more real they become and the more they engage our interest and our sympathy for themselves to the point that, in a great work, the images of art take on a life of their own. The very success of the medieval poet's fiction, therefore, will tend to distance us from any reality that is not of his own making.

I do not mean that Chaucer was at odds with his time or with his audience—at least no more so than any great poet. He shared the tastes and beliefs of the men of his day. I *am* suggesting that his creative gifts carried him, in spite of himself, beyond anything taught to him by the old clerks he read and sometimes translated of whom he always speaks with affectionate if not precisely reverent regard. Although he set out to place his art in the service of truth, he came to realize something equivocal in the truth of his poems that led him ultimately to retract the best of them in the moving conclusion of the *Canterbury Tales*. With hindsight we can see that the doubts leading to the Retraction were always present, but these doubts in no way detract from the greatness of the works. On the contrary, Chaucer's effort to reconcile the "auctorite" of his age with the "experience" of his inner vision is precisely what makes his poetry great.

This study traces the metamorphoses of Chaucer's conception of poetry as these are reflected in his works. It begins with a conventional ideal portrait of what a poet should be and Chaucer's early efforts to attain that ideal; it goes on to uncover ironic images of the poet embodied in the various tellers of the Canterbury tales; the Miller, the Man of Law, the Wife of Bath, the Pardoner, the Prioress. In writing the *Canterbury Tales* Chaucer came to master the art of illusion but at the same time to regard with growing skepticism its potential for expressing moral truths. The relationship between teller and tale often comments poignantly on the inadequacies of poetry, and each teller shows some new face of the poet's strumpet Muse. Chaucer is neither "one of us" nor "one of them"—his Protean being is distributed throughout his works, and it is there, not in critical preconceptions about the nature of poetry, that we must seek to embrace it.

FIGURE 2

The author narrating his work.
From Guillaume de Deguileville's *Pèlerinage de la vie humaine*
(B.M. MS Add. 38120, f. 1r)

CHAPTER I

Portraits of the Poet
and His Early Works

O SEE the ideal image of a poet through the eyes of a
medieval audience, we may look at the reproduction of
the famous frontispiece of the Corpus Christi College manuscript
of *Troilus and Criseyde* (Figure 1). The manuscript was made in
the early fifteenth century, and both the text and the picture may
have been copied from an even earlier manuscript personally com-
missioned by John of Gaunt.[1] Chaucer is portrayed "standing in a
sort of pulpit"[2] with the audience grouped in standing and sitting
positions at his feet. Various attempts have been made to identify
the figures, but with the exception of the couple standing immediately to the poet's right hand (i.e., left in the picture), who are
almost certainly Richard II and Queen Anne, the identifications, if
indeed any were intended, are uncertain.[3] However, there can be
no doubt that the artist has portrayed his idealized conception of
the most dazzling and powerful group of people in England.
Moreover, the idealization is not limited to the magnificent surface. Through his handling of detail, color, and composition, the
artist expresses an idea about the relationship between poet and
audience.

The fact that a poet should appear in so exalted a company reflects, as P. M. Kean has observed, a new esteem and status accorded in the late fourteenth century to court poets like Machaut

and Froissart in France, Chaucer and Gower in England: "The poet (certainly not a portrait of Chaucer, but a typical figure) is not distinguished from his audience by his dress."[4] I fully agree that the poet in the portrait is "a typical figure" and that the style of his costume resembles that worn by his auditors. Nevertheless, it is still more important to understand how the artist has set the poet apart from the audience, even in dress. He is bareheaded while the people listening to him are covered with different kinds of elaborate headdress—hats, hoods, and diadems. His costume is notably unadorned in contrast to the golden belts, collars, and borders seen on several of the other figures. His gown is without color. Some color may have rubbed off,[5] but even in its original state, the gown must have contrasted with the sumptuous golds, reds, and blues in which his listeners are arrayed. He is placed at the center and significantly above them. They are shown gravely listening (the faces in profile are meant to vary the design, not to suggest inattention). The figure of the poet and the composition of the group resemble a subject sometimes seen in religious art: a preacher addressing his congregation. The description of Chaucer's vantage point as a "pulpit" is, therefore, exactly right. The poet is not shown realistically reading from his book but speaking with his right hand slightly raised in the conventional gesture of a preacher, a modification of the traditional gesture of blessing. The same idea and many similar details may be seen in the first illustration of a manuscript (B.M. MS Add. 38120, f. 1r) of a popular religious allegory, La Pèlerinage de la vie humaine, by the Cistercian monk Guillaume de Deguileville (Figure 2).[6] The author-narrator, tonsured and wearing a cowl, stands in a pulpit to the left. The audience made up of laity, both men and women, in costumes suggesting noble rank, is seated below the pulpit with the exception of three prominent figures who are standing. The background is made up of trees, and to the right appears a chateau in an architectural style remarkably similar to that of the one in the Corpus frontispiece. The significance of both illustrations is the same. Both literally and symbolically, the artists have placed the authors, Guillaume and Chaucer, on a higher plane than the noble audiences they are instructing. Humble and mild in appearance, the poet of Troilus pursues an elevated calling.

The actual relationship between the poet and his noble audience presents a different picture. We can get some notion of it from a little scene in Chaucer's earliest narrative poem, the *Book of the Duchess*. The poem is an elegy for John of Gaunt's first duchess, Blanche of Lancaster, and Chaucer is recounting a dream in which he comes upon a knight dressed in mourning, who represents the duke, seated under a tree, lost in grief for his dead lady. For a time, the knight does not notice the dreamer's presence. When he finally does become aware of the dreamer standing awkwardly at his side with hood removed in a mute gesture of greeting, the knight apologizes with exquisite courtesy:

> "I prey the, be not wroth.
> I herde the not, to seyn the soth,
> Ne I sawgh the not, syr, trewely."   (519–521)

We should note, however, that the knight addresses the dreamer with the familiar pronoun "the," while the dreamer replies with the respectful "yow." In fact, the knight's courtesy serves to remind the dreamer (and the poet's audience) of Chaucer's true place in the world. "Loo! how goodly spak thys knyght," observes the dreamer, "As hit had be another wyght" (529–30). We might gloss freely: "He spoke to me as if he were just a fellow creature, as though we were equals." The tone of the black knight's apology is precisely that beautiful condescension with which the true aristocrat speaks to a servant.

Of course, the *Book of the Duchess* is only a fiction in which Chaucer presents himself not as a poet but as a slightly obtuse intruder in a dream world that he cannot make out. Nevertheless, the contrast between this image of Chaucer and that of the *Troilus* frontispiece brings out a real irony in Chaucer's situation as a court poet. The son of a bourgeois is placed in an equivocal position when he writes for a courtly audience, and especially when he confronts his audience, as we know Chaucer did, by reading his works aloud. If he is to be a poet according to the ideal conception of the artist, he must impart wisdom to his audience, and they are bound to look up to him as an authority. Yet, since he comes from an inferior class and acts in the ordinary business of life as their servant, he is expected to defer to their taste and judgment. If he

wants to instruct his audience, he must do so without ever seeming
to forget his place. He is not free to write what he pleases but must
choose those forms and subjects most acceptable to his audience.

The part Chaucer plays in his earlier poems as an outsider and
bemused observer in a wonderful but intimidating dream world,
therefore, translates into fiction the reality of his status as a young
man making his way at the English court. When Chaucer ventures
to offer instruction, it is always with a seemingly ingenuous self-
satire that dispels any hint of presumption. The dialogue between
the dreamer and the black knight in the *Book of the Duchess* already shows the manner Chaucer affects in addressing his audience.
In the poem, the dreamer with the utmost diffidence questions the
black knight about the cause of his grief and gently offers philosophical counsel to assuage it. But the dreamer cannot understand,
and the knight is forced to explain to him, as to a child, not simply
what he has lost but what that loss means. It is the patron who
becomes the instructor of the poet. Chaucer puts on a mask calculated to disguise and make light of the role that is traditionally
the poet's. Recent criticism has seen this mask as a brilliant artistic
stratagem, the persona of a "naive narrator." The mask is indeed
a kind of persona, but one used in everyday life, not simply in
fiction.[7] For Chaucer it expresses the essential truth of the relationship between himself and his audience. It is that other image of the
poet addressing his audience as preacher that is the fiction.

The two images of Chaucer, the picture and the book, give us
a perspective on the problem of a supremely gifted, ambitious, and
widely read young English poet writing for a feudal court, which
still spoke French as a second language and imported most of its
culture and literature from across the channel. The poet of the picture has the dignity and authority of an epic singer, one who
appears as Virgil did to Dante an "honor and light among poets,"
an author whose glory outshines even that of his imperial patron.
The book shows another kind of singer,

> Deferential, glad to be of use,
> Politic, cautious, and meticulous;
> Full of high sentence, but a bit obtuse;
> At times, indeed, almost ridiculous—
> Almost, at times, the Fool.

Chaucer's problem in composing his "love songs" for his aristocratic audience is not unlike Prufrock's in trying to break through the jaded forms and conventions of his society to make some significant statement: "To say: 'I am Lazarus, come from the dead,/ Come back to tell you all, I shall tell you all.' " That is the task of an epic poet, a Virgil or a Dante. But Chaucer was obliged to speak through other voices. To obtain a hearing from his audience, it was necessary for him to talk of courtly love and, preferably, to cast his poems in the forms of the love-vision and love-debate practiced by Machaut and Froissart, the most fashionable poets of the day. There is no reason to suppose that either the subject or the form was uncongenial to Chaucer, yet to follow in the footsteps of Machaut and Froissart imposed limitations as well as a challenge. A brief sketch of their works and of the *Roman de la Rose,* from which they and Chaucer alike drew their inspiration, will show what those limitations were and why it would have been impossible for anyone, even Chaucer, to attain epic stature by writing dream visions.

The *Roman de la Rose* is a work of epic proportions and deserves to be called a great poem though its laurels have faded. Written in the thirteenth century, it is a vast allegory of 21,000 lines, which encompasses practically the whole of the literary and intellectual traditions of the Middle Ages. Its central fiction was invented by the first of its two authors, Guillaume de Lorris. In a dream, a young man enters an ethereally lovely garden where he encounters a group of dancers, splendidly arrayed, who personify the values cherished by feudal court society, among them Gladness, Courtesy, Beauty, Wealth, Largesse, and Youth. Significant among them is the God of Love. Love is, in fact, the exclusive occupation of this allegorical court whose members are introduced as couples and lovers. As he wanders through the garden, the young man comes upon a fountain inscribed with the words: "Here died the beautiful Narcissus." It is the fountain of love. At the bottom, the young man sees two crystals in which the entire garden is reflected, but he loses his heart to a single rosebud that seems to enclose within itself everything that is desirable and worth possessing in this magical garden world. As he attempts to seize the rosebud, however, the young man is struck by the arrows of the God of Love who now becomes his lord and master and instructs him in the art of love. True love is not the simple act of plucking the object of desire. It requires self-discipline and long suffering, very much like the religious discipline of a penitent. After the God has taught the lover his commandments and how to endure his woes with hope, the dreamer, become lover, enters upon the struggle to obtain the rose in which he is opposed by its guardians who seek to drive him away and supported by allies who aid his cause. These represent psychological, social, and moral forces that prompt the lady to bestow or to withhold her favor. Guillaume de Lorris's poem breaks off just when the lover's plight seems most hopeless. The rosebud and the character called Fair Welcome, who personifies admission to the presence of the loved one, have been imprisoned in the Castle of Jealousy. We cannot tell how Guillaume would have ended his poem, but he created a myth of ideal love that continued to please courtly society for more than three centuries. What distinguishes Guillaume's poem from those of his many imitators is that in portraying the sincere frustrations and agonies of the lover he also raises questions and doubts about whether the ideal is only a phantom. At the end we cannot be sure whether this garden is a true paradise or a hell in which the goal of desire, like the fruit of Tantalus, is forever beyond reach.

Guillaume's poem, which comes to little more than 4,000 lines, was carried on some forty years later by Jean de Meun, an author of very different temperament. Jean turned Guillaume's allegory into an encyclopedic satire that touches on every topic that occupied men's minds in the thirteenth century. He develops a number of Guillaume's minor characters and adds some new ones, all of whom express their views about man and society in discourses that run on for thousands of lines. No summary can do justice to the sheer range of Jean de Meun's intellect and learning, but what emerges from these long speeches is the picture of a world corrupted by commerce and deceit, a world in which nearly everyone is out for what he can get, and in which most men love only themselves. The most representative figure of this world is a character invented by Jean de Meun, False-Seeming, who tells us that he may be found in the guise of all estates and professions but by his own preference in ecclesiastical robes. False-Seeming boasts that he and his kind have undermined the Church and rule the world, and his claims gain support from the complaints of two other important characters, Reason and Nature, both daughters of God, who denounce mankind for abandoning them. Yet Jean's satire does not become bitter; for it is charged with an energy and humor that is shared to some extent even by his two most debased characters, False-Seeming and "La Vieille," an old prostitute who delivers an amusing lecture with many examples on how to succeed in love (that is, from her point of view, how to wrest the maximum profit from one's lovers). Jean never quite loses the thread of Guillaume's story, but he turns the lover into a comic figure, sometimes sullen and petulant, often bewildered by the contradictory counsels of his loquacious helpers. He is finally permitted to win his rose, but his conquest is portrayed wittily and unromantically as the act of defloration. Dressed as a pilgrim, the lover penetrates the sanctuary of the rose with his trusty staff from which dangles his pilgrim's scrip.

Jean de Meun is a poet in the ideal sense of the *Troilus* frontispiece. Although in the poem he never appears in his own person (he continues the fictive "I" of Guillaume's dreamer), he speaks through the characters of Reason and Nature and most eloquently through Nature's priest Genius who preaches a sermon to Love's barons.[8] The illuminators of the *Roman* picture Genius elevated above his auditors in a composition similar to that of the frontispiece.[9] The high point of Genius' sermon is his description of the Park of the Good Shepherd, which, he says, is the true Paradise of which the garden of Mirth that entrapped the dreamer is only a sham imitation. The Park contains the fountain of life, which Genius contrasts with the deadly fountain of love where Narcissus perished.

Jean de Meun and Chaucer are kindred spirits, and Jean's comic vision exercised a more pervasive and lasting influence on Chaucer than the world-view of any other poet. However, the *Roman de la Rose* exhausted the possibilities of the form it created. Chaucer's dream visions are full of ironic humor and serious philosophy, but to match the scale of Jean's achievement and to find outlets for a creative talent that far surpasses the French poet's, Chaucer had to discover new forms. Jean de Meun is first and foremost a dialectician, and it probably amused him to make a lover's dream-quest for a rosebud the focus of a grand debate about man's place in a fallen world in the course of which many speakers have their say and tell many tales to exemplify their ideas. Chaucer would do something similar with the pilgrimage to Canterbury, but the allegorical landscape of the *Roman* becomes the English countryside with landmarks like the Tabard Inn, and Jean's personifications come to life as the Friar, the Pardoner, and the Wife of Bath. Instead of a dream-allegory Chaucer finally shapes a real world, at least one with the power to convince us that it is real; yet that world retains much of the symbolic value of Jean's universal satire.[10]

Jean de Meun was not dependent upon courts and addressed himself to an audience of intellectuals, which included the University of Paris. His impact on medieval literature was extensive, but poets writing primarily for aristocratic circles modelled their works on the love-vision of Guillaume de Lorris. None of Guillaume's French imitators, however, recaptured his freshness and earnestness. They missed the otherworldly quality of Guillaume's garden, the perilous beauty which makes it such a seductive and questionable place, and saw only the superficial elegance of the settings, the formal conversations, and the rules of conduct legislated by the God of Love. The poems of Machaut and Froissart are clever exercises in convention, short enough to provide an evening's light entertainment. They hold up the flattering image of a *beau monde* composed of noble, sophisticated, and charming characters in which the audience might see itself reflected. The God of Love or some one of his servants keeps a feudal salon where one meets only the very best company. Pleasure explains the entrance requirements to Froissant in a poem called the *Paradise of Love:*

> Il y a contes, dus et rois,
> Chevaliers et de toutes gens,
> Dont li arrois est beaus et gens,
> Car qui n'est de moult gentil estre,
> Il ne poet a mon signour estre
> Ne estre escris en son registre.[11]

There are counts, dukes, and kings, knights, and all sorts of people whose array is beautiful and noble, for whoever is not of very noble condition cannot belong to my lord nor be enscribed in his register.

Among Machaut's contributions to the genre was the introduction of his patrons as characters in the story, casting the Duke of Berry, the King of Bohemia, and the King of Navarre in the roles of Love's courtiers and arbiters. In the *Judgment of the King of Bohemia,* the King is asked to decide an ingenious "question of love." A lady whose knight has died has an argument with a knight whose lady has forsaken him. Which one is worse off? The King of Bohemia gives his verdict in favor of the knight, but in another poem, the King of Navarre reverses the judgment. Obviously the interest in these poems does not lie in portraying human emotions or character but in providing cases, like hypothetical cases at law, to exercise a familiarity with literary language and convention shared by the poet with his audience. Poetry like this was never meant to be "popular"; it is designed to appeal to an exclusive coterie that prides itself on its ability to discriminate between the sensibilities and language of the noble lover and the *villein.*

The sententious and didactic strain so characteristic of most medieval poetry is by no means absent from the French love-visions. The lover's every move is liable to be analyzed and turned into a lesson in genteel manners. However, this is far from the kind of moral instruction meant to guide the poet's distinguished audience in the serious conduct of their personal and public affairs. On the contrary, these poems provide a welcome escape into an imaginary realm where love is the only business of life, and love itself is removed from actual human passion and treated as though it were a complicated game like chess. For Machaut and Froissart, the art of poetry was a highly refined diversion, and their very considerable creative talents found expression in other forms—in Machaut's magnificent religious music and Froissart's famous *Chronicles of France, England, and Spain.*

Chaucer is the first poet to write courtly visions in English, and for his audience it must have come as a novelty to hear poems of this type read in the vulgar tongue of their own country. In the *Book of the Duchess* Chaucer sets out to rival Machaut and Froissart, at times translating their very words into his native idiom, but from the first he aims at a more universal significance. In a sense, he seeks to restore to the genre some of the depth and range of the first great model, the *Roman de la Rose*. Although he does not presume to teach the "art of love" or to preach on any subject, he nevertheless attempts to fulfill the poet's ideal goal of moral instruction in the guise of the audience's humble servitor. He has the gift of making his visions seem more like the dreams we really experience and of making his characters speak with real voices, but what chiefly distinguishes the *Book of the Duchess* and the still more original *House of Fame* and *Parliament of Fowls* from the works of Machaut and Froissart is not the superior "realism" for which they have been justly praised, but their intellectual content. Unpretentiously, often with disarming humor, Chaucer's early visions raise philosophical questions about life and death, fame and fortune, right love and wrong love. To some extent all three show the influence of Boethius's *Consolation of Philosophy*.[12]

The opening of the *Book of the Duchess* combines a series of motifs copied, at times almost verbatim, from Froissart, Machaut, and Guillaume de Lorris: a sleepless narrator, an Ovidian fable, the onset of sleep and a dream-awakening to a lovely spring morning. The audience is prepared to hear an allegory of love. Instead they are presented with a tale about death. A figure in black, in stark contrast with the lush earth that has cast off its winter mourning, is overheard uttering a complaint, not to Love or to a pitiless lady, but to pitiless Death who has taken the lady.[13] The rest of the poem, except for the brief ending, consists of a long dialogue between the man in black and the dreamer. The dreamer, unable to grasp what the black knight has lost or what that loss means, attempts kindly and awkwardly to console the knight until the stark fact of death is finally driven in upon him:

> "She ys ded!" "Nay!" "Yis, be my trouthe!"
> "Is that youre los? Be God, hyt ys routhe!"   (1309–10)

There is nothing left to say—the dreamer awakes to a striking clock, and in the brief coda reflects upon the wonderful quality of the dream that he will essay to put "in ryme." Even in outline, it is evident that this dream-elegy not only tells a moving story but raises questions about the nature of a happiness that proves so transient.

In the *House of Fame* Chaucer dreams that he finds himself within the Temple of Venus on the walls of which he sees depicted the sad story of Dido and Aeneas. Emerging from the temple, the dreamer is snatched up into the heavens by a gigantic golden eagle who informs his terrified passenger that Jupiter is rewarding his poetic labors in Love's honor with a trip to the court of the goddess Fame. There he will learn tidings of love that will provide him with new matter for his poetry. During the ascent (because Fame is air she dwells in the upper regions of the sky), the eagle lectures the queasy poet on such unpoetic subjects as the physics of sound. The trip is a comic version of the celestial journey taken by predecessors like Dante. The court of Fame turns out to be just like an earthly court, and, as I have argued elsewhere, the company Chaucer encounters in the adjoining House of Rumor— sailors, pilgrims, pardoners, and messengers—is reminiscent of the people Chaucer would have encountered every day of his waking life on the wharves of London.[14] The *House of Fame* has been classified as a "love-vision," but it contains a bit of everything. It is a boisterous, funny, and reflective poem that gets progressively farther away from the subject of love.

The *Parliament of Fowls* is more truly a love-vision, but like Jean de Meun's part of the *Roman* it expands the categories of love to include types that differ from courtly love and are even antithetical to it. It begins with a paraphrase of a famous Neoplatonic dream vision, Cicero's *Dream of Scipio,* in which every kind of earthly love is rejected except love of the common good. It proceeds through another Temple of Venus to a grand image of Nature presiding over the annual mating of the birds. A dispute among three courtly eagles over the same female leads to the bird "parliament," during which the speakers exhibit amusingly the variety of ideas about love and rhetorical styles that prevail among the different classes of men.

A just appreciation of the complexity and subtlety of these early poems has been among the accomplishments of Chaucer criticism during the last two decades. Today there are enough articles and books about them to offer the reader his choice among a variety of interpretations. It is not my purpose to explain what in my opinion is their meaning. I wish rather to place them in the perspective of Chaucer's later and greater works, and when we do this, there can be no question that Skeat was right in publishing them under the title of "Minor Poems."[15] Moreover, I would argue that to Chaucer himself they were tentative expressions of great but as yet unfulfilled literary ambitions. Such an attitude is implicit and at times explicit in the poems themselves. Among the questions they raise are ones that concern the poet himself. What is his mission? Specifically, to what subjects and what themes should he address himself? As Robert Payne has stated, "the nature and functions of art and the justification of the artist" is "a continuing minor theme" in every one of his earlier works.[16] The fact that in both the *House of Fame* and the *Parliament* the ostensible reason for the poet's dream is his need for new subject matter is evidence that in writing these poems Chaucer was seeking new themes. Although Chaucer the poet has not sought in vain, it nevertheless remains true that the promises made in the poems to his fictional persona are largely disappointed.

Both the *House* and *Parliament,* and to a lesser degree also the *Book of the Duchess,* end on a note of irresolution and anticlimax. The *House of Fame* is of course unfinished. The poem breaks off at the very moment when "A man of gret auctorite" is about to make an important announcement. There has been much speculation about the identity of this man and about what he might say. It has been suggested that he is Boethius or even Jesus Christ. These guesses seem to me highly improbable because I do not think that the *House of Fame,* for all of its learning and philosophy, is the sort of poem that can bear the weight of a definitive moral from any such authority. Chaucer, I believe, was not ready to make such a statement and knew it. It may be that the *House of Fame* is unfinished because Chaucer could think of nothing for the "man of gret auctorite" to say.[17] In the *Parliament of Fowls* the narrator awakens and goes on reading his old books, hoping

> to rede so som day
> That I shal mete som thyng for to fare
> The bet.

Presumably he is hoping for a vision that will enable him to write a better poem. The awakening of the dreamer in the *Book of the Duchess* is the perfect ending because it brings with it, at least for the dreamer and the audience, the consolation and emotional uplift appropriate to the elegy. Nevertheless, here too there is no attempt to draw a final moral. The dreamer simply resolves to put his remarkable dream into verse, "As I kan best." Some critics have observed that the moral, if there is one, has been tactfully put into the mouth of the ghost of the dead king in the story over which Chaucer fell asleep:[18]

> "Awake! let be your sorwful lyf!
> For in your sorwe there lyth no red. . . .
> To lytel while oure blysse lasteth!"   (202–203, 211)

If this is a message to the bereaved John of Gaunt and to the reader, it is one of eloquent simplicity.

"The lyf so short, the craft so long to lerne," so begins the *Parliament of Fowls*. One expects the old adage to be applied to the art of poetry, not, as it actually turns out, the art of love, but the art of poetry is never far from Chaucer's mind in composing these so-called "love-visions." We detect in the *House of Fame* and the *Parliament of Fowls* the enormous impression made on him by the discovery of Dante. But "Dante in Inglissh," as Lydgate called the *House of Fame,* has a very different sound and effect from the *Divine Comedy,* and as I have pointed out the destination, the court of Fame, is very different from the Paradiso. Chaucer flies reluctantly and humorously in the eagle's claws "Wyth fetheres of Philosophye" (974).

The *House of Fame* is not epic but mock-epic, and yet epic seriousness is clearly what Chaucer is reaching out for, not only in this but in his other dream visions. In the *House of Fame* and the *Parliament of Fowls* the poet remains the passive observer and the transmitter of other voices. He paraphrases Virgil:

> "I wol now singen, yif I kan,
> The armes, and also the man . . . ,"   (143–144)

but he is unprepared to rival Virgil. "Yif I kan"—that is the humble Chaucerian, not the Virgillian, signature, and it sets the modest tone of these early poems. They contain the promise of what is to come.

During the 1380s Chaucer's poetry undergoes an extraordinary change and development. From internal evidence we can deduce that he must have begun his great romance *Troilus and Criseyde* sometime in 1382. *Troilus* is followed by the incomplete *Legend of Good Women*, Chaucer's first and not entirely successful attempt at telling a series of stories in a narrative frame. His adaptation of Boccaccio's *Teseida*, which eventually became the Knight's Tale, belongs to the same period, probably a little before or after *Troilus*. It is likely that by 1387 he had begun the *Canterbury Tales*. Not only is it a very prolific period but one of great variety and, of course, full maturity. Around 1380 Chaucer is still a fourteenth-century court poet, far surpassing Machaut and Froissart in imagination and depth, but nevertheless still the practitioner of what, with the exception of Jean de Meun's part of the *Roman*, was a minor form. By the end of the decade he has already become one of the great poets of all time.

Whatever reasons we see determining this rare phenomenon, the growth of a major talent, one factor we must reckon with is Chaucer's consciousness, indeed his self-consciousness, about his art and the direction it will take. All of the early dream visions, including the *Book of the Duchess,* imply a fondness for that fashionable genre but also a sense of dissatisfaction with it. Both affection and dissatisfaction underlie the parody of the conventions of the dream vision. These sentiments are present in the chorus of snoring sleepers in the Cave of Morpheus, in the eagle's lecture on the mechanics of sound, and in the speeches of the goose and the duck. We can see the limits of the courtly vision in the plethora of allusions to greater works of literature and philosophy. There are moments of true grandeur—the vision of the earth as a pinprick in the *House of Fame* (906–907) and the music of the spheres in the *Dream of Scipio* (another major work, like *Aeneid* I–IV, given in summary) as recounted in the *Parliament* (57–63). At such points Chaucer briefly rises to epic heights.

The poem that turns out to be the masterpiece begins unpretentiously enough. There is, to be sure, the naming of the hero, Troilus the son of Priam, and the invocation of a kind of

Muse, the dreadful fury Tisiphone, an appropriate companion of what is to be a tragic tale, but then the tone modulates to comedy as the narrator introduces himself as a priest of the God of Love. The teller of the tragic love story keeps on reminding us that he has no personal experience in love, and, indeed, we are told later that his work is only an unsentimental, almost painfully literal translation of an ancient Latin history.

The dream visions have prepared us for the disarming, self-deprecatory tone of the narrator, but even he is aware that, for all his "unliklynesse," he is engaged on a great task, and addresses the audience with a passion and seriousness that is new. There is never any question that this is meant to be a major work and that the narrator speaks from the chair in which the artist of the frontis-piece has portrayed him. However, only at the very end, when the author is saying farewell to his work, do we realize fully in what company Chaucer hopes that it may be considered:

> Go, litel bok, go, litel myn tragedye,
> Ther God thi makere yet, er that he dye,
> So sende myght to make in som comedye!
> But litel book, no makyng thow n'envie,
> But subgit be to alle poesye;
> And kis the steppes, where as thow seest pace
> Virgile, Ovide, Omer, Lucan, and Stace.   (V. 1786–92)

The farewell to the book, conventional as it is, bears Chaucer's personal touch. The characteristic humorous modesty is present in the adjective "litel"—the little book of more than 8000 lines—and in the slightly ludicrous image of the little book kissing the foot-steps left by the great poets. There is an anxious, proprietory, again almost humorous affection expressed for this "litel myn tragedye," sent out into the world like a favorite child with the paternal admonition to make no envy and to know its place. Chaucer is underplaying his hand, but the lack of pretentiousness and the humor should not disguise the pride in his work and the place he claims for it. E. T. Donaldson is absolutely right: "This is the modesty convention again, but transmuted, I believe, into some-thing close to arrogance."[19]

The last line may remind us of the scene in Limbo where the

great poets of antiquity invite Dante to join their select circle. Dante's way of putting it may be less subtle than Chaucer's, but the essential idea is the same. The scene in Limbo is the starting point of Ernst Curtius's monumental *European Literature and the Latin Middle Ages*. What Curtius says of Dante can just as well be applied to Chaucer: Dante's list includes Virgil, of course, Homer, Horace, Ovid, Lucan, and to this number Curtius adds Statius, who cannot be present in Limbo because he is waiting for Dante on the slopes of Purgatory:

> The six writers represent a selection from the antique Parnassus. Dante's bringing them together to form a "school" epitomizes the medieval idea of Antiquity. Homer, the illustrious progenitor, was hardly more than a great name to the Middle Ages. For medieval Antiquity is Latin Antiquity. But the name had to be named. . . . To the whole of late Antiquity, as to the whole of the Middle Ages, Virgil is what he is for Dante: "l'altissimo poeta." Next to him stands Horace, as the representative of Roman satire. . . . Ovid . . . wore a different face for the Middle Ages than he does for us. In the beginning of the *Metamorphoses*, the twelfth century found a cosmogony and cosmology which were in harmony with contemporary Platonism. But the *Metamorphoses* were also a repertory of mythology as exciting as romance. Who was Phaeton? Lycaon? Procne? Arachne? Ovid was the *Who's Who* for a thousand such questions. . . . Furthermore, all these mythological stories had an allegorical meaning. So Ovid was also a treasury of morality. . . . Lucan was the virtuoso of horror and a turgid pathos, but he was also versed in the underworld and its witchcraft. . . . Statius, finally, was the bard of the fratricidal Theban War, and his epic closes with homage to the divine *Aeneid*.

Curtius concludes the section with a grand metaphor: "The Latin Middle Ages is the crumbling Roman road from the antique to the modern world."[20]

If we compare Dante's and Chaucer's lists, the only discrepancy is the omission of Horace by Chaucer. Perhaps there was no room for Horace in the pentameter line, but a more likely reason is that Horace was not, like the others, the author of a long narrative poem. All the poets in Chaucer's list wrote long historical poems. The *Metamorphoses* can be included because, even though it is not precisely "history" in the same sense as the others, it does, as Curtius says, provide a cosmogony and cosmology, it starts with the creation and ends with the beginnings of the Roman Empire. As for the Theban and Trojan wars, they were as "historical" in Chaucer's mind as the wars between Caesar and Pompey celebrated by Lucan.

We may conclude, therefore, that Chaucer and his audience regarded *Troilus and Criseyde,* like these forebears, as a long historical poem on an epic theme. We call it a "romance," but I doubt that any medieval poet and his audience would have recognized the modern distinction between epic and romance. The romance is the legitimate offspring of the epic. In the twelfth century there is a sudden spate of romances that are adaptations of ancient history and epic: the *Roman de Troie,* the *Roman de Thebes,* the *Roman d'Enée.* In these poems battles alternate with a new love interest. Benoit de St. Maure, the author of the *Roman de Troie,* makes Achilles fall romantically in love with the Trojan princess Polyxena, and it is by using Polyxena as a lure that the Trojans succeed in killing him. Benoit also invented the story of Troilus and Cressida, which became the main source of Boccaccio's *Il Filostrato,* which is in turn the main source of Chaucer's *Troilus.*

For Benoit, Boccaccio, and other writers of such "epic romances" love is every bit as grand and instructive a theme as war, an attitude shared by Spenser who declares in his Proem to the *Faerie Queene:* "Fierce warres and faithfull loves shall moralize my song." The themes of love and war are, indeed, closely connected, and, though Chaucer's poem is primarily a love story, the war determines the course of that story and provides a pervasive and meaningful background for it.

Chaucer declares near the beginning of the first book that he does not intend to tell about the Trojan "gestes," that is, their deeds of war. His theme is the double sorrow of Troilus. However, the story of Troilus is an epitome of the war, for there is an intimate connection between the fate of Troy and the fate of the hero who bears the name of the city. Chaucer makes it clear that the same

forces of destiny govern the fortunes of both. Both stake everything upon a woman and both are betrayed in the end. Troy is
betrayed by Criseyde's father Calchas who deserts to the enemy
and helps the Greeks to bring about the downfall of the city
through treachery. Troilus is betrayed by Calchas's daughter who
gives herself to the Greek chieftain Diomede. The lesser events
prefigure the pattern of the greater.

It was taken for granted by the medieval audience that the
purpose of the works of the ancient poets was didactic, and Chaucer's *Troilus,* from the medieval point of view, shares with its
great predecessors a moral and philosophical import. One of Chaucer's fellow writers, Thomas Usk, calls Chaucer "the noble philosophical poete in Englissh," unquestionably basing his estimate
on *Troilus,* and this is precisely the reputation Chaucer himself
would have wished his poem to attain. In a famous stanza at the
end, he dedicates the work to his friends, the "moral Gower" and
the "philosophical Strode," another indication of the spirit in
which he meant the poem to be read.

By definition then, the major work will take a form established
by the ancients: a long narrative poem on an historical theme dealing with fundamental philosophical and moral issues. It attempts to
instruct the audience by presenting the lessons of the past in a
noble and dignified manner. That, in any case, is the poem Chaucer
wanted to write when he set to work on *Troilus.* Whether the poem
he actually wrote fulfills those conditions is another question.

CHAPTER II

The Theme of Love
in Troilus

IN *Troilus and Criseyde* the narrator at last steps into the pulpit
that is the poet's rightful vantage point, but from the very
first he is presented ironically—a further development of the
humble and naive persona of the dream visions. He introduces
himself to his audience as one who serves the "God of Loves
servantz," borrowing the Pope's title "servus servorum dei," and
like a priest he proceeds to lead his audience through the formula
of a "bidding prayer" for lovers in various stages of bliss and woe.
Also like a priest, he has no personal experience of sexual love,
in his case because of what he calls his "unliklynesse." Though he
dare not plead to Love for his own salvation, he hopes to advance
his soul by pleading the cause of others. It is a strange advocate of
Love who dedicates himself to serving his Lord by choosing to
tell a tragic tale of true love betrayed!

As he warms to his subject, the poet continues to assume a
priestly role, glossing the text of his tale like a preacher. Thus
when Troilus blasphemously denies Love in the Temple of Pallas,
the narrator breaks in to preach a little sermon against pride. He
argues that Love is, first, irresistible, and, secondly, virtuous, and so:

> Now sith it may nat goodly ben withstonde,
> And is a thing so vertuous in kynde,
> Refuseth nat to Love for to ben bonde,

> Syn, as hymselven liste, he may yow bynde.
> The yerde is bet that bowen wole and wynde
> Than that that brest; and therfore I yow rede
> To folowen hym that so wel kan yow lede.   (I.253–259)

Throughout the first three books, the narrator addresses his audience as a defender of the faith in this all-powerful and virtuous love, and throughout the last two books he tries to preserve its crumbling image against the inexorable facts of his story. Small wonder, then, that it comes as a shock when this same narrator at the end gives advice that seems flatly to contradict the counsel he gave at the beginning:

> And loveth hym, the which that right for love
> Upon a crois, oure soules for to beye,
> First starf, and roos, and sit in hevene above;
> For he nyl falsen no wight, dar I seye,
> That wol his herte al holly on hym leye.
> And syn he best to love is, and most meke,
> What nedeth feynede loves for to seke?   (V.1842–48)

C. S. Lewis squarely faced the contradiction and rejected the ending as a conventional palinode, deeply serious, deeply moving, but absolutely irrelevant to the meaning of the poem. *"Troilus,"* Lewis insisted, "is what Chaucer meant it to be—a great poem in praise of love."[1] Few critics writing after Lewis have been able to face and dismiss the contradiction so bluntly, and interpretation of the poem has been preoccupied for over thirty years with the problem of reconciling the ending with the main body of the poem. These interpretations have tended to take one of two opposed positions, either that the praise of human love in the early books is ironic,[2] or that Chaucer is somehow trying to praise *both* human love and divine and to reconcile them by showing how both emanate from the same source.[3]

Most of the critics take for granted a premise long ago stated vigorously by Kittredge: *"Chaucer always knew what he was about"* [italics Kittredge's].[4] That is to say, if we can discover Chaucer's purpose we can understand his poems. The same conviction underlies Lewis's assertion that the poem *"is* what Chaucer *meant* it to be." The criticism that holds the praise of love to be ironic is just as positivistic, in its way, about the poet's intention; it assumes, indeed, that Chaucer wrote always with one purpose and therefore could not have *meant* to portray sympathetically a form of love that he explicitly rejects at the end of the poem and elsewhere, for example in the Parson's Tale. Assumptions about a writer's intent seem to me a convenient and necessary step in determining his meaning, and I have myself been making such assumptions in the preceding chapter about Chaucer's purpose in writing his vision poems.

However, as the disagreements about *Troilus* illustrate, arguments from intent to meaning are inevitably circular. If modern criticism has anything to teach us, it is to be wary of interpretations based too narrowly on assertions of the author's intent, whether uttered by the author himself in the course of his work or elsewhere, or by a critic professing to speak for him.[5] This is emphatically not to argue that the author's intentions are irrelevant to what a poem means to us, but simply to say that his intentions, whether explicit or implied, are not necessarily equivalent to the meaning of the work of art.[6] Moreover, what a poet "is about" or what he "means" cannot always be reduced to a simple declaration of purpose. A poet is not bound by his initial intent, or, to put it somewhat differently, he may discover a broader and deeper intent in the process of composition, or he may not even be aware of what he truly intends. Intent can certainly be ambiguous, and great works of art often do generate contradictions that need not be resolved in the interest of logical consistency but should be frankly admitted as elements of their texture and meaning. The division among the modern critics of *Troilus* may thus proceed from a division in the poem itself.

"Without Contraries," Blake declared, "is no progression." In the same work (*The Marriage of Heaven and Hell*) Blake offended generations of Miltonists still to be born by asserting, "The reason Milton wrote in fetters when he wrote of Angels & God and at liberty when of Devils & Hell is because he was a true Poet and of the Devil's party without knowing it." Chaucer's *Troilus* seems to me a poem of Contraries, and I want to advance the proposition that Chaucer was of Criseyde's party without knowing it—that is to say that Chaucer in composing *Troilus* did *not* fully know what he was about and was a true Poet *because* of, not in spite of, this fact.[7]

The *Troilus* seems to me to be one of those works like *Hamlet* that moves us not because of the clarity of its moral vision but because it forces us to share the doubts and difficulties involved in making moral choices, in committing ourselves to some point of view. To declare that Chaucer definitely commends or condemns human love or even to say that in some measure he does both falsifies what I find to be most readers' experience of the poem. What I feel myself is a profound split on Chaucer's part between what his intellect as a medieval moralist tells him ideally should be and what his feelings as a poet tell him actually is true.[8]

I think he set out to write a didactic work that would impose a clear moral pattern on Boccaccio's love story. The *Troilus* takes up the themes that were casually treated in the *Parliament of Fowls*. It portrays and contrasts different kinds of love. The theme of *Troilus* is the two loves that have been and will continue to be the chief concern of Chaucer and his audience. To borrow an expression from Pandarus, they are "love celestial" and "love of kynde" (I. 979). "Love of kynde" is in itself no simple or single phenomenon. There are many forms of earthly love. One of these is the idealized form that is a product of medieval civilization to which modern criticism has affixed the epithet "courtly." But essentially we have two ideals, one human, one divine. These are not separated and confined to different parts of the poem, one taking up the main part, the other being dragged in only at the end. The entire poem turns on the relationship of these ideals.

For Pandarus, the practical man, they are easily accommodated to each other. Each has its proper time and season. Youth is a time for love of kynde. "Elde" is reserved for love celestial. As far as Criseyde is concerned: "It sit hire naught to ben celestial/As yet" (I. 983–984). His advice to her is *carpe diem*. Criseyde, in a more ladylike way, shares Pandarus's attitude. "I am naught religious" (II. 759), she tells herself—I haven't taken any vows. She really has no inclination to retire to a cell to pray and to read the lives of the saints (II. 117–118), and so she lets herself be persuaded to take a chance and find happiness in love of kynde. And she finds it as is quite clear from her words to Troilus when at last they are in bed together: "Welcome my knyght, my pees, my suffisaunce!" (III. 1309). The word "suffisaunce" turns up four times in the poem, three of them in speeches by Criseyde.[9] It occurs seventeen times in the third book of the *Boece* where it translates forms of *sufficientia*.[10] The third book of Boethius turns around the question of what constitutes man's true happiness, and so does Chaucer's poem. What in fact is man's "suffisaunce," his sovereign good, the end toward which he strives? This seems to me the central question that Chaucer has raised and done his best to answer.

For Pandarus and Criseyde it is clearly love of kynde. Love celestial, as Pandarus's worldly remark implies, is a distinct second-best—highly respectable and virtuous but something to be deferred until the time when man is no longer capable of experiencing the joys of human love. *Carpe diem* contains the recognition that human love has its term. It cannot last forever, but as a good pagan, Pandarus regards it as a sin not to take advantage of the limited happiness that life has to offer.

For Troilus it is another matter. He has intimations of something much finer than *carpe diem*. He sees in love the means not simply for enjoying life but for transcending it, a way of being born anew and thereby defeating time. And up to a point this is what happens to him. We meet him first as a shallow young cynic, see a sudden blinding illumination, and witness his gradual regeneration in which one can trace the pattern of contrition, penance, and finally absolution. For Troilus his love for Criseyde is from the very first both a physical and a spiritual experience. What he comes to possess in Book III is not simply the heaven of Criseyde's body but the heaven of her grace, her forgiveness of his former sins. The experience, as I think Chaucer makes very clear, does transform him and change him from a comic figure into someone we can finally admire and take seriously. He becomes a character capable of tragedy.

Troilus differs from Pandarus and Criseyde in this respect. As a pagan, he too seeks the highest good through love of kynde. He has no other way. The pagan gods, though he respects and fears them, cannot become the objects of ideal love, and this is consistent with all we know of pagan mythology. For the Olympian gods do not partake of our suffering and mortality, in short, of our humanity. Humankind for them can never be more than objects for their pleasure. That is one reason why mortals like Cassandra reject the love of the gods and why the affairs of the gods and mortals always seem to end tragically. The pagan does not know a god who is also human. For Troilus, therefore, there is no alternative but to try to turn a human being into a god.

This is the thesis of Father Dunning's essay "God and Man in *Troilus*." Dunning finds the basis of Troilus's tragedy in the religious character of his love for Criseyde. Troilus's "fundamental error in his understanding of human love," in Dunning's words, is "overcharging it beyond the limits of human nature."[11] What we see in Troilus is a yearning for a love that will transcend human nature, and such a love cannot take for its object an earthly mistress: Criseyde, though extraordinarily lovable in human terms, is not worthy of such a love as this. To quote Dunning once more, "It is because [Troilus's] conception of love in the poem has been represented at the highest natural level that the only conclusion possible is the conclusion which Chaucer, in fact, gives: only God can match such constancy in love."[12]

It is not that human love is sinful or degrading. On the contrary, it is capable of ennobling us and of giving us for brief moments a fulfillment that comes so close to perfection that it is easy to mistake it for perfection itself. The higher good need not cancel out the value of the lesser—rather, the lesser gives us some foretaste of what the higher must be like. The bliss of love for a mortal woman contains an intimation of love for the human God.

This, I believe, is the lesson that Chaucer wished to pass on to his audience and to us. Human love in that remote pagan world is presented as a prefiguration of the infinitely greater love open to the Christian. The poem does not force us to make an easy choice between good and evil but between an imperfect and a perfect good. The praise of love in the first three books is not ironic. The love extolled there, a love within the limits of our understanding, is derived from the love that surpasses our understanding. Human love is treated with sympathy then, but for the Christian who does have a choice between the two loves, there is no question as to which is to be chosen. The one is blind, feigned, and transient. The other is complete and eternal. To argue that Chaucer praises both kinds of love does not allow us to escape the fact that at the end the reader is asked to make a choice, and the right choice is made relentlessly clear.

However, if this is indeed what Chaucer intended—to lead us at the end to renounce "the blynde lust, the which that may nat laste" and to turn our hearts on heaven—I feel that he has failed in his didactic purpose. The greatest irony of *Troilus* is that it succeeds only in fixing our hearts more firmly on the imperfect human love. Moreover, I believe that this is because Chaucer himself, though intellectually committed to his Boethian and Christian moral, is emotionally committed to the human reality he has created. Instead of turning us from the world, Chaucer only attaches us to it more strongly than ever before, though with a greater understanding of what it is we love.

It is not as if we had not been forewarned all along. Chaucer's irony foreshadows the moral on every page. We know that both Troy and Troilus are doomed. We learn this from history and mythology. The fate of Thebes, alluded to at various points in the story, tells us what the destiny of Troy must be. The swallow who awakens Pandarus on a lusty Mayes morwe and the nightingale who sings romantically the same evening by Criseyde's window were transfigured through blind and horrible lust. We hear— ironically it is through the mouths of Pandarus and Criseyde—the Boethian theme: "O brotel wele of mannes joie unstable!" (III. 820) and "worldly joie halt nought but by a wir" (III. 1636). In the very heart of the love scene in Book III, we learn through the storm that howls through the night and the inexorable rising of the morning star and the sun that Troilus and Criseyde are in the grip of forces that they cannot control. We see through the hyperbole of Criseyde's oaths—her professions that her love will last till the sun falls from its sphere and until every river returns to its source—how pathetically frail such resolutions are. In a hundred ways we have been prepared to accept the moral. And when it comes we find—at least I find it so—that it is unacceptable. And ultimately I think it is also unacceptable to Chaucer the poet.

The brevity and fragility of love of kynde enhance its value for us, make us feel all the more the urgency of *carpe diem*. I do not believe such an attitude is sentimental or especially modern, influenced by the fact that for most of us love celestial is no longer the reality it represented for most of Chaucer's audience. The reason is rather that at all times, in the fourteenth century as now, art, and literature in particular, through its nature, immerses us in the experience of *this* world and lacks the means of making the next real to us in any terms other than through the image of the one in which we live.

What we bring away from *Troilus* is not the final disillusionment and emptiness of human love but its transient sweetness. And that sweetness grows out of the process of change that ultimately destroys love. Throughout *Troilus* Chaucer links the cycle of love with the great cycles of nature, and especially the change of the seasons. In this he follows both a medieval convention and universal experience. We cannot dissociate the fragrance of spring flowers from the winter that has preceded them and will come again. It is our experience of the one that confers value on the other. Thus it is that the feast of Palladion receives its beauty and poignancy from the desperate situation of the Trojans, the treason of Calchas, and our knowledge that the theft of the statue will bring about the destruction of Troy:

> And so bifel whan comen was the time
> Of Aperil, whan clothed is the mede
> With newe grene, of lusty Veer the pryme,
> And swote smellen floures white and rede . . .
> (I. 155–158)

The image of Troilus and Criseyde in each other's arms is the honeysuckle twined about the hazel (III.1230–32)—coincidentally the very image of the love of Tristan and Isolde in the lay of *Chevrefeuil*. We cling to what we possess in the knowledge that we cannot have it forever.

The desire of Troilus to possess it forever destroys him. The narrator has cited an old saying: "The yerde is bet that bowen wole and wynde/Than that that brest." Troilus turns out to be the stick that breaks. Criseyde who can be content in the brief present moment is more like Nature herself—she is the stick that bends. Troilus survives for only one season of love, passing from winter to spring and summer, and back to winter again. Criseyde has already survived one winter when we meet her in widow's black, and the weakness, the flexibility of her character paradoxically gives her the strength to survive.[13] Trying to encourage Troilus, Pandarus cites the fable of the reed and the oak (II. 1387–89). A worthless reed will bend with every blast, but a great oak, though it comes slowly, will fall once and for all with a crash. He means that Criseyde will be like the oak, but ironically it is Troilus who is the oak and Criseyde the reed. Her love for Diomede may diminish her worth in the eyes of many readers, but her essential quality has not changed. She gives herself to Diomede for the same reasons that she gave herself to Troilus: the honeysuckle requires a tree to wrap around. As Criseyde says, a rootless plant will soon die (IV. 767–770), and so she strikes new roots. Her relationship with Diomede is not ideal or courtly, but my point is that life has values that are neither ideal nor courtly, and so has Chaucer's poem.

Chaucer clings just as tenaciously to the quality of life as his heroine. We can detect it even in the epilogue at the very moment when the moralist is condemning blind lust and worldly vanity. Professor Donaldson makes a splendid observation about the language of the epilogue. "The lines," he says, "in which [Chaucer] condemns the world poignantly enhance the very thing that he is repudiating."[14] He quotes the lines:

> and thinketh al nys but a faire
> This world, that passeth soone as floures faire.
>
> (V. 1840–41)

The rhyme forces us to compare the meanings of "fair." What remains is not only, or even primarily, the lesson of vanity fair but the fact that the flowers are fair.

This is by no means the only touch in which Chaucer betrays the ambivalence of his moral position. Consider the quality of the adjective "litel" in this "litel spot of erthe" with all the affection that implies for the earth along with the recognition of its limitations. It is an echo of "Go, litel book, go, litel myn tragedye." The "litel erthe" is embraced by the sea—the image of two lovers like Troilus and Criseyde. And what of the "yonge, fresshe folkes, he or she?" The effect of "fresshe" and of the linking of "he or she" is to enhance, as Donaldson has said, the very thing Chaucer is repudiating.

Whether Chaucer deliberately contrived this effect or whether he simply allows it to happen is a difficult question that cannot be finally answered, certainly not within the context of *Troilus* alone. What one can say is that such lines both create and define the ambivalent emotions with which the ending of the great poem leaves many of its readers. If Chaucer, as I have suggested, fails in his didactic purpose, it was because he understood, perhaps subconsciously, that such a limited goal had never been his true purpose in the first place.

The works that follow *Troilus,* the *Legend of Good Women* and the *Canterbury Tales,* do indicate a growing awareness on Chaucer's part that there is a fundamental difference between the points of view of the poet and moralist. The moral Gower is first and foremost a moralist. The fifteenth century rated him as Chaucer's equal. We do not read him very much today because for us the value of literature does not reside primarily in its condemnation of vice and encouragement of virtue. In Chaucer the vocation of the poet is far stronger than that of the moralist, but this is not to deny the latter his voice. Indeed, the greatness of *Troilus* and of much else in Chaucer's poetry comes from a struggle between the moralist who calls for judgment and the artist who refuses to judge, a struggle in which the artist usually prevails. The questions about the purposes of art posed in the early dream visions are certainly not resolved in *Troilus,* and they are not abandoned. Chaucer addresses them again in his next poem, the most self-conscious assessment of his art, which responds indirectly to *Troilus:* the Prologue to the *Legend of Good Women.*

CHAPTER III

The Paradise
of Earthly Love

IN THE *Legend of Good Women,* written after *Troilus and Criseyde* around 1386–87,[1] Chaucer returns one last time to the dream vision and to the religion of love. In the Prologue he dreams that he is accused by the God of Love of heresy for his translation of the *Roman de la Rose* and the writing of *Troilus* because both of these works are held by Cupid to be slanders of women. Alceste, who appears as the God of Love's queen and the prototype of the good woman, intercedes for the poet and obtains his pardon on the condition that he compose a series of lives of Cupid's saints, women who were martyrs for love. The Prologue is followed by nine legends, the last unfinished. It seems that the work was set aside for the *Canterbury Tales* although Chaucer did take it up again at least once to make an extensive revision of the Prologue.

Scholarship on the *Legend* was for many years almost exclusively concerned with a debate over which of the two Prologues came first. With more recent critics it has become conventional to discuss the G text, the one most commonly thought to be the revision, and to dismiss the question of priority by saying that it makes little difference because both Prologues say essentially the same thing. I agree that G is the later version, but I shall base my interpretation on F because that is the version that reflects the stage of Chaucer's development between *Troilus* and the *Canterbury Tales*. Moreover, contrary to most recent opinion, I feel that the changes Chaucer made in G significantly alter both the tone and meaning of the Prologue. G reflects a later stage in Chaucer's development, a question to which I shall return at the end of the chapter.[2]

My primary concern is with the relationship of the *Legend of Good Women* to the two great poems that come before and after it with which, for all its wit and charm, the *Legend* must suffer in comparison. Why after the profound exploration of human character and the heartrending lessons of *Troilus* did Chaucer go back to the love-vision and renew, or pretend to renew, his allegiance to the God of Love? Although, in disagreement with Professor Robinson, I suspect that much of the *Legend* was written tongue-in-cheek, I certainly do not regard it as a frivolous poem.[3] The Prologue to the *Legend* suggests a profound if ultimately unsatisfactory answer to the troublesome questions the reader is left with by the Epilogue of *Troilus*, and it already expresses the major theme on which the *Canterbury Tales* opens. It makes a transition between the tragic conclusion of *Troilus* and the comedy of the General Prologue.

The idea of the *Legend* came to Chaucer as he was completing *Troilus*. In the Epilogue he offers a tongue-in-cheek apology to the ladies in his audience for any offense he may have given by telling about Criseyde's infidelity:

> Bysechyng every lady bright of hewe,
> And every gentil womman, what she be,
> That al be that Criseyde was untrewe,
> That for that gilt she be nat wroth with me.
> Ye may hire giltes in other bokes se;
> And gladlier I wol write, yif yow leste,
> Penelopeës trouthe and good Alceste.   (V.1772–78)

If, as is often suggested, Queen Anne or some other great lady did in fact commission Chaucer to perform penance by writing about good women, the poet himself provided the idea in the last two lines of that stanza. The joining of Alceste's name with Penelope's means that Chaucer had been looking over the catalogue of

virtuous pagan women in St. Jerome's *Epistle Against Jovinian,*
the same passage that was to become the source of Dorigen's lament
in the Franklin's Tale (V. 1367–1456). Jerome had written, "Al-
cestin fabulae ferunt pro Admeto sponte defunctam; et Penelopes
pudicitia, Homeri carmen est" (stories tell that Alceste died in
place of her husband Admetus, and Homer sings of Penelope's
virtue).[4] The echo of Jerome in *Troilus* is evidence that the tract,
which was to become so important an influence on the *Canterbury
Tales,* also helped to inspire the *Legend of Good Women* and that
Chaucer had been doing research on "good women" while he was
still working on *Troilus.*[5]

Thus Chaucer was already looking ahead to the poem he would
write next and may well have been thinking of a poem like the
Legend when in the farewell to "litel myn tragedye" he wishes that
God may give him the power to write "some comedye" (V. 1786–
88). These lines have been interpreted as a prophecy of the *Canterbury Tales,* but there is no evidence that the plan of the Tales had
begun to take shape. If Chaucer had a specific comedy in mind the
evidence points to the *Legend of Good Women.* In view of the
lugubrious endings of the legends themselves—desertion and sui-
cide—it may seem perverse to call the poem a comedy, yet I think it
really *is* a comedy in Dante's sense. It should not be forgotten that
when we first encounter the heroines of the *Legend,* we see their
heavenly apotheosis, not their earthly misfortune. As a reward for
being faithful in love, they have all been translated to the court of
Cupid and Alceste, the reigning deities of love, whom they follow
as the martyrs in the Book of Revelations follow the white lamb.
What we see in the Prologue is surely the Heaven to which Cupid's
martyrs go, or at least, if not the place itself, the company that
dwells there. At the end of F, the God of Love tells Chaucer:

> I moot goon hom (the sonne draweth west)
> To paradys, with al this companye.   (563–564)

The *Legend* is, therefore, a comedy in the technical sense that it
ends happily, but of course the idea of a Paradise for martyrs like
Cleopatra and Medea is comic in itself. The many analogies between the religion of love and Christianity help to create the
light and irreverent tone that runs through both the Prologue and

the legends, which keeps us from taking the sufferings of the un-
fortunate heroines too seriously.

The comedy, however, also has a serious side, and the humor
does not prevent the poem from suggesting an answer to the disil-
lusioning stanzas that conclude *Troilus*—to the hero's condemnation of "the blynde lust, the which that may nat laste" and to the
narrator's advice to shun "This world, that passeth soone as floures
faire." The answer, in its simplest terms, is that the flowers pass
only to be reborn, like the daisy, and that the virtue of a faithful
woman also has a generative power. Chaucer knows that the same
flowers do not return each spring as he knows that it is literally impossible for a mortal woman like Alceste to return from the underworld. Nevertheless, the daisy and the story of Alceste point to the
restorative power of Nature herself, which is a form of grace,
holding out comfort to Chaucer as a man and as a poet against the
bitterness of betrayed love. The flowers and the ladies who fill the
meadow in Chaucer's vision represent the coming of spring and
with it a consolation more potent than the consolation of philosophy.

In the Prologue, especially the F version, Chaucer draws heavily
upon the theme of resurrection that has always been implicit in the
reverdie, the conventional spring opening of the love-visions. Cupid's martyrs are resurrected after their passion, the daisy is resurrected after the winter, Alceste is resurrected from Hades, and,
most significant of all, the poet's own creative power, exhausted by
the labors and the painful emotions of his tragic romance, takes on
a new life and a new direction. With the *Legend,* Chaucer is back
to searching for a subject and more than ever concerned with the
problem of what the poet should write. Robert Payne has made a
brilliant and convincing case that poetry, its functions and its
justification, *is* the chief subject of the Prologue."[6] I would add that
the need to come to terms with his art arose from the rejection of
"love of kynde" at the end of *Troilus* and the failure of that rejection to convince most of his readers and, as I have maintained, the
poet himself. For better or for worse, Chaucer had to recognize
himself as the poet of "love of kynde" and not of "love celestial."
The Prologue to the *Legend* represents his return to earth from the

eighth sphere and is his attempt to justify himself as the only sort of poet he ever could be—the poet of "kynde."

The Prologue begins with a lengthy passage in which Chaucer defends his preoccupation with books by declaring that they are our only means of knowing about things that we cannot witness with our own eyes, like the joys of heaven and the pains of hell:

> A thousand tymes have I herd men telle
> That ther ys joy in hevene and peyne in helle,
> And I acorde wel that it ys so;
> But, natheles, yet wot I wel also
> That ther nis noon dwellyng in this contree,
> That eyther hath in hevene or helle ybe,
> Ne may of hit noon other weyes witen,
> But as he hath herd seyd, or founde it writen.   (1–7)

The idea is developed for a number of lines with the conclusion:

> Wel ought us thanne honouren and beleve
> These bokes, there we han noon other preve.   (27–28)

This is the most indirect of all the openings of Chaucer's vision poems, yet just as in the case of the beginnings of the others, a thematic relevance to what follows can be established. As Professor Payne has pointed out, the passage introduces the familiar Chaucerian topic of the importance of "books" (*auctorite*) and "experience" for the poet's craft and the difficulty of reconciling the two.[7] The passage is a variation of Chaucer's pose as a poet who lacks experience and whose knowledge, especially in matters of love, comes to him almost entirely through books. In *Troilus* he apologizes constantly to his audience for his inability to do justice to the experience of the lovers. Only by following his "auctor" can he describe the "hevene" of Troilus and Criseyde in the third book.

The beginning of the *Legend,* therefore, brings up a general topic that is crucial to a consideration of Chaucer's poetry, but it also introduces it with a specific example that looks back to *Troilus* and forward to Chaucer's vision in the Prologue: the "joy in hevene and peyne in helle." We are concerned not only with a question of how a poet writes but what it is he writes about. Heaven and Hell are without question the two most relevant subjects for any medieval poet, yet no mortal man has ever been there. Or possibly there is just one man. Chaucer's curious way of putting it—"noon *in this contree*"—makes one wonder whether he might not have been thinking of a man from another country who *had* been there: Dante. If there is any poet who succeeds in fusing the points of view of the artist and the moralist, it is Dante. The *Divine Comedy* had been an important influence on Chaucer's *Troilus,* and the spirit in which Chaucer treats the ending owes more to Dante than to Boccaccio. For the final stanza he adapts a beautiful prayer from the Paradiso: "Thow oon, and two, and thre, eterne on lyve." The opening lines of the *Legend* are like a quizzical footnote to that moving appeal to the Trinity. It is as though Chaucer, having come down from those heights, were asking himself, how can we be sure there really is a heaven? The answer is: by reading books. But that answer raises a second question. How can we trust what we read in books? As his disciple Henryson put it with reference to Chaucer's own *Troilus:* "Quha wait gif all that Chauceir wrait was trew?"

The Prologue to the *Legend* gives an answer to the second question. The poet's experience may confirm what he has read, even the limited experience of a poet like Chaucer who has never seen either Dante's Paradise or the earthly heaven of the lovers in the third book of *Troilus.* What Chaucer obtains through his dream is, as I have pointed out, a vision of Heaven, though not, to be sure, the one Dante saw. The pseudo-Heaven of Cupid's saints is an earthly one closely connected with Nature, yet it resembles the celestial one in certain ways and bestows a measure of grace upon true believers like an errant love poet who is pardoned for his misdeeds. Chaucer's vision gives him cause to continue believing and to continue writing. More than that, he learns to accept the fact that every poet must write about whatever of heaven is revealed to him, not necessarily about the heaven revealed to Dante. Chaucer's vision of Cupid's Paradise is distinctly second best, yet it, too, has its assurances and rewards, and it is not unfit to be a subject for poetry.

The narrator is wrong that books are the only evidence to sustain our faith. He thinks of his studies as a religious discipline, and of truancy from his books as an act of apostasy:

On bokes for to rede I me delyte,
And to hem yive I *feyth* and full *credence*,
And in myn herte have hem in *reverence*
So hertely, that ther is game noon
That fro my bokes maketh me to goon,
But yt be seldom on the *holyday*,
Save, certeynly, whan that the month of May
Is comen, and that I here the foules synge,
And that the floures gynnen for to sprynge,
Farewel my bok, and my *devocioun!*

(30–39, my italics)

Yet his visit to the meadow is also an act of worship, and even though the narrator does not make the connection, we are meant to see, I think, that his devotion to his books and his devotion to the daisy are complementary. Experience confirms authority.

Just as books tell us about Heaven, so does the daisy. With the white petals surrounding the golden center, she is the day's eye, the sun (184); and like the sun, which "dies" each night to be "reborn" the next morning, the closing and unfolding of the daisy's petals symbolizes the cycle of death and resurrection. The religious symbolism of the daisy is especially notable in the language and imagery of the F Prologue, as in the following passage that was cut from G:

She is the clernesse and the verray lyght
That in this derke world me wynt and ledeth.
The hert in-with my sorwfull brest yow dredeth
And loveth so sore that ye ben verrayly
The maistresse of my wit, and nothing I. . . .
Be ye my gide and lady sovereyne!
As to myn erthly god to yow I calle,
Bothe in this werk and in my sorwes alle.

(84–88, 94–96)

Also in F, Chaucer wishes to be present at

the resureccioun
Of this flour, whan that yt shulde unclose
Agayn the sonne, that roos as red as rose.   (110–112)

This passage, too, was omitted from G, and I shall consider possible reasons for these omissions below. For the present, I wish to point out that in what is now commonly accepted as the original form of the Prologue, Chaucer presented the daisy as an emblem of rebirth in the world of nature. The daisy confirms what we have been told in books: "That ther ys joy in hevene." In the *Legend* one of the fading "floures faire" becomes the light and inspiration of Chaucer's poetry "in this derke world."

Alceste is Cupid's queen and the dominant figure in the *Legend* because her willingness to die in her husband's place makes her the type of ideal love.[8] That is what she represents to Troilus when he rejects Cassandra's charge that Criseyde has betrayed him:

> As wel thow myghtest lien on Alceste,
> That was of creatures, but men lye,
> That evere weren, kyndest and the beste!
> For whan hire housbonde was in jupertye
> To dye hymself, but if she wolde dye,
> She ches for hym to dye and gon to helle,
> And starf anon, as us the bokes telle.   (V.1527–33)

However, it is not Alceste's death but her return to life that perfectly suited Chaucer's purpose in the *Legend*. The resurrection of her flower the daisy along with the rising of the sun is a symbolic reenactment of Alceste's return from darkness into light. Chaucer's treatment turns her into a spring goddess like Persephone. She is clothed in "real habit grene," and her crown of pearl with a center of gold fretwork, as Chaucer remarks, "Made hire lyk a daysie for to sene" (214–224). She *is* the daisy, and like the flower on this May morning, she is a personification of spring. Her consort, the God of Love, is dressed to match in a silk garment,

> enbrouded ful of grene greves
> In-with a fret of rede rose-leves,
> The fresshest syn the world was first bygonne.
> (227–229)

Portrayed in this fashion, the couple cannot help but remind us of the King and Queen of the May. Although most of our knowledge of May Day celebrations comes from Renaissance sources, the

custom is ancient and was certainly familiar to Chaucer.⁹ The F
version of the Prologue is set on "the firste morwe of May" (in G
it takes place "Whan passed was almost the month of May").
Chaucer has obviously gone out to pay his observance to May and
in his dream runs into a May Day procession engaged on the same
business. Chaucer would not need to know anything about fertility
cults in order to understand the symbolism inherent in the King
and Queen of the May and the green of their costumes. Cupid and
Alceste resemble Zephyrus and Flora, "god and goddesse of the
floury mede" (174). As King and Queen of Love they represent
the generative force that causes the fields to bloom and sets the
birds to mating.

In the Prologue Alceste acts out her roles as a saint and as
goddess of spring by interceding for the poet and making him fruitful. More than in any of the earlier visions there is a poignancy in
the comic self-portrait of the narrator as a man of books, out of
touch with the life that is going on all around him. He uses an
autumnal image for himself that discords with the flourishing
spring meadow. He is a poet come late to the harvest that has been
reaped by others:

> For wel I wot that ye han her-biforn
> Of makyng ropen, and lad awey the corn,
> And I come after, glenyng here and there,
> And am ful glad yf I may fynde an ere
> Of any goodly word that ye han left.   (73–77)

In Cupid's Paradise, Chaucer is an intruder, the serpent in the
garden. The God of Love tells him: "Yt were better worthy,
trewely,/A worm to neghen ner my flour than thow" (317–318).
But through the goodness of Alceste he is restored to grace and
given a new subject for his poetry. When he finally does identify
Alceste with the daisy, he finds a new way to praise his favorite
flower, and at the end he is sitting down to the task of composing a
long poem in honor of love. Alceste has made the lines Chaucer
addressed to the daisy come true:

> as an harpe obeieth to the hond
> And maketh it soune after his fyngerynge,

Ryght so mowe ye oute of myn herte bringe
Swich vois, ryght as yow lyst, to laughe or pleyne.
                                                    (90–93)

This is the sense that we can get out of the Prologue by reading
it as believers and closing our eyes to the humor and irony. But the
humor and irony cannot be ignored, and they inject a current of
skepticism about the ultimate value of this earthly paradise, about
the saintliness of its saints, and about the veracity of the books that
vouch for them. First of all, whatever "faith" in earthly love is
generated by the Prologue is severely undermined by the legends
with their caricatures of villainous men and gullible women. They
certainly do not "Spek wel of Love." Chaucer is simply telling the
story of *Troilus* all over again with the sexes reversed. The increasing flippancy of the narrator's tone in the legends has often
been remarked. Critics have underrated the quality of the legends
as poetry and the sympathy of Chaucer for his heroines; nevertheless, the plunge from the dream vision world of the Prologue into
the Ovidian world of wars and seductions in the legends is a cold
one. In the Prologue the charm and beauty of the spring passages
and of the genuinely impressive appearance of Alceste and the God
of Love is undercut by the suggestion that Cupid's accusations
against Chaucer, particularly his objections to *Troilus,* are absurd
and trivial.

The God of Love's majesty starts to diminish as soon as he begins to speak. He sounds like any pompous feudal nobleman, a
point made very clear in Alceste's long harangue on the duties of
a lord to his subjects in which she tells him that he should not act
"lyk tirauntz of Lumbardye" (374). But is not this precisely how
the God of Love does act toward his subjects throughout medieval
love poetry? Alceste is a delightful figure, but what makes her
delightful is that her saintliness is qualified by her humanity. Like
the Wife of Bath, she is both sententious and imperious, and
though she stands up for Chaucer, her defense of him is humiliating. The best she can say in his behalf is that he either didn't
know what he was doing or was ordered to write the offending
works by someone he could not disobey (something that she is
about to do herself):

And eke, peraunter, for this man ys nyce,
He myghte doon yt, gessyng no malice,
But for he useth thynges for to make;
Hym rekketh noght of what matere he take.
Or him was boden maken thilke tweye
Of some persone, and durste yt nat withseye.

(362–367)

The accusation of incompetence or toadying may be more damning to a poet than the charge of heresy. When Chaucer tries to speak up in his own defense to say that he wrote *Troilus* to further the cause of love, she cuts him off:

Lat be thyn arguynge,
For Love ne wol nat countrepleted be
In ryght ne wrong; and lerne that at me!   (475–477)

For anyone who has read and understood the *Roman de la Rose* and *Troilus,* the God of Love is preposterously wrong; yet, there is also a comic truth in Alceste's statement that, right or wrong, it is no use arguing against him.

If the Prologue to the *Legend* has any lesson to teach Chaucer or the reader, Alceste's statement about Cupid's infallibility comes as close to expressing it as anything. Whatever reservations we may have about the god, his saints, and his heaven, we must make the best of it. Chaucer's own reservations are implicit throughout the Prologue, but he too makes the best of it by writing a gracious recantation. Moreover, if we take Chaucer's advice to young folk at the end of *Troilus* absolutely literally, the God of Love has a case and Chaucer is guilty. The Prologue does correspond to a genuine effort by Chaucer the poet to make his peace with the kind of love and the kind of poetry he had renounced. Even Alceste's defense that Chaucer did not know what he was doing is not entirely beside the point. If I am right that the problems that readers and critics have with the Epilogue of *Troilus* stem from Chaucer's own difficulties in forcing a Christian moral upon the story, he never truly was a renegade to Love's law. We might say that the spirit of the Epilogue in *Troilus* is not fully consistent with the letter of what is being said. Chaucer's heart was not fully in it, or, looking at it another way, his heart was too much in it. With whatever ironic reservations, Chaucer *does* return to the fold in the *Legend,* and the theme of resurrection in Nature is something that can be taken seriously. The metamorphosis of Alceste into the daisy is more than a charming myth. It suggests that the constancy of human lovers like Troilus and Alceste is part of a cycle of life. Like the daisy that reappears every spring and the sun that rises each morning it is a sign against death, a light "in this derke world."[10] The legends of Christian martyrs are not the only subject through which a Christian poet may express his faith. "Love of Kynde" is also a mystery that confers an earthly martyr's crown, symbolized by the petals of the English daisy, white on top (for purity) with a reddish underside (for martyrdom):

> Cibella maade the daysye and the flour
> Ycrowned al with whit, as men may see;
> And Mars yaf to hire corowne reed, pardee,
> In stede of rubyes, sette among the white.   (531–534)

In the praise of Alceste, the queen who returned from the underworld, and her symbol the daisy, Chaucer takes the first tentative step toward writing the comedy for which he had invoked God's aid in *Troilus.* The comedy is to be a celebration of life and the renewal of life on earth. Yet the symbols through which the theme is developed, for which Chaucer draws upon classical mythology and the French "marguerite" poems, are far removed from the life they celebrate. They manifest a powerful creative impulse that has as yet found no outlet except in intellectual and symbolic form. They express an idea of comedy, but they fail to provide Chaucer with a comic subject to write about. At the end of the Prologue the poet is back where he started from, in his library poring over still another old book. The legends themselves are tepid redactions of oft-told tales, enlivened by flashes of Chaucerian warmth and humor; as vehicles for a comic vision they prove totally inadequate.[11]

The essential idea of the Prologue to the *Legend* is expressed more naturally and effectively in the first eighteen lines of the General Prologue to the *Canterbury Tales.* The opening of the General Prologue, too, is full of literary echoes and is very far from being a realistic description of April in the English countryside. Nevertheless, the difference between the Prologue to the *Legend* and the General Prologue is that in the latter Chaucer begins to create a world that takes on an actuality of its own totally different from the world of dream visions or the recreation of the ancient world in *Troilus.* The scene that starts to unfold in the *Canterbury Tales,* no matter how much it may depend on books, corresponds to the experience of fourteenth-century England.

As I shall be arguing in the chapters on the *Canterbury Tales,* Chaucer's ideas about the relationship between art and life, between experience and authority, kept on changing. It is not surprising, therefore, that he came to have second thoughts about the Prologue to the *Legend.* We cannot know exactly why he decided to rework the Prologue, but the revisions reveal a considerably tougher, less idealistic cast of mind. Most of the passages on which I have based my interpretation of F were cut or altered in G, and I have pointed out a number of these changes in passing. The apostrophe to the daisy is eliminated. Instead of wishing to be present at the daisy's "resurrection" (110), Chaucer wants simply "Upon the freshe daysie to beholde" (92). The time of the vision is changed from the first of May to the end of May. Cupid no longer says that he must return "To paradys" (564) but simply bids the poet farewell (541). In short, the religious imagery on which my reading is based was largely eliminated. These changes were observed long ago by D. D. Griffith and explained by him as resulting from an increasing devoutness in Chaucer's religious convictions that led him to regard this kind of imagery as essentially blasphemous.[12] I would account for the changes in exactly the opposite way. The F Prologue is by far a more moral and religious poem than the G version. Far from being blasphemous, the religious diction and imagery in F are meant to suggest a divinity in Nature that mirrors and confirms Christian belief. The F Prologue is a testament of faith in "kynde" and attests to the continuation of a genuine moral purpose in Chaucer's poetry. On the other hand, the F Prologue also contains an underlying skepticism that such a faith in nature is well-founded and that poetry of this kind has any real moral justification.[13]

That skepticism becomes dominant in G. The daisy in G is

simply another flower instead of a heavily weighted symbol of regeneration. The suggestions that the God of Love and his entourage
represent a kind of Paradise are pruned away or toned down.
Chaucer expands the God of Love's speech to include a literary
passage (268–307) that heightens the absurdity of Cupid's accusations against Chaucer and makes the authority of books all the
more suspect. The God of Love recites a list of books in Chaucer's
"cheste" that presumably tell about good women, and these contain
works, especially Jerome's *Epistle Against Jovinian,* on which
Chaucer drew for the antifeminist portions of the Wife of Bath's
Prologue. What the passage shows is that the God of Love, like
many critics, does not know or does not understand the books he
is citing (and by analogy doesn't know or understand the *Roman*
and *Troilus*), and that authority can be twisted to serve whatever
purpose an author has in mind. The titles in this passage suggest
that G belongs to the period of the Wife of Bath's Prologue and
the Merchant's Tale, both of which make use of some of these
works and both of which are concerned more with the abuses than
with the uses of authorities.

The differences between F and G do not indicate any change in
Chaucer's fundamental religious convictions or new scruples about
a conventional kind of imagery that other poets would continue
to use after him. They do show a loss of faith in the defense of
poetry he had tried to make when he first set out to write a comedy
of earthly love. By the time he came to revise the Prologue to the
Legend, Chaucer's doubts about the moral function of poetry had
grown considerably. The experience of writing the *Canterbury
Tales* was leading him to experiment with fictions like the fabliaux
that are difficult to reconcile with the moral purpose of art, and
he grew to be less tolerant of critics like the God of Love who insist that poetry must serve a worthy cause whether that cause be
"love of kynde" or "love celestial."

When he first wrote the Prologue to the *Legend,* however,
Chaucer himself still subscribed to some such view of a poet's
duties. He had always regarded himself as a love poet, a clerk of
Venus. In all of his works he had labored to make love poetry
serve a higher purpose, and in the F Prologue he presents us with
an elaborate apology for his art and its main subject. But Chaucer's

return to the fold was temporary. The legends of Cupid's saints turned out to be an artistic blind alley, and he abandoned them for the more universal statement of the theme that underlies his praise of the daisy and of Alceste: "Whan that Aprill with his shoures soote. . . ."

CHAPTER IV

Portrait of the
Christian Community

*t*HE CREATIVE ENERGY we find in the Prologue to the *Legend* could no longer be contained by the mythology of dreams. The winged god and his queen and their attendant troop of ladies are like those creatures of poetic fancy that Yeats came to call his Circus Animals: "Those stilted boys, that burnished chariot,/ Lion and woman and the Lord knows what." The figures of romance and dream vision are the Circus Animals of a medieval love poet, and they had held Chaucer's imagination much as Irish myth and legend captivated the early Yeats. The modern poet's question about the symbols of the dream that had enchanted him can help us to grasp the essential difference between Chaucer's Prologue to the *Legend* and the Prologue to the *Canterbury Tales:*

> Those masterful images because complete
> Grew in pure mind, but out of what began?

The images of myth and dream are masterful products of the poet's art, but in another sense they master or dominate the poet because they present him with a ready-made beauty absent from his own fragmented experience. Nevertheless, as Yeats came to acknowledge, experience is the seed from which the vision grows in the poet's mind. The archetypal images of myth enable the poet to transmute and transcend experience in a purer and more pliable medium, but a time comes when he is abandoned, not by the vision, but by the painted images in which the vision has been veiled, a time when the poet begins to construct his vision out of the bits and scraps of his own observation. The modern poet's Circus Animals give way to the inventory of a "rag-and-bone shop":

> A mound of refuse or the sweepings of a street,
> Old kettles, old bottles, and a broken can,
> Old iron, old bones, old rags, that raving slut
> Who keeps the till.

Chaucer's dream meadow, the God of Love, and the nineteen ladies in his company are replaced by the Tabard Inn, the Host, and the twenty-nine pilgrims. The fragmented images that comprise the medieval poet's new vision—such objects as a gold brooch, a milk-white purse, a glass reliquary containing pigs' bones —contrast sharply with the symbolic daisy and Alceste's crown of pearl, but it is not, as in Yeats, a bitter contrast. The objects of the General Prologue, like the people who possess them, remain to some degree idealized; they are qualified by adjectives like "fresh," "clene," "newe," "sheene." To that extent, at least, the visionary gleam has not faded. But these objects belong to a world of social, commercial, and political action, in short, the world of Chaucer's experience. The scene that unfolds teems with the life of fourteenth-century London.

I would not deny that Chaucer's earlier poetry is also rooted in experience, nor am I reviving the old idea that Chaucer's pilgrims are real people and the pilgrimage, a record of an actual event. Naturalism was always an essential element of Chaucer's style; the gossipmongers in the House of Rumor, the quarreling birds in the *Parliament*, Pandarus and Criseyde have their source in the same world as the Canterbury pilgrims. Anyone can feel the life inherent in the most courtly of Chaucer's fictions. Moreover, much in the General Prologue harks back to the past. Its structure—an opening spring passage, a series of portraits, and the introduction of a guide —owes a great deal to the *Roman de la Rose*.[1] The pilgrims are social and moral types, and a surprising amount of detail in the Prologue has been lifted straight out of books. The pilgrimage to

Canterbury has a symbolic level; it is the journey of life that all men must travel.

All the same, when these qualifications have been made, the scene in the General Prologue makes a radical break with Chaucer's earlier poetry. The subject of a pilgrimage, including descriptions of the dress, complexions, conversation, table manners, horses, beards, and noses of his travelling companions, is a remarkable change for a poet who had always insisted that all of his matter came to him out of books or through some wonderful dream. Chaucer's constant apologies for his lack of experience were a wry acknowledgment that the experience of a customs collector could be of no conceivable interest or importance to his courtly audience. In the General Prologue, on the other hand, it is as though the narrator were obsessed with getting in all he has seen or heard, no matter how trivial or vulgar, lest "he moot telle his tale untrewe." He still apologizes for his ineptitude and for the coarseness of the language of some of his fellow pilgrims, but his experience is the only authority he alleges, and he overwhelms us with it.

Lines 1–11 of the Prologue make a link between Chaucer's earlier poetry and the scene about to unfold at the Tabard. The reverdie is a conventional signal for the beginning of a dream vision or a love affair. The verse is in the high literary style of similar spring passages in *Troilus* (e.g., I.155 ff., II.50 ff.). A series of convoluted clauses, the personification of April and March, the classical allusion to Zephyrus, the astrological placing of the sun, the relatively high incidence of poetic diction drawn from romance vocabulary (e.g., *licour, engendred, inspired, corages*), all identify the courtly style and set up the expectation of a courtly subject. These are the lines for which one can cite such a great number of literary analogues.[2] The turning point comes with line 12, which introduces the main clause of the 18-line period: "Thanne longen folk to goon on pilgrimages." In the remaining lines the ideal landscape of romance gives way to the medieval world where pilgrims are journeying to distant shrines and more particularly the English countryside where folk "from every shires ende" converge upon Canterbury. Arthur Hoffman has pointed out the movement of the entire passage "from the broadest inclusive generality to the firmest English specification, from the whole western tradition of the celebration of spring . . . to a local event of English society and English Christendom."[3] That movement is marked by a stylistic shift from literary language in such a line as "Of which vertu engendred is the flour," which sounds almost like French, to the homely Anglo-Saxon quality of "To ferne halwes, kowthe in sondry londes" or "That hem hath holpen whan that they were seeke." The latter will be the dominant style of the Prologue, but the company of sundry folk moves out from a background of universal nature and literary tradition. It is a way of declaring that the cosmic powers to which poet-dreamers and chivalric lovers respond are also at work in the borough of Southwerk.

The impulse that moves the birds to mate and men to seek out holy places links the pilgrims with two great themes of medieval romance, "love of kynde" and "love celestial" as I have called them in *Troilus,* or, as Hoffman puts it, "the two voices" that echo through the Prologue: the voices of St. Venus and St. Thomas.[4] Hoffman shows how the pilgrims are both differentiated and connected by the way each, in his own way, responds to the call of one or the other or sometimes both of these voices. Like the heroes of chivalric romance, each one, impelled by love, from the highest kind to the most debased, is making his own journey of life.

The pilgrims are questers, but they are Englishmen and for the most part common folk, not knights and ladies of ancient Troy, Rome, or Camelot, and there is another crucial difference between them and the figures of romance although both heed the same voices. The romance hero seeks a personal perfection apart from society. He typically starts out by separating himself from the fellowship of knights to pursue a secret ideal or adventure. When Troilus is smitten by Criseyde's eyes, he leaves his troop of young followers to contemplate his new destiny in the privacy of his bedchamber. Similarly, the Chaucerian dreamer is a lonely and often wistful figure seeking after some new knowledge or vision. The Canterbury pilgrims, however, have joined together in their quest. They are "sondry folk, by aventure yfalle/In felaweshipe," and Chaucer is "of hir felaweshipe anon." The *Canterbury Tales,* unlike Chaucer's earlier works, is concerned not only with individuals and their personal goals but with a community of people and the effect upon the community of individual strivings. The pilgrims, it is often said, make up a cross-section of medieval society, but they are more than that. Their fellowship is a microcosm of a Christian community; the motive of their pilgrimage, to be healed of spiritual sickness, is the end toward which any Christian society is ordered; the works of the pilgrims reveal the religious, social, and economic conditions that tend to promote or to disrupt that order. The pilgrims are members of a single body, and the health of that body is the subject of the Prologue.

We learn in the Prologue that the body is sick. Chaucer could not know that the disease was mortal and that the old feudal order was slowly dying through the civil wars, the corruption in Church and State, and the beginnings of capitalism in the waning Middle Ages, but he was able to portray the symptoms as they appeared in everyday life. Ideally, the Christian community is structured so that each man performs the task to which God has assigned him to assure the physical or spiritual welfare of the whole. That order is being gradually eroded by the desire of most of its members to promote not the common profit but their own welfare and status. The Church has been infected by the commercialism of the Commons. Both Church and Commons try to emulate the pride and ostentation of the Nobles. As a result, the society is in ferment and offers a rich field for ironic observation of the gap between ideal and reality.

Chaucer is, of course, by no means the only writer to perceive the sickness. The topos of "the world upside down" is the common cry of late medieval literature.[5] Chaucer's friend John Gower bitterly denounces the evils of his day; he is a *Vox Clamantis* (the title of his long Latin poem), one of many such. Gower's biographer, John Fisher, may well be right that Gower's influence was partly responsible for turning Chaucer's poetry in the direction of social themes.[6]

Chaucer is unique, however, because he does not denounce the vices of the age but portrays his world with irony but also with affection through the persona of the narrator. The narrator displays a *genuine* enthusiasm for the pilgrims regardless of what he perceives or fails to perceive of their shortcomings, an enthusiasm the reader may share. This is no ordinary random assortment of folk; it is the most remarkable group of individuals ever assembled because each of them is in some respect the best of his kind. The pilgrims are representative of their classes and professions, but they are far from average. They represent their type in some superlative degree. The Knight is a "verray, parfit gentil knyght," the Physician, a "verray, parfit praktisour." The Parson is the best parish priest there may be; the Friar is the best beggar in his order. From Berwick to Ware—from one end of England to the other—there wasn't another Pardoner like this one. Such phrases can be found in all of the portraits. Not only are the pilgrims all wonderful people—practically every detail about them arouses the narrator's sense of wonder. It does not matter whether it is a thing of beauty like the Squire's curls or something in itself repulsive like the Cook's "mormal" (a running sore on his shin), all details are itemized almost lyrically from the Miller's nose, to the wart at its tip, to the tuft of hairs on the wart. Everything is in its place and everything is for the best in this best of all possible worlds.

One of the excellent arrangements in this world is that everyone in it occupies a place in a social hierarchy although sometimes it is not easy to calculate the exact order of precedence. The narrator has tried to list the pilgrims in order of social rank, but at the end he apologizes to the audience for any blunders he may have committed:

> Also I prey yow to foryeve it me,
> Al have I nat set folk in hir degree
> Heere in this tale, as that they sholde stonde.
> My wit is short, ye may wel understonde.   (743–746)

As usual in Chaucer's poetry, the narrator's ingenuous confession of his inability to judge is open encouragement to the reader to use his own judgment. In the Prologue, the values by which society judges degree (values that the majority of the pilgrims would accept without question) are precisely the values that are destroying the true order, an order the reader must detect for himself.

Even the most prosaic details the narrator gives us about the pilgrims are not the plain fact they appear to be but are really value judgments, and with rare exceptions, favorable ones, colored by his enthusiasm for his travelling companions and for the world in general. We can share his delight, but his lack of discrimination invites us to discriminate and to judge the difference between a "verray, parfit gentil knyght" and a "verray, parfit praktisour." Such verbal echoes and the recurrence of certain kinds of detail—the appearance and dress of the pilgrims, the horses they ride, the objects they carry, the things they love, the ways in which they earn a living—enable us to make comparisons and to evaluate the pilgrims and everything we are told about them. The reader's task is to perceive and sort out the intricate network of relationships among the portraits. Hoffman has traced one important strand in the motivations given to the pilgrims by "the two voices." Ruth Nevo has followed out another by noting "Mammon" as another kind of motivation. She classifies the pilgrims according to the sources of their income and their attitudes about money and finds discrepancies between their social positions and their moral characters.[7]

The most comprehensive standard of judgment we may apply is that of "worth" in general, thereby borrowing Chaucer's own thematic word "worthy," which appears nine times in the portraits and occurs in the first line of the first portrait: "A Knyght ther was, and that a worthy man." As applied to the Knight (three times), the word retains special associations of valor appropriate to a soldier (as in "The Nine Worthies"), but it also connotes a more general excellence. As an honorific epithet, "worthy" is clearly becoming elastic in Chaucer's time; it is applied, with varying shades of irony, to the Friar, Merchant, Franklin, and Wife of Bath.[8] The recurrence of the word raises the question: in what sense are these pilgrims "worthy?" What is their true worth? And, further, what constitutes worth? What are the values of these people and of their society, and are they genuine values? The word is thus not only a way of describing the pilgrims: the pilgrims define the word. Chaucer's portraits are an essay in "worthinesse."

In order to bring out the judgment of the individual pilgrims and of their social order, a judgment implicit in the entire Prologue, I shall make my own arrangement of portraits, beginning with the three that define "worth" in its highest moral sense: the Knight, the Parson, and the Plowman. It is no accident that these three ideal portraits represent the traditional three estates.[9] Taken together they show what the feudal order ideally should be. What that order actually was in Chaucer's time may be shown by comparing the remaining portraits both with the ideal and with one another, taking in order first the Commons and then the Church.

The Knight and his son the Squire are the only representatives of the Nobility. To be sure, socially the Knight ranks at the bottom of his own class; his humble bearing and, indeed, his presence among this motley group of pilgrims are far removed from the pride and ostentation of the Nobility. Nevertheless, his status as a professional soldier ("Ful ofte tyme he hadde the bord bigonne") and the precedence accorded him by both the narrator and the Host are evidence of his noble condition. Far more important, however, is the fact that the Knight embodies the values that should ideally accompany noble rank, the values of chivalry summed up for us in one line: "Trouthe and honour, fredom and curteisie." The Knight's worth is summed up in the record of his campaigns, the crusades he has fought in every distant corner of the medieval world. For Chaucer and many of his contemporaries, who had at best a vague knowledge of what was going on in distant places like "Lettow," "Algezir," and "Tramyssene," the crusades could still symbolize righteous wars of good against evil. The Knight was "Ful worthy. . . . in his lordes werre," a line usually taken to refer to the King's French wars. If that is the case, Chaucer's dismissal of the wars he did know something about in a single line tells us what he thought about them. England's fortunes in the Hundred Years' War were at a low ebb, and the Black Prince's great victory over the French at Poitiers (a battle in which the Knight could have participated that is conspicuously not mentioned) was already thirty years past when Chaucer was writing the *Canterbury Tales.* The inference is that he regarded wars among Christians as unworthy of a Christian knight. Thus the Knight, whose appearance without armor or weapons and in his rust-stained battle-shirt suggests a penitent, is presented as a *miles Christi.*

The Parson and Plowman come close to the end of the list of portraits, far down on the social scale. They are followed only by the five rascals, the Miller, Manciple, Reeve, Summoner, and Pardoner. The Plowman actually occupies the lowest rung on the social ladder and may owe his position ahead of the Miller to the fact that he is with the Parson (as the Yeoman's portrait comes early because he is in the company of the Knight). Since the Parson and Plowman are brothers, the Parson must come from peasant stock and yields place to the Wife of Bath. The first thing we learn about the Parson is that he is poor, "But riche he was of hooly thoght and werk." Here is the basic opposition of the two ways, material and spiritual, in which a man may be worthy. In the latter way the Parson is the worthiest of all and sets the highest standard for all of the pilgrims. He is also "a lerned man, a clerk," and he regards teaching as one of a priest's primary duties. He teaches both by word and by the most effective method of all, by example, for he is himself a model of Christian charity:

> This noble ensample to his sheep he yaf,
> That first he wroghte, and afterward he taughte.
> Out of the gospel he tho wordes caughte,
> And this figure he added eek therto,
> That if gold ruste, what shal iren do?
> For if a preest be foul, on whom we truste,
> No wonder is a lewed man to ruste;
> And shame it is, if a prest take keep,
> A shiten shepherde and a clene sheep.   (496–504)

The imagery of the shepherd and sheep is also taken from the Gospels, and as the Knight is the type of Christ the warrior against the Devil, the Parson is the type of Christ the Good Shepherd, keeping his sheep from the wolf.

The Plowman, in his way, too, practices the golden rule by giving what he has to give, his work and sweat:

> He wolde thresshe, and therto dyke and delve,
> For Cristes sake, for every povre wight,
> Withouten hire, if it lay in his myght.   (536–538)

The brief portrait stresses the idea of work. The Plowman is "A trewe swynkere and a good," and he pays his tithes "Bothe of his propre swynk and his catel." Like Piers the Plowman, in the poem by Chaucer's great contemporary, the Plowman is yet another type of Christ, the type appropriate to the common working man, and sets a standard of worth by which the other commoners on the pilgrimage may be measured.

Hoffman points out that the kinship between the Parson and Plowman, the fact that they are brothers, is symbolic of the brotherhood that should unite all men,[10] but that kinship may be interpreted in an even deeper symbolic sense. There is a complementary relationship between the professions they practice. The Plowman scatters his seed so that the bodies of men may be nourished by bread. The Parson scatters the seeds of doctrine so that the souls of men may receive spiritual nourishment. The symbolism is derived from the Parable of the Seeds (Mat.xiii, 24–30). Both the Parson and the Plowman are essential to the preservation of life—one to life in this world, the other both to life in this world and in the world to come. Thus they represent two of the basic kinds of work in feudal society performed by two of the estates, Church and Commons. The third kind of work, and the other estate, is represented by the Knight. His work is to ensure that the work of the Parson and Plowman may proceed in peace, to keep order and establish justice in the kingdom of earth.

Thus the three ideal portraits express the ideal of the whole society. But even the ideal portraits make it evident that the society has fallen on evil days. It is evident that the Knight, Parson, and Plowman are the exception and not the rule. The praise of the Parson is also an attack on the common abuses of other priests. We are told what the Parson did *not* do. He did *not* excommunicate those too poor to pay their tithes, he did *not* hire out his parish to a vicar in order to find a more lucrative living in London singing masses for the departed souls of wealthy burghers, he was *not* haughty and contemptuous toward sinners. The portrait tells us that in fact the gold was for the most part rusted, the shepherds were shiten, and the wolf was ravening in the fold.

The Plowman, living in peace and perfect charity, is a tacit reproach to the unruly peasantry of the late fourteenth century. It is a portrait of what Chaucer and his audience thought a plowman should be, and they could not help but contrast it with the mob that had burned, looted, and killed during the Peasants' Rebellion of 1381.

As for the Knight, he is already more a figure of the romantic past than one actively engaged in the affairs of the present day. That is why his chivalry can be demonstrated only by campaigns

fought in remote parts of the world. Even before the use of gun-
powder, the longbow had already made the knight almost as obso-
lete in late fourteenth-century warfare as a battleship in the late
twentieth. The great victories at Crécy, Poitiers, and Agincourt
were won more by the English bowmen than by the knights. The
nobility was fast becoming a ruling class without a useful function.
Chaucer's Knight must ride out on crusades, the way the knights
of romance ride out on adventures, because there is nothing left for
him to do at home except to engage in plunder and internecine
territorial wars among the great feudal overlords.

Nevertheless, the *ideal* represented by the Knight, the Parson,
and the Plowman was still potent in Chaucer's time, and whether
it ever existed in fact, it remains potent even today as a moral
standard. That is how we must regard it in the Prologue. As a civil
servant, courtier, and the brother-in-law of John of Gaunt, Chaucer
himself belongs very much to an emerging new order that we see
in the portraits of the other pilgrims. But he still loves and believes
in the ideal order, and it provides him with a timeless standard
against which to set the present.

The Merchant's portrait heads the order of the Commons and
shows in its most obvious form the commercialism of the bourgeois
class, whether they trade in law and land like the Sergeant of the
Law, in marriages like the Wife of Bath, or in grain like the Miller.
If the Knight typifies the old order, the Merchant typifies the new.
The image of him "hye on horse," expensively dressed from his
Flemish beaver hat to his well-clasped boots, lends him a command-
ing and aristocratic air. But everything about the Merchant, his
costume and his demeanor, are a front meant to inspire confidence
in his honesty and his solvency. He utters his opinions "ful sol-
empnely,/Sownynge alwey th'encrees of his wynnyng." We are
not really surprised when we are told:

> This worthy man ful wel his wit bisette
> Ther wiste no wight that he was in dette.   (279–280)

Is Chaucer here coming in as omniscient narrator to give away the
secret, or is it perfectly obvious to everybody, though literally
known to none, that the Merchant has overextended his margin and
is present on the pilgrimage to gain time from his creditors? The

ironic use of "worthy" in these lines and in the final couplet shows
how the word itself and the Knight's ideal of worthiness have been
debased in the figure of this worthy whose name the narrator does
not know:

> For sothe he was a worthy man with alle,
> But, sooth to seyn, I noot how men hym calle.
>
> (283–284)

The Sergeant of the Law and the Franklin, travelling together,
are both prominent and wealthy members of the middle class.
Chaucer tells us how the Sergeant uses his expert knowledge of the
law to become rich through buying up land but says nothing about
what he has done to promote the cause of justice. Like the Merchant, the Sergeant of the Law cultivates a dignified appearance,
and here, too, it is implied, though with greater subtlety, that the
appearance is not necessarily the reality:

> Discreet he was and of greet reverence—
> He *semed* swich, his wordes weren so wise.
>
> (312–313, my italics)

"Wise" like "worthy" is a thematic word in the Prologue, and we
may recall about the Knight that "though that he were worthy, he
was wys." The Sergeant of the Law is "war and wys." In each case
"wys" is qualified by the word with which it alliterates. The Lawyer's is a wary and superficial wisdom, useful in getting the upper
hand in legal disputes and business matters, not the wisdom that
indicates depth of knowledge or character. It is his *words* that are
wise, and he can manipulate them as he can the cases and the
statutes of the land, which he knows by rote memory, to create an
appearance of official zealousness:

> Nowher so bisy a man as he ther nas,
> And yet he *semed* bisier than he was.   (321–322)

His companion the Franklin is much more attractive. The portrait emphasizes his cheerfulness, his high style of living, and above
all his warmhearted hospitality. Here one might think is a medieval
Squire Allworthy. In fact, everything about the Franklin already
suggests the life and opinions of an eighteenth-century country

squire. There is even a hint of what would become rationalism in the Franklin's holding with the Greek philosopher Epicurus that "pleyn delit/Was verray felicitee parfit." No matter that this is a total distortion of Epicurean philosophy, it is an attempt to rationalize private life on one's own country estate—cultivating one's own garden—as the perfection of the human condition. The portrait of the Franklin is evidence that, while commerce and industry may uproot the social and political power-structure of England, the landed gentry continue in their ideas and ways as though immune to change. But in the Middle Ages the Franklin is still a new man, and again we require the standards of the Knight and the Parson to test his worth. The Franklin's is measured by the quality of his bread and ale and the quantity of fish and flesh consumed at his board. He is generous with his possessions, and his table is always set to receive guests. As in the Land of Cockayne, where fat partridges fly into the mouths of the carefree inhabitants, "It snewed in his hous of mete and drynke." Yet all the conspicuous consumption points to an aristocratic standard of living divorced from an aristocratic way of life. The portrait conveys a sense of softness and ease that is caught again in the one detail we are given about the Franklin's costume:

> An anlaas and a gipser al of silk
> Heeng at his girdel, whit as morne milk.   (357–358)

The Franklin thus affects an aristocratic appearance, but his dagger and milk-white purse will never be rust-stained like the Knight's gipon. They are for ornament rather than for use, symbols of rank that no longer serve their old function.[11] In fairness to the Franklin, it must be said that he has held a number of offices. He has been a knight of the shire (i.e., a member of Parliament), justice of the peace, sheriff, and county auditor. But the very language, "At sessiouns ther was he *lord and sire;*/Ful ofte tyme he was *knyght* of the shire," shows how the terms of the old feudal order have been borrowed to dignify new institutions. The Franklin is a man of charm and public spirit, but there is more than a trace of irony in the final line of the portrait: "Was nowher swich a worthy vavasour."

If the Franklin anticipates the British squirearchy, the five

Gildsmen look forward to the London tradesmen in the novels of Dickens. Their knives are mounted with silver not brass and like the Franklin's anelace are primarily for show. It is in their collective portrait—for they look so much alike in their fraternal livery that Chaucer does not individualize them except by professions—that we first hear of an important new influence that will help shape the future of the new order. The Gildsmen's wives take an interest in their husbands' careers for excellent reasons:

> It is ful fair to been ycleped "madame,"
> And goon to vigilies al bifore,
> And have a mantel roialliche ybore.   (376–378)

The gild-official's wife is addressed as a lady and walks at the head of the holiday procession, her train carried like a queen's by her husband's apprentices. Thus the tradesmen's fraternities emulate the chivalric orders flourishing at the same time, and in the gild-ceremonies, the women join their husbands in aping the manners of the aristocracy.

The Gildsmen have left their wives behind, but woman's "estate" is represented on the pilgrimage by the Wife of Bath. Besides the two nuns, she is the only woman in the group, but she feels at home in the company of men: "In felaweshipe wel koude she laughe and carpe." She, too, practices a trade; she is said to be an expert clothmaker. But her true profession is the art of love, and we learn how expertly she turns it to her profit. "She was a worthy womman al hir lyve," and her worth is measured by her five husbands.

The Wife of Bath is defying the old order in a more subtle way than any we have encountered among the other burgesses. The feudal society whose values are represented at their best by the Knight, the Parson, and the Plowman, is a man's world, and this is one of its great limitations. Women have no place in it except to keep house, to bear children, and to bring dowries to their husbands. The only other avenue open to a talented and intelligent woman is to enter the convent, which, as we shall see in the case of the Prioress, is no escape. The Wife of Bath, simply by her unescorted presence on the pilgrimage, is challenging male supremacy. She wants what most of the other pilgrims want—money, status, and pleasure—but her case is special because she is a woman. Her feminism is far more revolutionary than the Merchant's commercialism. The Merchant wants to climb in the hierarchy by making money. The Wife of Bath wants money and position, too, but she also wants freedom, and in rejecting the place assigned to her as a woman, she is attacking the very basis of the feudal order: the inequality that is believed to be the inheritance of all men at birth. Even though their hidden motives may be closer to the Merchant's, the bourgeois revolutions were to be fought on the principle that all men are created equal. I am not suggesting that Chaucer was aware of any potential political significance in the character of the Wife of Bath. What he does instinctively recognize and sympathize with, though he satirizes it too, is the Wife's refusal to accept a natural inferiority attributed to her by men less vital and less intelligent than she, a resentment that a vintner's son who had made his way as a courtier was surely in a position to understand. I shall return to these considerations in connection with the Wife of Bath's Prologue and Tale.

The Miller, Reeve, and Manciple, the last of the Commons, all belong to the servant class (the Miller, independent though he may be, is nevertheless, like the Cook, regarded as a menial by those who employ him). All three are also consummate rascals, but their dishonesty is no more than a crasser version of the sharp practices of some of the more socially prominent pilgrims, perhaps more amusing because it involves less hypocrisy, and they prey upon men who are richer and more powerful than they. Thus the narrator delights in the irony that the Manciple should steal with impunity from the shrewd lawyers who employ him:

> Now is nat that of God a ful fair grace
> That swich a lewed mannes wit shal pace
> The wisdom of an heep of lerned men?   (573-575)

It is indeed remarkable how universally the same vices are distributed. Lerned and lewed, masters and servants, city and country, all classes and professions provide examples of such wit, and the best of all may be found in the Church.

The medieval Church is a world caught between two worlds, mediating between the kingdoms of heaven and earth. The Church is opposed to the vanities of earth, yet to carry out its mission it must dwell in the earthly kingdom and adopt its ways. One approach to the ecclesiastics among the pilgrims is to see in them various degrees of compromise between worldly and spiritual values. The Parson stands alone as the one man who has made no compromise at all. He represents the ideal of the New Testament in its pristine form. In all the others we detect the encroachment of two corrupting influences—the class consciousness of the feudal nobility and the grasping materialism of the bourgeois classes.

To understand the Prioress, one must first understand how the convent she governs already represents a compromise. The idea of an order of nuns is to permit women to retire from the world to follow a spiritual vocation. But the convent also lent itself to the practical needs of the feudal nobility. The law of primogeniture produced not only a large number of landless younger sons but an excess of unmarried daughters, for a nobleman must marry for land and property. When a girl did not find a worldly husband, the logical alternative was to espouse the heavenly bridegroom. Besides draining off unmarriageable daughters, the convent also functioned, as it often still does today, as a finishing school. While Madame Eglentyne's house may not have operated formally as a school, it undoubtedly provided the younger sisters with all the elements of an upper-class education. The irony is all the greater inasmuch as the nuns did not have a chance to practice the social graces beyond the walls of the convent unless, like the Prioress, they went on a pilgrimage.

Madame Eglentyne obviously comes from an excellent family, and this is undoubtedly an important reason why she was elected Prioress. The other reasons are that she is a very kind and gracious woman and does all the right things beautifully. She sings the holy office "ful weel." She speaks her convent French "ful faire and fetisly." The portrait abounds in words like "ful," "weel," "semely," "fetisly." Her style is summed up in the description of her impeccable table manners. In everything she does, she is at pains to imitate the manners of the court and to set a good example for the sisters. Her "conscience and tendre herte" is evidenced in the tears she sheds for a dead mouse or, worse, the death or suffering of one of her little lap dogs. Keeping pets was against the rules of the order, but such a petty breach of discipline hardly requires a dispensation! It might be observed that the dogs, which the Prioress fed "With rosted flessh, or milk and wastel-breed," probably fared better than the Plowman. But the irony is not that the Prioress lacks human feeling—she would be appalled if she knew that people were hungry—but that, for all her social pretensions, she has no contact with the world of the Parson and Plowman. She does not know real human misery, and in *this* sense she does live completely out of the world.

The motto of her gold brooch—"Amor vincit omnia"—evokes an old Chaucerian theme. Nature, it would appear from a series of delicate romantic touches, has created the Prioress for "love of kynde," but society has obliged her (of course with her full consent) to dedicate herself to "love celestial." Which love is meant by the motto? Professor Lowes, who raises the question, also supplies the perfect answer: "I think she thought she meant love celestial."[12] Her refinements seem so spontaneous, her tenderness so natural, and her infractions of discipline so trifling that they affect us like the innocence of a child, and, in fact, there is something childish about this largish woman who delights in so many little things. The Prioress can hardly be called corrupt, but she *is* shallow. She is more concerned about the proper way of singing the divine service than about the meaning of the liturgy. The "curteisie" on which she places such great value is the outward form and lacks the substance of the Knight's "trouthe and honour, fredom and curteisie." Poor Madame Eglentyne has not made the best of either of the two worlds that she holds in delicate balance.

If the Prioress is characterized primarily as a lady instead of as a nun, the Monk is described as a lord. His aristocratic tastes are shown in his love of horses and hunting. Hunting is a more flagrant breach of rules than any of which the Prioress is guilty. She leaves her convent to make one pilgrimage; the Monk is practically never in the cloister. She keeps lap dogs; he has "Grehoundes . . . as swift as fowel in flight." Her gold brooch is almost a religious object like the rosary from which it is suspended. The Monk's hood is fastened with a gold pin, significantly in the form of a love-knot. The Prioress's brooch merely raises the shadow of a doubt about the depth of her religious commitments. The love-knot suggests a more drastic breaking of vows, hinted at also in possible double-entendres in the references to the Monk's passion for hunting: "venerie" (166), "prikasour" (189), "prikyng" (191).[13] Where the Prioress may be guilty of a few petty infractions of discipline, the Monk directly criticizes the rules of his order as antiquated. He is a progressive monk, dedicated to "the newe world" of the fourteenth century. The Church must undergo an "aggiornaménto" to keep up with the times:

> This ilke Monk leet olde thynges pace,
> And heeld after the newe world the space. . . .
> What sholde he studie and make hymselven wood,
> Upon a book in cloystre alwey to poure,
> Or swynken with his handes, and laboure,
> As Austyn bit? How shal the world be served?
> (175–176, 184–187)

In the last line he unthinkingly rejects the very basis of the monastic ideal, which was to withdraw from the world, and his idea of serving the world is to go hunting! "Therfore he was a prikasour aright." Nevertheless, one can like the Monk because he is such a sturdy and virile fellow and so completely unconscious of the irony in what he is saying. If we can sympathize with the Prioress's warm heart, we can respond to the Monk's hot blood:

> He was a lord ful fat and in good poynt;
> His eyen stepe, and rollynge in his heed,
> That stemed as a forneys of a leed. (200–202)

When we turn from the Monk's eyes to the Friar's, we encounter a chillier look though the impression may be deceptive:

> His eyen twynkled in his heed aryght,
> As doon the sterres in the frosty nyght. (267–268)

Like everything else about the Friar, his eyes are merry and superficially attractive, but they are as cold as the frosty night. The Friar lacks every trace of the warmth and humanity that partially redeem the Prioress and the Monk. In the portrait of the "worthy lymytour," we have already approached the portrait of the worthy

Merchant, which follows next in order. The Friar is himself pro-foundly bourgeois and consorts with franklins, "with worthy wom-men of the toun," and "al with riche and selleres of vitaille." It is from such people that he milks contributions, but he also regards them as his proper associates:

> For unto swich a worthy man as he
> Acorded nat, as by his facultee,
> To have with sike lazars aqueyntaunce.
> It is nat honest, it may nat avaunce,
> For to deelen with no swich poraille.   (243–247)

Here is a more flagrant rejection of the ideal than the Monk's in-genuous "How shal the world be served?" It was to help such "trash," as the Friar calls them, that Francis created his order. The Friar's viciousness masquerades as virtue. He shows his generosity in providing dowries for the young women he has cast off. It is a tribute to the sweetness of his manner that "thogh a wydwe hadde noght a sho, . . . Yet wolde he have a ferthyng, er he wente." There may be an allusion to the poor widow (Mark xii,42) whose mite is worth more than all the rest because it is her all; perhaps she also gave her penny to the Pharisees. The Friar plays an in-strument and is celebrated as a singer of ballads. The epithets for him are "merye," "sweete," and "plesaunt":

> Ful swetely herde he confessioun,
> And plesaunt was his absolucioun.   (221–222)

The most damaging accusation that can be brought against the Friar is that he uses the sacrament as a sales device. As he himself says, he is licensed to hear confession, so that it is no longer neces-sary to go to church to be confessed by a priest. The Friar will bring confession "right into your own home." He carries trinkets—little knives and pins—that he passes out to housewives like a travelling salesman with "a personal gift for you." He assigns an easy penance to anyone from whom he expects a fat tip. The mod-ern reader should not misunderstand the possible consequences of such practices. By encouraging false or imperfect confessions, the Friar is helping to send some of his clients to Hell. The merry air, the pleasant greeting pronounced with an elegant lisp, the smile at the door of this solicitor can bring death to the soul.

The Summoner and Pardoner are the last of the several pairs and groups among the pilgrims. They symbolize, respectively, the sickness and impotence that have infected the medieval Church and, indeed, the whole society. Hoffman points out how their sterile relationship complements the fruitful brotherhood of the Parson and Plowman. The Summoner, who calls sinners before the ecclesiastical court, is perverting God's justice; the Pardoner, who sells fake absolution, is perverting God's infinite mercy. That is to say that between them they are preying upon the basic motives that have brought the pilgrims together and unite all men in the Christian community: the fear of God's punishment and the hope of His forgiveness. As Hoffman says, "the Summoner and Pardoner . . . suggest the summoning and pardoning, the judgment and grace which in Christian thought embrace and conclude man's pilgrimage."[14]

The Summoner's ghastly skin disease is the outward sign of his inner sickness. His "fyr-reed cherubynnes face" ironically resembles the cheeks of an angel in one of the painted statues in medieval churches, but the Summoner is a fallen angel, and in fact resembles the devils in scenes of the Last Judgment. The Pardoner's appearance is also symbolic of his inward state. The high-pitched voice, the fact that he has no beard "ne nevere sholde have," all details about his appearance confirm the narrator's observation: "I trowe he were a geldyng or a mare." The Pardoner is a eunuch, and his impotence matches the impotence of the pardons he sells. His pardons can no more give eternal life than he is capable of giving physical life even if they were to bear the Pope's seal. His fraudulent relics are a further symptom of the decadence of the medieval church. There is something necrophilic about the fascination exercised during the late Middle Ages by the skulls, bones, hair, blood, and teeth of the martyrs. Like many of the objects described in the Prologue, relics were used as symbols of status. The wealth of the great medieval shrines depended upon the fame of their relics, and little parish churches "at every shires ende" might seek to emulate great ones like Canterbury by purchasing "relics" from men like the Pardoner. Like the pardons, these relics are symbolic of the Pardoner himself. He and his stock appropriately bring to an end the catalogue of pilgrims because they express in its most outrageous form the discrepancy between ideal and reality, the sham and the false pretensions that can be observed in so many different forms in nearly all of the portraits except for those of the Knight, Parson, and Plowman.

The Pardoner is a confidence man like the sinister figure in Herman Melville's last and darkest novel who appears in so many different disguises that he appears to have no fixed identity and ultimately comes to symbolize loss of identity in a society where all are in disguise and everyone is a confidence man. But Chaucer's pilgrims, even the most depraved among them, retain their identities and their worth. The overall impression of the Prologue is not one of sickness and evil but of humanity. The narrator's undiscriminating enthusiasm for the pilgrims is the basis of irony, but it is also the basis of a warmth and sympathy that is denied to none of the pilgrims, not even the Summoner and the Pardoner. In the last analysis they are all worthy men and good fellows.

The Summoner

> was a gentil harlot and a kynde;
> A bettre felawe sholde men noght fynde.
> He wolde suffre for a quart of wyn
> A good felawe to have his concubyn
> A twelf month, and excuse hym atte fulle.   (647–651)

The irony in these lines is transparent, but they also show that the Summoner is pathetically human. He is a repulsive man from whom children turn in fear, and he needs companionship. The price for keeping one's wench a year is not just the price of a quart of wine—it means sharing the wine with the Summoner and being his table companion and good fellow. It means recognizing his humanity as we, too, are forced to recognize it. The idea of fellowship has brought the pilgrims together. They need one another, and within their corporate identity the best and the worst of them find their individual identities. For all its decadence, the society is still a cohesive one, and their holiday is a joint celebration. The Summoner exemplifies the festive spirit:

A gerland hadde he set upon his heed
As greet as it were for an ale-stake.   (666–667)

The Pardoner is the most isolated of all the pilgrims, but even he is something of a "good felawe." The beginning and end of his portrait picture him singing. He sings the anthem before his sermon "the murierly and loude" in order "To wynne silver," but the corrupt motive cannot cancel out the joyousness of the song. Nor can his unsavory relationship with the Summoner spoil the effect of his opening song, " 'Com hider, love, to me.' " Arthur Hoffman has beautifully captured the sense in which the simple words of the popular melody express the profoundest meaning of the Prologue:

> The Summoner cannot finally pervert, and the Pardoner's impotence cannot finally prevent; the divine justice and love are powerful even over these debased instruments— *Amor vincit omnia.* Beyond their knowing, beyond their power or impotence, impotently both Pardoner and Summoner appeal for the natural love—melody of birdsong and meadows of flowers—and both pray for the celestial love, the ultimate pardon which in their desperate and imprisoned darkness is their only hope: 'Com hider, love, to me!'[15]

Hoffman here touches upon the essentially Christian character of Chaucer's art, which balances judgment of sin with love for the sinner. However, the complexity of such a response may be beyond the capacity of most readers, and, indeed, to respond consistently in such a balanced way may be beyond human capacity and possible only to God. One can grasp the need for such a response intellectually and feel it in Hoffman's criticism, but in the actual experience of *reading* the Prologue, readers will tend, I believe, either to judge the pilgrims or to love them wholeheartedly. They can be looked upon as types of virtues and vices, as they are treated in the works of some critics, or, more commonly I think, they are regarded simply as characters in a work of fiction whose virtues and vices are immaterial because what matters to us is their existence. For a medieval audience, conditioned to the kind of unequivocally moral poetry written by a lesser poet like Gower or even a great one like Langland, poetry that minces no words in denouncing evil, it would have been even more difficult than for us to attain the complexity of Chaucer's vision. Chaucer's Prologue, therefore, is liable to the charge that, by medieval standards, it is not moral enough because it fails to make judgment explicit. By modern standards, that is its greatness as a work of art. Great fiction has the power of making the reader suspend moral judgment along with the sense of disbelief. He becomes absorbed in the imaginary characters *for their own sake* and not for the sake of some truth or moral that can be learned from them.

Moreover, as I have maintained for *Troilus,* the author himself may become absorbed in the world and the characters he has created until he is no longer able to reclaim convincingly the moral purpose for which he created them. They have taken on a life of their own. The same thing happens to Chaucer in the *Canterbury Tales* except that this time he gives way to his fictional world and allows it to take its own course. He has drawn the portrait of a whole society and composed his essay on worthiness, but in doing so he creates a world that becomes autonomous. In the conclusion of the Prologue, Chaucer steps back and allows the pilgrimage to proceed without any guiding moral purpose and, for the most part, without the controlling voice of the narrator.

When the portraits are finished, the narrator apologizes to his audience for any errors he may have made in ranking the pilgrims and for the vulgar character of some of the pilgrims and the low words they used in their tales. The apologetic narrator whose wit is short is a familiar figure from *Troilus* and the dream visions, but this is a different kind of apology. Before, Chaucer has always professed his own lack of experience and skill that prevent him from doing justice to his subject. This time the subject itself is the cause of embarrassment. There is no skill involved at all. Chaucer is merely truthfully repeating all that he has seen and heard and thereby asking the audience to participate in the fiction that this is a real pilgrimage and that these characters really exist. His only excuse for telling the story is that it is a true one. Though this may seem like the most ancient of narrative ploys, its originality in Chaucer's time should not be underestimated. It amounts to a departure from the medieval belief, to which lip-service is paid in the crudest of fabliaux, that a story is worth telling only if it has a lesson. The only comparable instance in the Middle Ages where a series of stories is justified simply by the fact that someone told them is Boccaccio's *Decameron*. About the frame story of the *Decameron*, Professor Singleton has written:

> The framework of the *Decameron* is the effort to justify and protect a new art, an art which simply in order to be, to exist, required the moment free of all other cares, the willingness to stop *going anywhere* (either toward God or toward philosophical truth).[16]

The same words could apply just as well to the new art of the *Canterbury Tales*. Through the invention of the frame story, Chaucer is able to escape his moral obligations as a poet. He succeeds in detaching himself from his fiction more completely than he ever has before. The narrator intervenes once more in the Prologue to the Miller's Tale and returns to tell his own tales of Sir Thopas and Melibee. Except for these instances, we are not aware of his voice again before the Retraction. The pilgrims take over, and the narrator simply merges with the group. Chaucer thus escapes both from his persona and from his court audience. In their place, we have a series of fictional narrators and a fictional audience, the pilgrims themselves reacting to one another's tales. It is no longer an aristocratic audience but one made up of people from all walks of life, and the tales they tell are no longer limited to aristocratic genres like the romance or dream vision but include every kind of story. In short, what Chaucer has done is to give himself license to write exactly as he pleased.

And so Chaucer the pilgrim turns the stage over to his surrogate, the Host, who will, hereafter, play the part of "governour" and "juge." An innkeeper is not unlike a writer of fiction. He, too, must know how to deal with all kinds, to know the way men think and talk, and also to like them, because a good host should love his guests the way a good writer loves his characters. Both are professional entertainers. The Host has all the imposing presence, good humor, and appealing dishonesty found in the portraits of the other middle class pilgrims:

A fairer burgeys is ther noon in Chepe—
Boold of his speche, and wys, and wel ytaught,
And of manhod hym lakkede right naught.
Eek therto he was right a myrie man.   (754–757)

"Merry," "mirth," "play," "disport" are the key words at the close
of the Prologue, and it is the Host who uses them in making his
sales-pitch to the pilgrims. His motives are transparent. He would
like to get this crowd of well-paying customers back for another
night on their return from Canterbury. But he is not doing it just
for the money. Good business can also be good fun, and the Host
himself loves a good story. His own criteria for the tale that will
win the prize are a compact statement of the medieval aesthetic:

> This is the poynt, to speken short and pleyn,
> That ech of yow, to shorte with oure weye,
> In this viage shal telle tales tweye
> To Caunterbury-ward, I mene it so,
> And homward he shal tellen othere two,
> Of aventures that whilom han bifalle.
> And which of yow that bereth hym best of alle,
> That is to seyn, that telleth in this caas
> Tales of best sentence and moost solaas,
> Shal have a soper at oure aller cost.   (790–799)

"Sentence," instruction, and "solaas," entertainment, are the crucial terms. Harry Bailly's idea of art like all his ideas is conventional. Ideally the best art should both instruct *and* entertain, but as
we shall see, in practice one or the other of these goals tends to
predominate. The Host's terms will be useful to us in discussing
the tales. It should be pointed out, however, that, although no man
is more sententious than the Host, his entire manner as well as his
words tell us that the primary motive behind the storytelling will
be "solaas." The true purpose of fiction is "to shorte with oure
weye,/In this viage," whether it be the journey to Canterbury or,
in a larger sense, "il camin di nostra vita." Inadvertently the Host
has described the purpose of Chaucer's new art.

CHAPTER V

The Order of
Chivalry

tHE KNIGHT'S TALE is one of a few earlier works that Chaucer incorporated into the *Canterbury Tales*[1] It is undoubtedly the poem Alceste in the Prologue to the *Legend of Good Women* describes as

> al the love of Palamon and Arcite
> Of Thebes, thogh the storye ys knowen lyte.
> (F 420–421)

There is no evidence to support an old theory that Chaucer extensively revised the tale in order to adapt it to its new setting.[2] On the contrary, the one obvious change is such a crude bit of patchwork as to indicate that Chaucer went to no great pains to fit the tale into its dramatic context. Near the beginning the narrator says that it would take too long to tell of Theseus's battles with the Amazons and of his wedding with Ypolita:

> I have, God woot, a large feeld to ere,
> And wayke been the oxen in my plough.   (886–887)

This is the rhetorical device called *occupatio*, common enough in romances, by which the storyteller calls attention to parts of the tale he is omitting; the homely metaphor of the large field of matter to be plowed by the feeble oxen of the poet's genius is just the sort of disingenuous apology we would expect from the narrator of *Troilus*.[3] Then come four lines that have clearly been added:

> I wol nat letten eek noon of this route;
> Lat every felawe telle his tale aboute,
> And lat se now who shal the soper wynne;
> And ther I lefte, I wol ayeyn bigynne.   (889–892)

That is the extent to which Chaucer considered it necessary to disguise the fact that the Knight's Tale is an older work that is quite implausibly long for the road to Canterbury. The mention of the prize supper, the only such reference in any of the tales or links, probably means that the passage was hastily written not long after the Prologue and that Chaucer was anxious to get on with new material, and content to let the old stand as it was.

Of course nobody minds, and the tale is admirably suited to the Knight. However, the fact that the tale existed before the Knight should make some difference in the way we interpret it. Criticism that treats the tale as a dramatic development of the Knight's character conveniently ignores this fact. The tale was not made for the Knight, but the Knight for the tale.

The distinction is important because it enables us to look at early works like the *Palamon and Arcite* or the Life of St. Cecilia, which became the Second Nun's Tale, from two perspectives, first as independent works and second as parts of a greater whole. For although the text remains essentially the same, the act of assigning it to one of the pilgrims and associating it with other tales puts it in a new light. We learn something about Chaucer's development as an artist because the placing of the old tale allows Chaucer tacitly to make a new estimate of his former achievement. The poet of the Miller's Tale is no longer the same poet who wrote the *Palamon and Arcite*. By pairing them within the framework of the *Canterbury Tales,* Chaucer can let the old and the new comment upon and qualify one another. Assigning the *Palamon and Arcite* to the Knight and following it with the Miller's Tale is a more creative act than any revision could have been.

To look at the Knight's Tale from these two viewpoints will also give us our first indication of the potential effect of the frame upon all the individual stories that it contains, a potential that Chaucer discovered gradually and learned to exploit fully during the thirteen years that he worked on his masterpiece. What T. S. Eliot says of the poetic tradition applies just as well to the works of any single poet or to a single long work like the *Canterbury Tales:*

> . . . what happens when a new work of art is created is something that happens simultaneously to all the works of art which preceded it. The existing monuments form an ideal order among themselves, which is modified by the introduction of the new work of art among them. The existing order is complete before the new work arrives; for order to persist after the supervention of novelty, the *whole* existing order must be, if ever so slightly, altered; and so the relations, proportions, values of each work of art toward the whole are readjusted.[4]

I am not arguing that the *meaning* of the tale changes when Chaucer assigns it to the Knight; on the contrary, the interesting fact is that the meaning remains constant but acquires new significance in the new context. E. D. Hirsch draws the important distinction between meaning and significance:

> *Meaning* is that which is represented by a text; it is what the author meant by his use of a particular sign sequence; it is what the signs represent. *Significance,* on the other hand, names a relationship between that meaning and a person, or a conception, or a situation, or indeed anything imaginable. Authors, who like everyone else change their attitudes, feelings, opinions, and value criteria in the course of time, will obviously in the course of time tend to view their own work in different contexts. Clearly what changes for them is not the meaning of the work, but rather their relationship to that meaning.[5]

With this clarification we may adopt Eliot's statement as one of the aesthetic principles underlying the *Canterbury Tales.* None has its "complete meaning alone." The arrival of the Miller's Tale forces us to readjust the relations, proportions, and values of the Knight's Tale to the whole; the introduction of the Reeve's Tale again brings about a new order, and so it goes, whether spontaneously or by the author's design.

If we ask ourselves what place the *Palamon and Arcite* held in the old order before the supervention of the *Canterbury Tales*, the work to which it bears the most meaningful relationship is *Troilus and Criseyde*. Both are based on works by Boccaccio. Both are chivalric romances set in pagan times under the dispensation of the pagan gods. The destruction of Thebes is part of the "romaunce" that is being read to Criseyde and her friends when Pandarus first comes to call. The two works are concerned with the problems of fortune and destiny; astrology plays a significant part in both; both depend heavily on Boethius for their philosophical coloring. In sum, *Troilus and Criseyde* and *Palamon and Arcite* have similar subject matter and similar themes. Both attempt to interpret the human condition by seeing love and change as principles of a cosmic order.

Yet the style of the two poems is radically different. Although the *Troilus* is half again as long as the *Filostrato* and the Knight's Tale less than a quarter of the length of the *Teseida*, it is the latter that seems to move far more slowly. The *Troilus* is constructed as a series of highly dramatic scenes, and the reader becomes deeply involved with the characters. Thus not only Troilus and the narrator, but also the reader, may fall in love with Criseyde. No reader is likely to fall in love with Emelye because Chaucer has deliberately refrained from bringing her fully to life. She is never, unlike Criseyde, permitted to become more than the type of the ideal courtly heroine. That Palamon should mistake her for Venus is entirely understandable.

Chaucer, however, pays a price for the believable characters that make *Troilus* so appealing to the modern reader. The ideal of cosmic order, a universe bound by love, is overwhelmed by the confusing human reality. The pain and desolation that we share with Troilus is not redeemed by the Christian ending. We cannot really follow the hero to the stars and attain his celestial perspective. All that is permanent in the world is the process of change itself. Stability lies beyond our world in the eighth sphere and with God who sits in heaven above. Chaucer has tried to raise us to that

level, but as I have said before, for most readers I do not think
he succeeds.

The contrasting style of the Knight's Tale can, I think, be
explained as Chaucer's attempt to hold the troubling sense of
humanity in abeyance. The characters are kept at a distance so that
we continue to view them as types of the qualities they represent.
Palamon, Arcite, and Emelye are the human counterparts of
Venus, Mars, and Diana, who in turn represent Love, War, and
Chastity. The conflicts among the characters figure forth warring
forces, and the resolution of the plot is an instance of the universal harmony reconciling discordant elements. The lines of action are mathematically plotted, and the figures go through their
motions like dancers in a classical ballet. The patterns are richly
embodied and elaborated in a wealth of descriptive and sensuous
detail so that the poem has been aptly compared to a tapestry. But
the intricacy of detail is never allowed to obscure the figure in the
carpet.

Two passages will illustrate the complementary relationship
between *Troilus* and the Knight's Tale. Each presents the pageant
of a noble knight riding in a procession—in the one case, Troilus
returning from battle beneath Criseyde's window, in the other,
King Emetrius making his entry into Athens. The two passages
are linked by several verbal similarities. Both Troilus and Emetrius
ride a bay horse and are compared to Mars "the god of armes" and
"of bataille." Troilus is "Al armed, save his hed, ful richely."
The hundred knights attending Emetrius are "Al armed, save hir
heddes, in al hir gere,/Ful richely." But here is the first passage
in its entirety:

> This Troilus sat on his baye steede,
> Al armed, save his hed, ful richely;
> And wownded was his hors, and gan to blede,
> On which he rood a pas ful softely.
> But swich a knyghtly sighte, trewely,
> As was on hym, was nought, withouten faille,
> To loke on Mars, that god is of bataille.
>
> So lik a man of armes and a knyght
> He was to seen, fulfilled of heigh prowesse;

> For bothe he hadde a body and a myght
> To don that thing, as wel as hardynesse;
> And ek to seen hym in his gere hym dresse,
> So fressh, so yong, so weldy semed he,
> It was an heven upon hym for to see.
>
> His helm tohewen was in twenty places,
> That by a tyssew heng his bak byhynde;
> His sheeld todasshed was with swerdes and maces,
> In which men myght many an arwe fynde
> That thirled hadde horn and nerf and rynde;
> And ay the peple cryde, "Here cometh oure joye,
> And, next his brother, holder up of Troye!"
>
> For which he wex a litel reed for shame,
> Whan he the peple upon hym herde cryen,
> That to byholde it was a noble game,
> How sobrelich he caste down his yën.   (II.624–648)

This passage was chosen by Charles Muscatine as an example of the "courtly" style: "[Troilus] moves, so far as we can see him alone, in an aura of the courtly style. In this Chaucer handles him functionally; in the insubstantial realm of the idealizing imagination he uses nonrepresentational forms."[6] While the passage certainly idealizes and isolates Troilus, I would add the qualification that it does so within a naturalistic and dramatic perspective. Troilus enters at the "end" of the street leading past Criseyde's palace. We see him through the eyes of the cheering crowd and through the eyes of Criseyde at her window. The details—the wounded horse, the helmet hanging by a "tyssew," the shield bristling with arrows—idealize the hero but also make him quite real and convey the humorous suggestion, somewhat undercutting the idealization, that like his horse he is wounded—by Cupid's arrows. However, Muscatine's comments apply absolutely to the description of Emetrius, a pure example of the courtly style:

> With Arcita, in stories as men fynde,
> The grete Emetreus, the kyng of Inde,
> Upon a steede bay trapped in steel,
> Covered in clooth of gold, dyapred weel,
> Cam ridynge lyk the god of armes, Mars.

His cote-armure was of clooth of Tars
Couched with perles white and rounde and grete;
His sadel was of brend gold newe ybete;
A mantelet upon his shulder hangynge,
Bret-ful of rubyes rede as fyr sparklynge;
His crispe heer lyk rynges was yronne,
And that was yelow, and glytered as the sonne.
His nose was heigh, his eyen bright citryn,
His lippes rounde, his colour was sangwyn;
A fewe frakenes in his face yspreynd,
Bitwixen yelow and somdel blak ymeynd;
And as a leon he his lookyng caste.
Of fyve and twenty yeer his age I caste.
His berd was wel bigonne for to sprynge;
His voys was as a trompe thonderynge.
Upon his heed he wered of laurer grene
A gerland, fressh and lusty for to sene.
Upon his hand he bar for his deduyt
An egle tame, as any lilye whyt.
An hundred lordes hadde he with hym there,
Al armed, save hir heddes, in al hir gere,
Ful richely in alle maner thynges.
For trusteth wel that dukes, erles, kynges
Were gadered in this noble compaignye,
For love and for encrees of chivalrye.
Aboute this kyng ther ran on every part
Ful many a tame leon and leopart.   (2155–86)

Here there is no perspective of street, palace, crowd, or heroine.
The detail is both more elaborate and more opulent. Emetrius himself is less the center of attention than the richness of cloth, the
sparkling of jewels, and the brightness of color. The white eagle
and the tame lions and leopards are like heraldic beasts on a coat
of arms, no part of a naturalistic description. However, the most
important point to be made about this portrait is that it describes
a minor figure in far more visual detail than we are ever given
about either Palamon or Arcite. Yet the matching portraits of
Emetrius and Lycurgus really are about Palamon and Arcite or
rather about the qualities and forces of which they are types. The
two descriptions blazon forth the beauty, splendor, and nobility of

chivalry on either side, and at the same time its potential for violent conflict, a conflict also inherent in the powers that dominate the destiny of the two heroes. Lycurgus is physically the type of a man under the astrological influence of Saturn, Emetrius, the type influenced by Mars.[7] Saturn will cause the death of Mars's knight Arcite for whom Emetrius and his party fight. The two kings, therefore, symbolize the hidden forces that determine the outcome and contribute in yet another way to the pattern Chaucer is weaving. By such stylized contrasts, we are led to understand that Arcite's tragic death is not without meaning, although Arcite never develops into a figure so rounded as to enable us to suffer with him as we can with Troilus.

This is not to say that one remains unmoved by Arcite's dying lament but moved more by the death of noble youth, beauty, and passion than by the death of the individual character. The very lyricism of the language, the repetitions and balanced phrasing, mitigates any of the pain we might feel at a personal tragedy:

> Allas, the wo! allas, the peynes stronge,
> That I for yow have suffred, and so longe!
> Allas, the deeth! allas, myn Emelye!
> Allas, departynge of oure compaignye!
> Allas, myn hertes queene! allas, my wyf!   (2771-75)

The lines sweep on to the rhetorical climax:

> What is this world? what asketh men to have?   (2777)

Here is the central question for which the tale is meant to provide an answer. For the dying Arcite it is the ironic truth exemplified in his bitter end:

> Now with his love, now in his colde grave
> Allone, withouten any compaignye.   (2778-79)

But Chaucer, when he wrote the story of Palamon and Arcite, wanted his audience to see more than this. The world is not irrational; it is a hierarchical order, a fair chain of being, in which every element is assigned to its proper place. The order of chivalry, "trouthe, honour, knyghthede,/Wysdom, humblesse, estaat, and heigh kynrede," mirrors the universal order and gives to it its most civilized expression. To make that order as clear as it is imposing, Chaucer has projected it upon a brilliant surface and painted it in a deliberately artificial style. In spite of the rich texture, we do not lose sight of the design because there is not the illusion of reality in which we can become involved as we do in *Troilus*.

The style of the tale is therefore the key to its meaning, as Charles Muscatine has demonstrated.[8] The countless instances of symmetry and balance—for example, the matching of Palamon with Arcite and of Lycurgus with Emetrius, the three temples of Venus, Mars, and Diana and the three prayers of the protagonists, the wedding of Theseus and Ypolita at the beginning and of Palamon and Emelye at the end—all convey the idea of pattern and order through artistic structure. Moreover, it is an order that repeats itself on different hierarchical levels.[9] On the human level we have Palamon, Arcite, and Emelye subject to Theseus, the type of the just ruler on earth. Theseus's role receives symbolic expression in the image of him seated at a window presiding over the tournament—"Arrayed right as he were a god in trone"—like God the Father ruling over his creatures. On another level, we find the pagan gods and their corresponding planets, feuding like the men below. Venus, Mars, and Diana are subject to Saturn as their human counterparts are subject to Theseus. Behind the pagan gods is the Prime Mover who is the author of the chain of being and the source of its harmony. Theseus's discourse on the Prime Mover articulates in Boethian terms the rationalism that has been implied all along by the style:

> The Firste Moevere of the cause above,
> Whan he first made the faire cheyne of love,
> Greet was th' effect and heigh was his entente.
>
> (2987–89)

The "cheyne" is an image both for the idea of order—a ladder descending by degrees from God—and for the idea of necessity—a power that binds all things to their proper place. Thus the chain both limits man and links him with God. He is bound by his mortality, yet he has the capacity for ideal love and heroic action. If we choose to regard only his limitations "This world nys but a thurghfare ful of wo" (2847), in Egeus's image, or in Theseus's image a dungeon, "this foule prisoun of this lyf" (3061). Yet such a view of the world is not incompatible with a more hopeful one, just as the grim tower in which Palamon and Arcite are shut up "Was evene joynant to the gardyn wal" (1060). The world is also a garden, and the vision of Emelye gathering flowers and singing, "as an aungel hevenysshly" is also a vision of a grace to be obtained in this life. Her marriage to Palamon reemphasizes the idea that the universal order is a bond of love:

> Bitwixen hem was maad anon the bond
> That highte matrimoigne or mariage   (3094–95)

Although we may never fully understand the workings of the Prime Mover, we may nevertheless have faith that all is for the best in a world that obeys the laws of chivalry. The tale thus presents a stoic and fatalistic but not a gloomy philosophy. The Knight's Tale is perhaps the best case that can be made for the chivalric ideal. But is it an adequate case? The disagreement about the tale and what it means, as sharp as the disagreement about the ending of *Troilus,* suggests that here, too, Chaucer has not made himself entirely clear—at least to modern critics.[10]

The tale also contains elements which I have ignored up to this point, that cannot be reduced to pattern or explained away by all of Theseus's philosophy. The idea of order is disturbed on the one hand by a sense of the ridiculous and, on the other, by a sense of evil. It is impossible to read with a straight face the quarrel between Palamon and Arcite over which of them loved Emelye first. When her angelic beauty gives rise to the technicality of whether Palamon first adored her as a goddess or as a woman, the idealization of the courtly style is taken so literally that we can no longer be serious about it. The common people excitedly debating about who will win the tournament as though it were any sporting event give a comic and realistic turn to the whole proceedings:

> Somme helden with hym with the blake berd,
> Somme with the balled, somme with the thikke herd;

Somme seyde he looked grymme, and he wolde fighte;
"He hath a sparth of twenty pound of wighte."
(2517–20)

And what are we to make of Venus the "queene of love" breaking into tears like a thwarted child "Til that hir teeres in the lystes fille" (2664–66)? In a more sinister way, the picture of the pillagers picking over the corpses on the battlefield (1005–8) and the clinical description of the efforts to save Arcite through bleeding, leeches, laxatives, and emetics (2743–58) strike an ugly note of discordant realism.

In what is to my mind the closest and the most perceptive reading of the tale, Elizabeth Salter finds in it a mixture of styles that reflects a divided purpose:

> In passing so swiftly from powerful expression to comment which is trivial, almost flippant, [Chaucer] seems to be using two voices; one reveals for us the pain latent in the narrative, the other, less sensitive, speaks with imperfect comprehension of that pain.[11]

My only quarrel with such a formulation would be that the flippancy is only seemingly less sensitive. The courtly and philosophical rhetoric that dominates the poem would seek to convince us that life is tragic but can be beautiful. The passages written in the lower style are a pervasive reminder that what passes for tragedy in the chivalric view of things can be at times funny, at times nasty. To ask in the Boethian language of Palamon,

> O crueel goddes that governe
> This world with byndyng of youre word eterne, . . .
> What is mankynde moore unto you holde
> Than is the sheep that rouketh in the folde?
> (1303–4, 1307–8)

is to abstract and distance the problem, in a sense to falsify the truth by dignifying it. To say in plain language about Arcite's painful death,

> And certeinly, ther Nature wol nat wirche,
> Fare wel phisik! go ber the man to chirche!   (2759–60)

makes us feel the indifference and cruelty of the gods more keenly than any apostrophe or analogy between mankind and "the sheep that rouketh in the folde."

I do not think that such touches ultimately diminish the total effect of the Knight's Tale. They form an undercurrent that only sporadically disturbs the calm, majestic surface. Some critics have made far too much of them, but of course they cannot help but raise a doubt whether this noble ideal of order is not just a splendid illusion created by art in a not entirely successful effort to mask intractable reality. I take such passages to be reflexes of Chaucer's native skepticism. At the time that he composed the tale, I think he sincerely wished to believe in the order to which he gave such eloquent form; yet, he could not resist qualifying that belief with his habitual irony. The *Palamon and Arcite* contains the distilled essence of Chaucer's courtly poetry, and along with *Troilus* represents the achievement of his middle period. It expresses the beauty, the romance, and the moral idealism of chivalry rationalized by Boethian philosophy. But the essence is by no means pure, and by sacrificing the human interest of *Troilus*, Chaucer did not make his lesson any more convincing.

That Chaucer himself recognized the limitations of his *Palamon and Arcite* is clear from the use he made of it as the first of the *Canterbury Tales*. Its teller becomes "a verray, parfit gentil knyght," who is an old veteran like Theseus. The virtues loved by the Knight—"Trouthe and honour, fredom and curteisie"—are the ones stressed in the tale. But, as we have seen in the Prologue, the Knight is an ideal figure out of the past. The feudal order he represents at its best is threatened by a new class that refuses to keep the place assigned to it in the great hierarchical chain. What the Knight's Tale expresses most faithfully is not the prevailing order but the nostalgic wish for an order that might have been once upon a time. At the time it was written, the tale was Chaucer's last word in an ancient tradition. As the Knight's Tale it becomes the beginning of something new. The Knight is rightly the first of a series of storytellers who try to answer the question "What is this world? what asketh men to have?" He answers it in a manner befitting his views and his station in life, which we may assume correspond to the views and class of the majority of the members of Chaucer's audience. But the pilgrim audience of the *Canterbury Tales* contains a diversity of views and conditions, and each of the pilgrim narrators, in his own way, provides in his tale a different answer to the same question. If the Knight had a final answer, he would have ended the game before it was even started.[12] But the Knight speaks for the old aristocratic order. The Miller is the first of those who speak for a new order. He is a new voice in Chaucer's poetry: unromantic, anti-intellectual, and amoral. His tale will make us reflect back upon the Knight's and help us to see much that is left out of the epic world of the Knight; in return, the existing monument, the *Palamon and Arcite* now become the Knight's Tale, gives us a perspective from which to judge the petty world of the Miller. In literature, the new order does not supersede the old but includes and qualifies it.

CHAPTER VI

The Comedy of Experience

*T*HE KNIGHT'S TALE tried to exemplify the truths that lie at the heart of the fourteenth-century feudal establishment. The conflict of human passions and the dire influence of warring planets constantly threatens to dissolve the world in chaos, but behind this apparent chaos lies an eternal, immutable hierarchical order. In the social and political realm this order is represented by the institution of chivalry, which gives form and beauty to the otherwise savage pursuits of love and war. Chivalry is patterned upon the grand cosmic design of the Prime Mover who has bound all elements in a "faire cheyne of love." Man's duty is to accept his lot within the universal order and make a virtue of necessity. In Theseus's words:

> whoso gruccheth ought, he dooth folye,
> And rebel is to hym that al may gye. (3045–46)

As the preceding chapter has maintained, the tale itself does not succeed fully in convincing the reader of the truth of these propositions, and in the dramatic framework of the *Canterbury Tales* they are immediately challenged. On the surface, the band of pilgrims, when we first encounter them at the Tabard, would seem to exemplify the Knight's ideal of order. For all their differences, the pilgrims seem bound by a "faire cheyne of love," united by the season and the common goal of travelling to the martyr's shrine. As though to cement their solidarity, the pilgrims have by unanimous consent submitted to another bond: the agreement to the storytelling contest. Rule and order are stressed in the legalistic language by which the bargain is sealed. The Host asks the company if they will stand by his "juggement" (778), they in turn ask him to pronounce his "voirdit" ("verdict," 787), and after the scheme has been explained to them swear oaths and ask him to act as their "governour" and "juge" (813–814). It is all very feudal and ceremonious, and to make sure that order prevails, Harry Bailly, the Prime Mover of the contest, arranges, by pinching off the end of the Knight's straw, that the noblest of the pilgrims tells the first tale.

However, barely has the Knight pronounced God's blessing on "al this faire compaignye," when the first of many quarrels erupts to shake this microcosmic fellowship and to subvert the principle of order. The generally favorable reception of the Knight's Tale sustains the spirit of harmony for a brief moment:

> Whan that the Knyght had thus his tale ytoold,
> In al the route nas ther yong ne oold
> That he ne seyde it was a noble storie,
> And worthy for to drawen to memorie;
> And namely the gentils everichon.   (3109–13)

The specification of the "gentils" already intimates the social comedy that is about to explode. A taste for courtly romance is, of course, a badge of class, and clearly the socially mixed pilgrim audience has responded to the Knight's Tale with varying degrees of enthusiasm. Harry Bailly takes personal pride in the Knight's success. He is enjoying his part as though he really were "a marchal in an halle" (752), officiating at some aristocratic entertainment. There will be no more drawing of lots; the Host himself will summon the contestants into the lists; and he calls next upon the Monk—the closest thing to a knight among the ecclesiastics. The Nobility having spoken, it is now the turn of an aristocratic representative of the Church.

But before the Monk has a chance to speak, the third estate breaks in with an arrogant display of feudal pride:

> By armes, and by blood and bones,
> I kan a noble tale for the nones,
> With which I wol now quite the Knyghtes tale.
>
> (3125–27)

The Miller launches what turns out to be a literary Peasants' Rebellion. His noisy vulgarity is the antithesis of the Knight's aristocratic reserve, but like the Knight he is a fighter and a champion. The Knight splinters lances; the Miller shatters doors by charging through them with his skull. His generally aggressive demeanor is made more martial by his sword and buckler, and he has already taken the lead in heading the procession of pilgrims out of town. If the Knight is introduced as a *miles Christi*, the Miller is presented as something of a *miles gloriosus*.

In his Prologue the Miller casts down his gauntlet in a literary challenge. He will "quite" the Knight with a "noble tale" of his own and insists on telling it there and then. Harry Bailly is appalled and soothingly pleads with the Miller to observe his proper place:

> Abyd, Robyn, my leeve brother;
> Som bettre man shal telle us first another.
> Abyd, and lat us werken thriftily.   (3129–31)

But the Miller will not be silenced. The Reeve makes a last-ditch attempt to stop him by appealing to the canons of decency:

> Lat be thy lewed dronken harlotrye.
> It is a synne and eek a greet folye
> To apeyren any man, or hym defame,
> And eek to bryngen wyves in swich fame.   (3145–48)

But the Reeve's motives in assuming the role of public censor are suspect, and the Miller gleefully turns *that* argument *ad hominem*.

The Miller has been a rebel against the Host's judgment, against the social order, and he is about to offend against propriety by telling a thoroughly indecent story. Yet our sympathies are entirely on his side against what we recognize instinctively as

the Host's snobbishness and the Reeve's sanctimoniousness, for
we know without having to be told that the Miller's drunkenness,
impudence, and coarseness have the license of the time and season. His rebellion is in harmony with the great annual revolution
Chaucer has described in the opening lines of the General Prologue. The pilgrims have a serious purpose in journeying to
Canterbury, and at the end the deeper meaning of their common
goal will be spelled out by the Parson. They are seeking "Jerusalem celestial," the city of God.[1] But their pilgrimage is also a
holiday, an escape from serious matters and from holy things. I
have commented above on the festive spirit of the company as it is
expressed even in the unsavory Summoner and Pardoner. The
festive note is also in the sound of the Miller's bagpipe. The time
is right for feasting and for licentious comedy.

Such comedy has the sanction of deep-rooted folk custom.
C. L. Barber has shown how the "form" of Elizabethan holidays
underlies the structure of Shakespearian comedy. The "Saturnalian
Pattern" is, as Barber points out, an ancient one:

> F. M. Cornford, in *The Origins of Attic Comedy,* suggested
> that invocation and abuse were the basic gestures of a nature
> worship behind Aristophanes' union of poetry and rail-
> ing. The two gestures were still practiced in the "folly" of
> Elizabethan May-game, harvest-home, or winter revel: in-
> vocation, for example, in the manifold spring garlanding
> customs, "gathering for Robin Hood"; abuse, in the cus-
> tomary license to flout and fleer at what on other days
> commanded respect.[2]

Renaissance festival and festive comedy go back to medieval tradition of parody, burlesque, and mock-defiance of authority. The
saturnalian spirit survived in the celebration of the great seasonal
feasts long after these had been integrated into the Church calen-
dar. They were occasions for drinking, dancing, and sexual license.
They could also be occasions for travesties of the solemn rituals of
the Church.

One of the most ancient of these customs was the institution of
the Boy Bishop who with the rest of the choir boys would take
control of the service on Holy Innocents Day at the reading of

the Psalm: *Deposuit potentes*—He has put down the mighty from their seats. A similar and far more riotous practice was the popular Feast of Fools usually celebrated on one of the days of the New Year season. Here the passing of the *baculus,* the celebrant's staff of authority, to the master of the feast touched off wild demonstrations and parodies of the divine service among the lower clergy. Another such institution, closely related in spirit, was the Feast of the Ass. According to one document, quoted by E. K. Chambers, at Beauvais:

> A pretty girl, with a child in her arms, was set upon an ass, to represent the Flight into Egypt. . . . The ass and its riders were stationed on the gospel side of the altar. A solemn mass was sung, in which *Introit, Kyrie, Gloria* and *Credo* ended with a bray. To crown all, the rubrics direct that the celebrant, instead of saying *Ite, missa est,* shall bray three times (*ter hinhannabit*) and that the people shall respond in similar fashion.[3]

An analogous institution is the Lord of Misrule who presided over the Christmas Revels at the court of the Tudors. The significance of such customs as the Feast of Fools or the Feast of the Ass and of the whole tradition of medieval parody has been given a profound explanation by Mikhail Bakhtin:

> Laughter was as universal as seriousness; it was directed at the whole world, at history, at all societies, at ideology. It was the world's second truth extended to everything and from which nothing is taken away. It was, as it were, the festive aspect of the whole world in all its elements, the second revelation of the world in play and laughter.
>
> This is why medieval parody played a completely unbridled game with all that is most sacred and important from the point of view of official ideology.[4]

Ritual thus generates ritual comedy.

The Miller in pushing himself to the fore is, therefore, claiming no more than the privilege of the Boy Bishop, the master of the Feast of Fools, and the Lord of Misrule. By challenging the Knight, the figure of authority, he follows the pattern of medieval comedy. His tale will be outrageous in the same way that the holiday revels were outrageous. Just as in his rudeness, aggressiveness, and profanity we can see an inversion of the qualities of the Knight, so the Miller's Tale can be looked at as a burlesque romance inverting the traditional values of feudal society. It is Chaucer's "festive comedy."

Insofar as the Miller's Tale has any specific target, it is the Knight's Tale. The two perfectly illustrate Per Nykrog's theory about the relationship between fabliau and chivalric romance: both treat essentially the same subject matter but from radically opposed points of view and in totally different styles.[5] In both tales we have two rivals competing for the favors of a lady. The wooing of Alisoun contains burlesque echoes of the wooing of Emelye. But the earthiness of the Miller's Oxford is at the opposite pole from the courtliness of the Knight's Athens, and instead of two noble kinsmen fighting over the hand of the sister-in-law of Duke Theseus, we have a pair of clerks trying to seduce a carpenter's country wife.

All this has been noted before.[6] It would be a mistake, however, to regard the Miller's Tale simply as a reply to the Knight's or as a travesty of chivalric ideals. The range of its comedy is much broader. It turns "up-so-doun" the idealism of the medieval world of which chivalry, as we encounter it in the Knight's Tale, is only one of the many forms of expression. The targets of the Miller's Tale could be described more generally as conventional attitudes toward sex, conventional attitudes toward learning, and conventional attitudes toward the Church. Naturally the tale has no such clear-cut divisions, and the three areas overlap; however, they will make a convenient basis for discussion, and I shall deal with each of these topics in turn.

To begin with sex. The fabliau reverses the asceticism that underlies both medieval Catholicism and the "religion of love." Though it is an oversimplification, one may say generally that the Church in the Middle Ages denigrates sex as a necessary evil and upholds celibacy as the ideal. Chivalry, even though it idealizes human love, does not do much better by the physical act of love. Chivalry envelops sex with a mystic aura and makes a cult of sentiment. The emphasis thus falls mainly on the courtship and desire. Romances are preoccupied with the psychology of divided lovers, rarely with the consummation of love, and in this respect the Knight's Tale is typical.

Much of the gaiety of the Miller's Tale comes from the inversion of these repressive attitudes. Sex is frankly presented as the *summum bonum* because it is the supreme *physical* pleasure, a natural satisfaction like food and drink, the highest expression of the joy of life. If we apply to the Miller's Tale Arcite's despairing question—"What is this world? what asketh men to have?"—the answer is easy: what men desire to have is summed up in Alisoun.

She embodies all the purely sensual pleasures. In her portrait she is closely identified with the objects of Nature. Her brows are black as a sloeberry; she is a more blissful sight than a peartree in bloom; her breath is as sweet as apples stored in hay. Most particularly she is compared to a series of young and graceful animals:

> As any wezele hir body gent and smal. . . .
> Therto she koude skippe and make game,
> As any kyde or calf folwynge his dame. . . .
> Wynsynge she was, as is a joly colt.
> (3234, 3259–60, 3263)

She is full of animal spirits, as fresh and wholesome as one of Nature's products, simply begging to be seen, heard, tasted, and especially to be touched. The cheap, shiny ornaments and silky materials she wears enhance her natural voluptuousness. The closing lines of the portrait make explicit the cumulative sex appeal of the imagery:

> She was a prymerole, a piggesnye,
> For any lord to leggen in his bedde.   (3268–69)

For Alisoun sex can be enjoyed as though the fall of man had never taken place, as though she really did belong to the animal world that is described happily mating in such lyrics as "Lenten is comen with love to towne."

Music is used throughout the tale with sexual overtones. When Nicholas plays upon his "sawtrie" there is an implied relationship to his playing upon Alisoun's body:

> He kiste hire sweete and taketh his sawtrie,
> And pleyeth faste, and maketh melodie.   (3305–6)

The same chord is struck when Nicholas and Alisoun hasten to bed: "Ther was the revel and the melodye" (3652). The imagery is humorous, but it is also intimately connected with the theme of Nature. The instinct that moves Nicholas and Alisoun is the same impulse that compels the "smale foules" that "maken melodye" in the Prologue. Like the birds, they too "slepen al the nyght with open ye," and in exactly the same sense.

The tale thus gives its blessing to any form of sexual indulgence that is simple and natural. On the other hand, it deals harshly with any violation of Nature, including all gratuitous refinements of pure sexual pleasure. Among the four protagonists, Alisoun's response to sex is the most healthy and natural, and I think it is significant that no mention is made at the end of any punishment for her. However, all three of her lovers go against Nature in some way and receive their appropriate rewards.

John's case is summed up in a line: "She was wylde and yong, and he was old" (3225). He is introduced as the stock character of the *vieux jaloux,* and Alisoun is justified in finding an outlet for her frustrated desires because John has sinned against Nature and common sense by marrying a young wife. This would be enough in most fabliaux to merit cuckolding. As the tale progresses, however, Chaucer alters the conventional character by making John appear almost pathetically trusting instead of jealous and suspicious. His emotions about his young bride are not represented as the senile lust of January for May but as a tenderness and protective feeling. He is more like a father than a husband. There is a strong element of fantasy in his love for Alisoun, and it is precisely this that makes him vulnerable to Nicholas's scheme. As soon as he hears of the flood, he can visualize the waves overwhelming his "hony deere." His first thought is for her: "Allas, my wyf!/And shal she drenche? allas, myn Alisoun!" (3522–23). He falls (literally as it turns out) not as a result of his jealousy but as a result of deluded sentiment.

The same point can be made, in a different way, of Absolon who has gazed into the well of Narcissus and fallen in love with his own image as a courtly lover. He is not really interested in Alisoun sexually but sentimentally as a stimulus to his absorption with his curls, his clothes, his breath, his serenading, and his acting. Not only does he play the part of Herod "upon a scaffold hye" (a bad case of miscasting)—he is playing a part all the time. The unnaturalness of his wooing is brought out by the emphasis on his effeminacy; the harder he works at the role of courtly hero, the more he resembles the courtly heroine. Like a lady, he is "daungerous" of vulgar speech and put off by such natural bodily functions as farting. The appropriate punishment for the courtly idealist is to discover reality by kissing his lady's ass.

Nicholas *is* genuinely interested in Alisoun's physical charms, but he too is undone by overelaborating the simple pleasures of sex. Not content with a straightforward seduction, he must turn his sexual triumph into a triumph of his art, a victory not simply of a young man over a jealous old husband, but of a clerk over a carpenter. He enjoys the execution of his plot as much as he enjoys Alisoun, and the chain of circumstances he has set in motion finally proves to be his ruin. He overreaches himself, and his cry for "water, water!" brings down the deluge even if only in the mind of John. To be branded in the rear end by fire is a punishment worthy of Dante for the false prophet of a second flood.

Thus John, Absolon, and Nicholas all bear witness to a lesson pointed out by the narrator:

> Lo, which a greet thyng is affeccioun!
> Men may dyen of ymaginacioun,
> So depe may impressioun be take.   (3611–13)

In context this bit of "sentence" applies to John whose passion for Alisoun causes him to visualize the terrors of the flood. However, "affeccioun" might be extended to include other obsessions that addle the brain and especially the "celle fantastik,"[7] the seat of the imagination. Absolon is under the spell of "love paramours." Of Nicholas we are told that "al his fantasye/Was turned for to lerne astrologye" (3191–92). Each suffers from an unnatural ruling passion that brings him to a bad end. In this respect the Miller's Tale is like a comedy of humors in which the characters are compelled by some idiosyncratic urge to violate a rational norm. Here the norm is represented by the simple satisfaction of man's physical appetites so richly provided for by

"Goddes foyson"—God's plenty. The portrait of Alisoun is an itemization of God's plenty, personified in one delectable female body. Here is everything that man could desire. But man always wants more than what he is given. Not content with the gift of physical pleasure, he wishes to enhance this pleasure through the dangerous use of the imagination. Dissatisfied with his earthly Paradise, he seeks knowledge of good and evil. In terms of the Miller's Tale he becomes inquisitive about "Goddes pryvetee."

This fatal curiosity brings up the second area where the Miller's Tale undermines the conventionally accepted scale of values. The celebration of man's animal nature is complemented by a distrust of his higher faculties. The reverence for book learning and philosophical inquiry so characteristic of the Middle Ages is lacking in the fabliaux. The heroes are frequently clerks, but this in itself indicates a certain irreverence toward the intellectual establishment. The clerk is admired because he is clever as a lover, not because he is clever at his books. It is Nicholas's misfortune that he tries to mix his intellectual and his fleshly interests.

The fabliau respects common sense and shrewd practical wisdom of the sort that is contained in maxims or proverbs. The Miller's Tale is full of such nuggets as

> Alwey the nye slye
> Maketh the ferre leeve to be looth.   (3392–93)

The pursuit of knowledge beyond such empirical observations lays traps for the theorist and the dreamer. One could go further and say that the fabliau opposes itself to the tendency of the medieval mind to see physical objects and everyday events as outward signs of an invisible higher reality—the exegetical impulse. In the fabliau, attempts to get to the bottom of the mysteries of life usually backfire.

In this respect also the fabliau can be contrasted with romance, and the Miller's Tale with the Knight's. All epic poetry—and romance is a form of epic—tries to justify the ways of God to man. It sees human action against the background of a higher order—a destiny or providence that has justly decreed that things should be as they are. Thus the pagan gods, the planetary influences, and the Boethian philosophy of the Knight's Tale all attempt to explain and rationalize the human condition as well as the outcome of the story.

In the Miller's Tale in place of the celestial machinery we have the astrology of hende Nicholas. Stargazing is for him a serious business, and no doubt he has faith in his Almagest and his astrolabe. The prediction of the second flood is only a brilliant hoax, but it has precedent in the bona fide attempts of astrologers to foretell the future, especially the advent of the ultimate catastrophe, the end of the world. However, to make the destruction of the world part of a stratagem to allow Nicholas to sleep all night in Alisoun's arms robs the idea of its terror. Doomsday jokes are probably archetypal. *Dr. Strangelove or How I Learned to Stop Worrying and Love the Bomb* is only a nuclear-age variation of the comic apocalypse. One reason Chaucer's audience delighted in the Miller's Tale was no doubt because it enabled them to stop worrying and to love the flood, the fire, or whatever it would be next time. Maybe Doomsday is only a prank played upon gullible men by mischievous clerks. When we laugh at the carpenter's terror, perhaps we are laughing not only at his folly but at our own in preparing daily for a judgment that may never come.[8]

Philosophy fares no better than science. The carpenter is ironically portrayed as a village Boethius who discovers in everyday happenings examples of man's fate. He takes a generally pessimistic view of life. As soon as he thinks that Nicholas is sick, John begins to fear that he might die. This depressing thought leads to a general reflection: "This world is now ful tikel, sikerly" (3428). Then the example clinching the point: John has that very day seen the funeral of a neighbor who was up and working only last Wednesday. The basic thesis and even the method of proof is not so very far removed from Theseus's Boethian speech at the end of the Knight's Tale:

> Of man and womman seen we wel also
> That nedes, in oon of thise termes two,
> This is to seyn, in youthe or elles age,
> He moot be deed, the kyng as shal a page;
> Som in his bed, som in the depe see,
> Som in the large feeld, as men may see;

Ther helpeth noght, al goth that ilke weye.
Thanne may I seyn that al this thyng moot deye.
(3027–34)

Theseus declares that man can never fully grasp the will of the Prime Mover but must nonetheless submit to it. John blames Nicholas's supposed illness on his foolish desire to know more than is good for him:

I thoghte ay wel how that it sholde be!
Men sholde nat knowe of Goddes pryvetee.   (3453–54)

John has stumbled upon the theme stated by the Miller in his Prologue:

An housbonde shal nat been inquisityf
Of Goddes pryvetee, nor of his wyf.   (3163–64)

If John had taken this lesson to heart he might have escaped his nemesis. There is a superficially pragmatic quality to some of his ramblings, but in fact they are the complacencies of a garrulous old man and are forgotten as soon as the clerk lets him in on the awful secret. Nicholas's prophecy fits in well with John's outlook. He is at bottom a believer in dark and malevolent powers, ready to pounce at any moment. Finding Nicholas in a trance, he immediately concludes that the clerk has been bewitched and recites a magic charm to ward off the evil spirits. His mind is a muddle of Christian doctrine, pagan superstition, and homespun philosophy, all of which conspire to persuade him: "This world is now ful tikel, sikerly."

The psychological effect of the Miller's Tale is to ridicule that picture and to prove it false. In the Knight's Tale Egeus, the old father of Theseus, describes the world as "a thurghfare ful of wo." In the Miller's Tale the world is a garden of delights. The original sin is, as always, to seek knowledge that we are better off without or, in terms of the tale, to pry into the secrets of God or of one's wife. Men bring their destiny upon themselves through vanity and folly. There are no secret agents or stellar influences. The even-handed justice of the fabliau is absolutely clear: the punishment always fits the crime.

Finally, I want to glance at the treatment of the Church in the Miller's Tale. One might wonder what the Church has to do with a fabliau, but if one looks closely, one finds its presence everywhere. Of course the Church played so pervasive a role in medieval life that it is necessarily part of any realistic picture. Nevertheless, the density of allusions to the Church, its rites, and its teachings is extraordinary. Separately these allusions seem unobtrusive and harmless enough, but they work together to produce a background of bustling religious life going its daily rounds oblivious of the intrigues that are hatching in and around the carpenter's house.

Each of the characters is involved in the affairs of the Church. Nicholas is presumably at the University studying for orders. Absolon is parish clerk. John happens at the time to be employed by a religious house at nearby Osney. Alisoun, immediately after she and Nicholas have reached their understanding, is pictured on a holiday going to mass, "Cristes owene werkes for to wirche" (3308). Absolon is right there with the incense dish, "Sensynge the wyves of the parisshe faste" (3341).

The characters are associated with a number of biblical figures. Absolon's name evokes the son of David who was characterized by medieval commentators as foppish and effeminate.[9] John and Alisoun become Noah and Noah's wife of the miracle plays. Absolon's complaint beneath Alisoun's window is a travesty of the Song of Songs.[10] Nowhere else in the *Canterbury Tales* are the oaths so strategically placed. Alisoun vows to be at Nicholas's will "by seint Thomas of Kent" (3291). Gerveys the Smith greets Absolon:

> What, Absolon! for Cristes sweete tree,
> Why rise ye so rathe? ey, *benedicitee!*   (3767–68)

Absolon asks for his kiss "For Jhesus love, and for the love of me" (3717). That way of putting it—"For Jhesus love, and for the love of me"—typifies the pattern of these references. They give an additional ironic twist to the action, the final touch of absurdity.

A question arises whether such comic touches are not calculated to alert the reader's moral sense. What precisely are we laughing at? A genuinely devout reader might not find anything funny in such allusions just as he might not be amused by a plot that is, after all, about adultery. One may sympathize, therefore, with a number of recent critics who have tried to find a "moral edge" in the tale while at the same time preserving its humor.[11] Is the tale perhaps meant to show the Christian reader that sin, just like the burlesque Vice characters of the morality plays, is not only wicked but ridiculous?

Such readings are clearly possible, but they go against the grain of Chaucer's humor and the humor of medieval "festive comedy." It is a brand of humor that still survives in most Latin countries (the films of Marcel Pagnol are a good example) where the Church is regarded with the same worldly, irreverent, but in the end sympathetic eye along with everything else under the sun. The sacred is seen from its temporal and human side. No doubt there is a vast distance between the spiritual and stylistic levels of the Song of Songs and the Miller's Tale. But Chaucer's comedy also implies their common humanity. The Canticle is, after all, on its literal level also a love song. In the low style of Absolon, "Awaketh lemman myn" sounds preposterous, but part of the fun is that the sacred words lose their awe when they are brought down to the level of the fabliau world.

The natural world celebrates its Maker in its own way. When Nicholas and Alisoun are in bed,

> Ther was the revel and the melodye;
> And thus lith Alison and Nicholas,
> In bisynesse of myrthe and of solas,
> Til that the belle of laudes gan to rynge,
> And freres in the chauncel gonne synge.   (3652–56)

The counterpoint of the melody made by the lovers in bed and the song of the friars in the chantry beautifully illustrates the comic balance Chaucer has achieved between the sacred and the profane. Each in his own way is performing the office of praise and sending up his *Te Deum*.

This balance of sympathy exists, to be sure, only for the moment. In the background the Church looms in the sanctity of its divine power, and the characters are absurd in their petty world of ephemeral pleasures. But the whole point of the Miller's Tale is that it provides an escape from the eternal and permits its audience to look briefly at the temporal world as though it were all that mattered. What is remarkable about the Miller's Tale is its *innocence,* a quality Chaucer never quite brings off again in any of his other fabliaux. The Parson's judgments are suspended in order to let us enjoy our holiday.

Chaucer himself seems to suggest in the person of the narrator that we should not take the Miller's Tale too seriously, and that it belongs in a different category from the expressly didactic tales. At the end of the Miller's Prologue, the narrator's voice is heard again, offering an elaborate apology to the reader for the painful duty of having to tell this objectionable story; any reader whose sense of propriety might be offended or who prefers not to waste his time on such foolishness is advised to

> Turne over the leef and chese another tale;
> For he shal fynde ynowe, grete and smale,
> Of storial thyng that toucheth gentillesse,
> And eek moralitee and hoolynesse.
> Blameth nat me if that ye chese amys.
> The Millere is a cherl, ye knowe wel this;
> So was the Reve eek and othere mo,
> And harlotrie they tolden bothe two.
> Avyseth yow, and put me out of blame;
> And eek men shal nat maken ernest of game.
>
> (3177–86)

Of course no one is taken in by this. It is an obvious come-on, and Chaucer's audience was hardly more squeamish than we are today. No doubt they enjoyed it all hugely, including the narrator's apology. The tacit understanding between the poet and his audience is that we are all men of the world able to enjoy a bit of disreputable fun, and this is basically the attitude taken by the majority of readers and critics ever since. Nevertheless, in raising the question of vulgarity and bad taste, Chaucer is sidestepping a more basic problem. The fabliaux can be defended as harmless amusement— "men shal nat maken ernest of game"—but is that the best that can be said for them? Is the Miller's Tale nothing more than a "jape" or a "nyce caas"—a foolish affair?

There is certainly more to be said for it than this, and it is possible to take festive comedy seriously without turning it into inverted morality. No matter how it starts out, in the end the Miller's Tale is something better than a sop to Momus or a holiday game. The vitality and earthiness of the Miller's Tale, the sheer pleasure expressed in the physical world, and the disregard for intellectual and spiritual ideals—all this is enormously seductive. These are not values entertained simply in play but genuine values. We do not merely laugh at the people and the pleasures in the Miller's Tale—we identify with them and love them until they may mean as much and more to us than the Knight's "trouthe and honour."

The Miller's Tale has its own truth, different from the Knight's —what Bakhtin calls "the people's unofficial truth."[12] The Knight's truth means fidelity to higher principle; the Miller's truth is fidelity to the vital principle of life. In the work of a major poet like Chaucer, the sheer artistry expended on the relatively simple plot of the Miller's Tale implies a new concept of art that goes beyond the one that sees a direct relationship between the value of a work of art and its "sentence." There is a profound meaning in the narrator's promise to tell everything that happened on the journey even if it means telling of churlishness and obscenity. His literalism is meant to seem naive, but it is also a defense of the artist's commitment not only to a moral or spiritual truth but to the representation of life as he sees it. On this plane of artistic truth the Knight and Miller and their respective tales achieve genuine equality. All creatures, no matter what superficial social or moral distinctions separate them, are equal in the eye of their creator if only they are imagined strongly enough.

In medieval life, ritual comedy is supposed to stay in its place:

> Throughout the year there were small scattered islands of time, strictly limited by the dates of feasts, when the world was permitted to emerge from the official routine but exclusively under the camouflage of laughter. Barriers were raised, provided there was nothing but laughter.[13]

However, the vitality of the celebrations is a measure of how deeply those emotions run for which laughter provides the only acceptable outlet. That is why holidays have a way of getting out of hand. Our knowledge of customs like the Feast of Fools comes largely from the efforts of bishops to reform the festivities. Some of the best accounts of May Day celebrations are to be found in Puritan tracts written against them. Once the spirit of license is set free, it transgresses the boundaries decreed for it, nor is it easily confined again.

Something like that must have happened to Chaucer as well. What starts out as "game" in the Miller's Tale releases creative energies more powerful than the poet may have imagined. The true Lord of Misrule is the artist himself, and the writing of fiction becomes a holiday during which the sanctions of everyday are suspended. The Miller's insistence that he be permitted to tell his tale turns out to be Chaucer's declaration of independence as an artist, the assertion of his freedom to write what he pleases. The apologetic narrator is Chaucer's old persona professing embarrassment at the turn of events. But it is really the Miller who speaks for Chaucer:

> By armes, and by blood and bones,
> I kan a noble tale for the nones.

I am not, of course, trying to maintain that the subversive spirit is foreign to Chaucer's earlier poetry. The goose and duck in the *Parliament of Fowls* and especially Pandarus strike discordant notes in their courtly surroundings; they anticipate the Miller's pragmatism, his gusto, and, in a more polite way, his concerns. However, in the Miller's Tale this spirit is given free play and allowed to dominate for the first time. A case could be made that the whole pilgrimage had to be invented for the sake of the fabliaux. The Knight's Tale of Palamon and Arcite was one that Chaucer had already told in his own person to his court audience. Many of the tales could well have been told as separate stories by Chaucer himself. But the Miller's Tale called for the creation of a new world of characters who make up a new audience and a new set of narrators. The *Canterbury Tales* is Chaucer's personal holiday from the business of being a noble philosophical court poet, and like all good holidays it gets out of hand. It will occupy him for the rest of his life. The Miller's Tale necessitates the Reeve's, and the Reeve's Tale leads to the Cook's, which was never finished possibly because Chaucer felt that it was time to put a temporary stop to the festivities. He makes good his promise that there will be tales of "moralitee and hoolynesse," but once the Miller has begun the game, things will never be the same. The result is a new kind of fiction, a representation of life with a Shakespearian fulness.

CHAPTER VII

The Comedy of Innocence

*t*HE REEVE'S TALE superficially resembles the Miller's festive comedy and is, of course, intended to "quite" it tit for tat. "Right in his cherles termes wol I speke," says the Reeve. He pays back the Miller's clever Oxford clerk, who seduces the old carpenter's young wife, with two Cambridge undergraduates, who stumble into a seduction of haughty Symkyn's wife and daughter. Like the Miller's Tale it is a funny, exuberant story. However, as recent criticism has demonstrated, on closer inspection the Reeve's Tale shows up to be a darker, more corrosive kind of comedy of a sort more nearly attuned to the modern sense of irony, which tends to be destructive rather than charitable.[1]

The theme of the tale is retribution.[2] The Reeve declares in his Prologue that "leveful is with force force of-showve." Aleyn tells John:

> ther is a lawe that says thus,
> That gif a man in a point be agreved,
> That in another he sal be releved.   (4180–82)

And the Reeve sanctimoniously concludes his exemplum of justice:

> And therfore this proverbe is seyd ful sooth,
> "Hym thar nat wene wel that yvele dooth";
> A gylour shal hymself bigyled be.   (4319–21)

However, it does not require much astuteness on the reader's part to see that the force of these proverbs rebounds upon the Reeve who exposes himself quite as much as he does his enemy the Miller. The art of the Reeve's Tale is more truly like the art of Conrad and James than anything Chaucer had written before because in it, for the first time, we are given a purely fictional persona whose biases are betrayed by his narrative. The Reeve is the first of the pilgrims to be developed in some depth, and in his tale, Chaucer discovers possibilities in the new form he has invented that will be fully exploited in the prologues and tales of some of the other pilgrims.

The original narrator of the Knight's Tale was Chaucer himself, and although the story is highly appropriate to the Knight, it can hardly be construed as a dramatic development of the Knight's character or as a satire of the Knight's obliviousness to the absurdities of his own chivalric story. The plot of the Miller's Tale is, again, highly appropriate to this "jangler" and "goliardeys," but the sophistication of that comedy is not consistent with the character of the coarse and drunken Miller. As I have said, the Miller and his Prologue provide a screen for the poet himself.

The Reeve's Tale is different. Of course, like all the tales, it requires a certain suspension of disbelief, and I don't mean to suggest that Chaucer has consistently tried to maintain the point of view of an actual reeve. However, the attitudes, values, and stylistic level in this tale are more than just appropriate to a reeve. They are credible as the expression of this particular reeve and, more than that, suggest a degree of imaginative participation by the teller in his tale. The Reeve's Tale is the story of a vindictive, salacious, and servile old man, exactly like the character we encounter in the Reeve's Prologue.

Some hints for this characterization are provided by the portrait in the General Prologue. We know that he is old because in youth he had been a carpenter and because the entire portrait conveys the impression of a seasoned veteran who has long ago established absolute power over his fellow serfs while ingratiating himself with his lord by playing the part of a faithful old family servant.[3] There is, furthermore, a skeletal and lurking quality in his appearance and manner that inspires terror in his subordinates and recalls uncomfortably a still more powerful bailiff—Death himself as he is sometimes personified in the art of the late Middle Ages.

It is ironically appropriate, therefore, that the vitality of the Miller's comedy should move the Reeve to sullen broodings about age and death. In an extraordinary monologue, addressed to no one in particular, the Reeve vents his bitterness at old age. The speech is cast in the form of a series of sententious reflections about old men in general so that the Host finally loses patience:

> What amounteth al this wit?
> What shul we speke alday of hooly writ?
> The devel made a reve for to preche.   (3901–3)

The Reeve's "sermonyng," however, bears his personal stamp, and has nothing to do with scripture. For a moment we are permitted a glimpse of the old man of the fabliaux as he sees himself, and it is not a pleasant view:

> But ik am oold, me list not pley for age;
> Gras tyme is doon, my fodder is now forage;
> This white top writeth myne olde yeris;
> Myn herte is also mowled as myne heris,
> But if I fare as dooth an open-ers,—
> That ilke fruyt is ever lenger the wers,
> Til it be roten in mullok or in stree.
> We olde men, I drede, so fare we:
> Til we be roten, kan we nat be rype;
> We hoppen alwey whil the world wol pype.
> For in oure wyl ther stiketh evere a nayl,
> To have an hoor heed and a grene tayl,
> As hath a leek; for thogh oure myght be goon,
> Oure wyl desireth folie evere in oon.
> For whan we may nat doon, than wol we speke;
> Yet in oure asshen olde is fyr yreke.
> Foure gleedes han we, which I shal devyse,—
> Avauntyng, liyng, anger, coveitise;
> Thise foure sparkles longen unto eelde.
> Oure olde lemes mowe wel been unweelde,
> But wyl ne shal nat faillen, that is sooth.
> And yet ik have alwey a coltes tooth,

As many a yeer as it is passed henne
Syn that my tappe of lif bigan to renne.
For sikerly, whan I was bore, anon
Deeth drough the tappe of lyf and leet it gon;
And ever sithe hath so the tappe yronne
Til that almoost al empty is the tonne.
The streem of lyf now droppeth on the chymbe.

                                        (3867–95)

It is as though the wholesome and appetizing images in the Miller's portrait of Alisoun had rotted and decayed. The sexuality underlying the "joly colt" has turned into the old man's "coltes tooth," a proverbial expression for youthful desires in an older person. For the image of "the newe pere-jonette tree," we have the "open-ers," a medlar pear that is put in the straw to rot until it becomes ripe. The image of the pear is phallic, but with the suggestion of impotence, just as is the image of the leek with its white head and green tail and the wine tap from which the stream of life is now only dripping. The entire passage is suffused with an old man's impotent rage and frustrated desires, and it confirms the accuracy of the Reeve's observation: "For whan we may nat doon, than wol we speke."

The Reeve's Tale affords its narrator such vicarious satisfaction through speech. It provides the Reeve with something more than revenge upon the overbearing Miller. It gives him a chance to take part imaginatively in the humiliation of his enemy through the sexual exploits of the two clerks. Sex in the Reeve's Tale is more graphic, coarser, and more animalistic than it is in the Miller's Tale. In the Miller's Tale, Alisoun's sexuality is idealized in language and imagery in terms suitable for her just as Emelye is idealized in the Knight's Tale. Malyne, on the other hand, is described as a softer version of her husky father, and there is no attempt to embellish her nubile points with flower imagery, whether it be lilies and roses, or primroses and piggesnyes:

This wenche thikke and wel ygrowen was,
With kamus nose, and eyen greye as glas,
With buttokes brode, and brestes rounde and hye;
But right fair was hire heer, I wol nat lye.   (3973–76)

The one romance touch, the "eyen greye as glas," is immediately undercut by the "buttokes brode."

Unlike Nicholas and Absolon, Aleyn and John have neither time nor occasion to employ courtly preliminaries. Debased as the chivalric idiom may be in the mouths of the characters of the Miller's Tale, it nevertheless carries with it a certain delicacy. Nicholas does not take Alisoun altogether for granted, and they both take the pretense of her "daunger" at least half-seriously:

> "Why, lat be," quod she, "lat be, Nicholas,
> Or I wol crie 'out, harrow' and 'allas'!
> Do wey youre handes, for youre curteisye!"
> This Nicholas gan mercy for to crye, . . .   (3285–88)

Aleyn does make one courtly speech.[4] As he is leaving, he promises,

> "But everemo, wher so I go or ryde,
> I is thyn awen clerk, swa have I seel!"   (4238–9)

But that promise seems all the more cruel in view of the triumphant boast addressed to (so he thinks) his friend:

> "Thou John, thou swynes-heed, awak,
> For Cristes saule, and heer a noble game.
> For by that lord that called is seint Jame,
> As I have thries in this shorte nyght
> Swyved the milleres doghter bolt upright.   (4262–66)

The lovemaking of Nicholas and Alisoun is briefly and charmingly described by means of imagery: "Ther was the revel and the melodye." The Reeve is more explicit:

> Withinne a while this John the clerk up leep,
> And on this goode wyf he leith on soore.
> So myrie a fit ne hadde she nat ful yoore;
> He priketh harde and depe as he were mad.   (4228–31)

Sex in the Reeve's Tale is the principal instrument in a savage class satire. The seductions are the means of crushing the pretensions of Symkyn and his wife to be superior to the other peasants in their village. The miller's wife is the daughter of the priest and boasts of a convent education. They hold their heads so high that no suitor is good enough for their daughter. Malyne is after all an heiress:

> This person of the toun, for she was feir,
> In purpos was to maken hire his heir,
> Bothe of his catel and his mesuage,
> And straunge he made it of hir mariage,
> His purpos was for to bistowe hire hye
> Into som worthy blood of auncetrye.   (3977–82)

Symkyn is so confident of his lofty status that he has actually managed to deceive a few readers and critics about it along with himself. It is true that he despises John and Aleyn with their strange provincial dialect and book learning, but it is a mistake to think that he also looks down on them (as is sometimes said) as simple rustics. The reverse is true. Although the boys are introduced as "povre scolers," they are the miller's superiors not only because of their education but because they can produce ready money to pay for their night's lodging: "Loo, heere oure silver, redy for to spende" (4135). We must not overrate Symkyn's prosperity. Whatever the miller's "greet sokene" (3987) amounts to, little of it comes in the form of hard cash. The parson's dowry consists of "many a panne of bras" (3944). In fact, the allusions to Symkyn's wealth are all sarcastic. His family shares the same room although not, as the narrator emphasizes, the same bed:

> His doghter hadde a bed, al by hirselve,
> Right in the same chambre by and by.
> It myghte be no bet, and cause why?
> Ther was no roumer herberwe in the place.   (4142–45)

These details are necessitated by the plot, but they also deflate any grandeur we might have looked for in Symkyn's ancestral dwelling. The miller's manner changes significantly as soon as John and Aleyn produce the money. Malyne is sent off to the village for ale and bread, and the miller roasts a goose—obviously not everyday fare. He personally makes the students' bed: "With sheetes and with chalons faire yspred" (4140). For Symkyn and his wife the

visit of the two young men is clearly a festive occasion, and they
imbibe liberally.

The students patronize the miller openly:

> "Al hayl, Symond, y-fayth!
> Hou fares thy faire doghter and thy wyf?"   (4022–23)

But in private, their contemptuous estimate of the family is plain
enough: "yon wenche wil I swyve" (4178). The victory of their
class attitudes is accomplished by "swyving" their host's wife and
daughter. This they regard as just recompense for the trick that has
been played on them, and they prove their superiority after all in
the business of nocturnal "grinding."⁵ In bed, where class distinctions are ultimately established, a clerk turns out to be the better
"miller" after all.

The narrator fully shares these class attitudes, and for him
Malyne is exactly what she is for Aleyn: a "wenche." He has little,
if any, pity to waste on her and nothing but scorn for Symkyn
whose roar of anguish betrays the enormity of his vanity at the very
moment that the bubble is burst:

> Who dorste be so boold to disparage
> My doghter, that is come of swich lynage?   (4271–72)

In its unromantic portrayal of sex and class conflict, the Reeve's
Tale is much closer to the French fabliaux than the Miller's.⁶ Although few of the French tales can match the richness of detail and
subtlety of the Reeve's, the latter represents the fabliau norm at
its best; the Miller's Tale is *sui generis*. However, in his characterization of the bitter Reeve, Chaucer has given the conventional attitudes of the fabliau a personal voice and thereby achieves a double
result. The tale develops the character of the teller, but at the same
time the teller becomes a commentary upon the character of the
fabliau genre.

First, what does the story tell us about the Reeve? The pleasure
taken in aggressive male sexuality (the escapade of the boys' horse
with the wild mares already prepares us for the night's activities) is
a further measure of the old man's frustration to which the Reeve

has confessed in his Prologue. The revenge motif in the tale, as several critics have observed, expresses the Reeve's own desire for revenge upon the Miller. He enjoys not only Symkyn's disgrace but the blood and violence of the ending:

> Doun ran the blody streem upon his brest.   (4276)

> And smoot the millere on the pyled skulle,
> That doun he gooth, and cride, "Harrow! I dye!"
> Thise clerkes beete hym weel and lete hym lye.
> (4306–8)

Less directly the tale also exhibits the Reeve's servile status. The better to cheat his lord and to maintain his authority over the other peasants on the manor, the Reeve has technically remained a serf although he could obtain his "freedom" at any time. That is the meaning of his shorn top: "His heer was by his erys ful round yshorn;/His top was dokked lyk a preest biforn" (589–590). He lends his master the money he has stolen from him and gets it back, no doubt with interest, but also with thanks and "a cote and hood"—a new livery. The Reeve's actual wealth and status are shown in his house, which stands apart surrounded by shade trees:

> His wonyng was ful faire upon an heeth;
> With grene trees yshadwed was his place.   (606–607)

But to get what he has, Oswald the Reeve has obviously had to swallow much of his pride. What enrages him in Robin the Miller is not only the personal insult but the Miller's swaggering independence. The Miller, as I have argued in the preceding chapter, is the voice of holiday misrule. The Reeve is the voice of the establishment and everyday "morality."[7] The savage fun at the naive pretensions of Symkyn, his nunnery-educated wife, and her father, the priest who thinks that "hooly chirches good moot been despended/On hooly chirches blood, that is descended," expresses true resentment toward the class aspirations that Chaucer has portrayed so variously in the portraits of the General Prologue, including of course the Reeve's own portrait. The Reeve's satire of

Symkyn's family says exactly what the Host has said to the Reeve in telling him to shut up and get on with his story:

> The devel made a reve for to preche,
> Or of a soutere a shipman or a leche.   (3903–4)

In this society, the cobbler should stick to his last.

In their scorn of the upstart, the Host and the Reeve ally themselves with the attitude of the ruling class. Ironically, their quickness to expose members of their own class who take on airs is a petit bourgeois imitation of aristocratic snobbery. The Host and the Reeve truly display the lackey mentality, and the Reeve's Tale, like the great majority of French fabliaux, is profoundly anti-bourgeois.

The notion that the French fabliaux are bourgeois in origin, which still has currency in the introductions to Robinson's edition, was dispelled in 1957 by Per Nykrog. Nykrog makes a convincing case that the fabliaux constitute, in fact, an aristocratic genre, which treats the parvenu middle class with relentless hostility. The social world of the fabliau is subject to a rigid caste system that discriminates against the bourgeois, the wealthy peasant, and especially the priest who leads the good life of the bourgeoisie.[8] Nykrog's study does not take into account Chaucer's fabliaux and raises an interesting question about them. Why, if the fabliau is really an aristocratic genre, are Chaucer's fabliau tales told by churls, bourgeois pilgrims, or debased ecclesiastics like the Friar and Summoner? There is definitely a social hierarchy of genres in the *Canterbury Tales,* the courtly and moral stories being told by elite pilgrims like the Knight, the Man of Law, and the Franklin, the ribald stories being assigned to the lower-class pilgrims. Is Chaucer portraying a fact of literary history that would seem to call Nykrog's evidence into question, or is he disguising the facts? The answer, I believe, is that although the fabliaux express aristocratic viewpoints, these attitudes are adopted at all social levels, exactly like aristocratic dress and manners. The Reeve's Tale is a case in point. When Chaucer warns us,

> The Millere is a cherl, ye knowe wel this;
> So was the Reve eek and othere mo,
> And harlotrie they tolden bothe two,   (3182–84)

he is also making a comment about the genre. "Harlotrie" *is* a churlish subject and delight in it is a powerful social leveller. No matter how sophisticated our response, our laughter at these stories *is* churlish laughter. For the most part, it is also pitiless laughter. We *join* the Reeve in anticipating and enjoying "deynous" Symkyn's fall, and consciously or not, we approve the Reeve's class attitudes while we read the story.

Let us, therefore, not be hasty in passing a harsh judgment on the Reeve, for we shall be judging ourselves as well. Critics have been saying some hard things about many of Chaucer's pilgrims, including the Reeve. The Reeve's Tale not only invites but seems to insist on such moral judgments:

> A gylour shal hymself bigyled be.
> And God, that sitteth heighe in magestee,
> Save al this compaignye, grete and smale!

The blessing, coming at the end of this tale, is of course ironic. God sitting in majesty like a judge is asked to "save" the pilgrims. But the narrator, who has been sitting in judgment over the characters of the tale, has shown no mercy. Just before he begins his story, the Reeve has said of the Miller:

> He kan wel in myn eye seen a stalke,
> But in his owene he kan nat seen a balke.

The allusion is to the Sermon on the Mount (Mat. vii. 1–4) and makes a singularly ironic introduction to this story of revenge. *Caveat lector!* We can easily detect the mote in the Reeve's eye while ignoring the beam in our own. The true lesson of Chaucer's new art is to refrain from moral judgment: Judge not, that ye be not judged.[9] The Reeve himself is treated by Chaucer with a humanity and understanding that contrasts with the Reeve's treatment of the characters in his tale. The proper response, and the proper punishment of the Reeve, is not dogmatic judgment but the laughter of Roger the Cook:

> The Cook of Londoun, whil the Reve spak,
> For joye him thoughte he clawed him on the bak.

CHAPTER VIII

The Man of Law
vs. Chaucer

$\mathcal{A}$ FTER A dramatic exchange between the Cook and the Host in which the Cook promises on some future turn to tell a story about a "hostiler" (a promise never fulfilled), there follow fifty-eight lines of the Cook's Tale—just enough to tantalize us. Then the first fragment of the *Canterbury Tales* breaks off. In the majority of manuscripts, the unfinished Cook's Tale is followed by the Man of Law's Introduction or by the spurious Tale of Gamelyn and then the Man of Law's headlink.[1] There have been several guesses as to why Chaucer left the Cook's Tale unfinished, and there is some question whether the Cook's Tale along with the Miller's and Reeve's was composed before or after the Man of Law's Introduction. Robinson assigns these three fabliau tales to "the early nineties,"[2] and one theory holds that the Man of Law originally began the storytelling with the Tale of Melibee.[3] All such theories must depend in large measure on conjecture. For myself, I cannot conceive that Chaucer ever allowed a plan designed "to shorte with oure weye" to begin with a long prose allegory. Furthermore, if Harry Bailly had the social tact to see that the Knight must tell the first tale (to the relief of all the company), we may credit Chaucer with the same good sense. The Miller's Tale is so direct a reply to the Knight's that I believe it to be the first of the *Canterbury Tales* to be written expressly for that frame. The preparation of the audience for the fabliau tales by the narrator's apologies in the General Prologue and the Miller's Prologue is another indication that Chaucer was conscious of introducing a novelty. Moreover, the presence in all three of these fabliaux of character portraits similar to those of the pilgrims in the General Prologue, and the absence of such portraits from other tales (except for the portraits of Chauntecleer and Pertelote) is strong presumptive evidence that these tales were written hard upon the portraits in the Prologue. As I have suggested before, it is possible that the idea of including fabliaux tales in a frame story may well have provided the inspiration for the creation of their tellers and along with them the world of the Canterbury pilgrimage.

I have taken some pains to set forth my views about the priority of the three fabliau tales in Fragment I because it raises a question of great importance for the future development of Chaucer's masterpiece. We know how the Miller's Tale was received by the pilgrim audience:

> Diverse folk diversely they seyde,
> But for the moore part they loughe and pleyde.
>
> (3857–58)

But how was it received by Chaucer's court audience, the audience of the *Troilus* frontispiece, and by such literary friends as the "moral Gower" and the "philosophical Strode?"

An indirect answer to that question may be found, I believe, in the Man of Law's Introduction and Tale. When called upon by the Host to tell the next story the Man of Law claims to be at a loss:

> I kan right now no thrifty tale seyn
> That Chaucer, thogh he kan but lewedly
> On metres and on rymyng craftily,
> Hath seyd hem in swich Englissh as he kan
> Of olde tyme, as knoweth many a man.   (46–50)[4]

He continues with a partial list of Chaucer's works that consists chiefly of stories from the *Legend of Good Women*, surprising us with several that Chaucer apparently never got around to writing. He praises Chaucer for avoiding stories about incest and alludes to two such tales with indignation. At last he declares that he will leave rhyme to Chaucer and tell a prose tale and immediately begins a prologue in rhyme royal.

Commentary on the passage has concentrated on several problems: the evidence of revision contained in the announcement of a tale in prose,[5] the character of the Man of Law implied by these remarks,[6] and a hypothetical quarrel that the lines may have precipitated between Chaucer and his old friend John Gower, who in the *Confessio Amantis* tells both the stories the Man of Law condemns.[7] Such questions, however, are subsidiary to a more basic one. Why should a lawyer of all people and at this stage of the journey deliver a pronouncement on Chaucer's works presumably without recognizing the poet among the pilgrims?

One has the uneasy sense of being excluded from a private joke that would be more readily intelligible to Chaucer's audience than it is to us. The Man of Law's portentous remarks do·not sound as though they were merely for "the nones." His discussion of poetry, especially when it is related to his Prologue and Tale and to the brief Epilogue that follows in several of the manuscripts, bears on the question I have asked about the reception of the fabliau tales and strongly implies an answer. Fragment II is a fresh start and makes us consider what sort of poet Chaucer had been in the eyes of his public and what sort of poet he would continue to be.

The narrator's apologies in the General Prologue and Miller's Prologue for the stories of the churls and their low words—which he regrets being forced to relate along with the rest—are of course meant to be taken humorously. When he warns the squeamish reader to "Turne over the leef and chese another tale," we realize that the poet, the real creator of all the tales, is pretending to thrust off on us the burden of a choice that he has already made. But the humor, though meant to be disarming, should not conceal from us the significance of the choice Chaucer did make between two alternatives that, to borrow the Host's terminology, we may call "the poetry of sentence" and "the poetry of solaas." The distinction is arbitrary, and, in theory, medieval aesthetics demanded that these two qualities of art should go hand in hand. Nevertheless, in practice, as the contrast between the Knight's Tale and the fabliaux of Fragment I demonstrates, one quality or the other tends to stand out. The tales of the Miller and the Reeve are not without their "sentence," but they are certainly not what the Man of Law and those who shared his taste would have recognized as "thrifty" stories. "Telle us a tale anon, as forward is," the Host reminds the Man of Law. The Man of Law's problem—what story to tell next —is also Chaucer's. By introducing a discussion of his former works into the frame story of a new work still in its formative stage, Chaucer prompts us to compare his previous achievements with the task on which he is currently engaged. He takes stock of what has gone before and perhaps looks ahead to what is still to come.

The Man of Law's doubts about his ability to tell a "thrifty" story may, therefore, reflect Chaucer's own uncertainty on the same score. He evidently had second thoughts about which story to assign to the Man of Law, for he replaced some prose tale (generally believed to have been the Melibee) with the Tale of Constance. The difficulty can hardly have been finding a new plot, for there was certainly no dearth of stories in the Middle Ages. However, it may very well have been a question of finding a *suitable* plot, that is, a plot that would suit both Chaucer and his audience, for the Man of Law's epithet "thrifty" (which applied to stories means "profitable" or "improving") implies a question of aesthetics. What constitutes a worthwhile story? The Lawyer's discussion of poetry can be construed as a humorous projection—with serious implications—of Chaucer's own search for fit materials to carry out the great plan of the *Canterbury Tales.*

To understand the exact nature of Chaucer's problem one must try to recapture the originality of that plan, not as it appears to us today, but as it first struck Chaucer's audience, and we ought not to assume that their response was as favorable as our own. We may be sure that the first installment of a new major work by the author of *Troilus* and the *Legend of Good Women* would arouse keen expectations and perhaps also severe apprehensions among the faithful followers of Chaucer's courtly poetry.

No doubt Chaucer's audience, like the pilgrim audience, "and namely the gentils everichon," were sensitive to such distinctions; and in the narrator's apologies, Chaucer is either anticipating or quite possibly answering criticisms of his new work. If when the passage in the Miller's Prologue was written, most of the tales of "moralitee and hoolynesse" to which the reader is referred did not yet exist, we may appreciate Chaucer's position. He had an obligation, like every conscientious medieval poet, to produce moral and religious works, and in Chaucer's case, "gentle" works as well. In beginning the *Canterbury Tales,* however, Chaucer had also incurred a commitment to the pilgrims whom he had brought to life and who in the Miller's Prologue start insisting on *their* right to be heard.

With such a perspective, we may see Chaucer in the Man of Law's fragment attempting to remain faithful to his commitment to write pious works but without abandoning his commitment to the human comedy he had begun. In the Man of Law's Tale and its links two different artistic impulses are at work. The handling of the Host and the Man of Law in the headlink and in the lively Epilogue to the tale continues the impulse toward realism, drama, and satire initiated in the General Prologue and developed in the fabliaux of Fragment I and its links. The tale itself, on the other hand, is an example of the moralized romance that takes us back to the Knight's Tale, the *Troilus,* and especially to the *Legend of Good Women.* This mode, predominantly courtly and didactic, was unquestionably the chief basis of Chaucer's reputation among his contemporaries and in the Renaissance. Of course in many works the distinction between moral seriousness and comic realism is by no means absolute. Nevertheless, a distinction exists, and for those members of Chaucer's audience who lacked his comic vision the two sides of his poetry must have been difficult to reconcile. Men like Scogan and Bukton, whose sense of comedy is clearly implied in the epistles Chaucer addressed to them, might appreciate the merits of Chaucer's new experiment with a frame story; but one may sympathize with other members of Chaucer's audience, men and particularly women of limited and established literary tastes, who would regard the lower characters in the General Prologue, not to mention their tales, with dismay.

The Man of Law's fragment may be considered Chaucer's response—half in earnest, half in game—to such an attitude. Having arrived at a point where two roads converged, Chaucer characteristically managed to travel both by writing a straightforward tale of "moralitee and hoolynesse" framed by links in which the point of view of those who insist that poetry deal exclusively with such subjects is deftly satirized. The result is paradoxical and ironic: a pilgrim who is shown to be something of a fool and perhaps also something of a knave turns out to have extremely straitlaced notions about literature and tells an impeccably moral tale. It is a response that Chaucer would not expect everyone to understand completely, least of all the very people who had provoked it. It would not have been the first time that he wrote to please his audience while managing, for different reasons, to please himself.

The Man of Law's discussion of Chaucer's works brings to mind an earlier critique of Chaucer's poetry, the God of Love's accusation in the *Legend* that Chaucer has written heresy and Alceste's patronizing defense of the poet, which includes, like the Man of Law's Introduction, a list of Chaucer's works. Cupid's charge that the *Troilus* is antifeminist almost surely reflects criticisms made either seriously or in jest by members of Chaucer's own circle who thought that they knew best what he should write about. In both works Chaucer is dramatizing, in a disarming manner, the difficulties of a poet who writes for a small and opinionated audience, specifically the problem of finding subject matter that will both satisfy them and please him. To articulate the case against him through fictional characters to whom Chaucer defers humbly and apologetically is a gracious way of acknowledging criticism, but as it turns out, it is also a manner of defense. For the humor is by no means all at the poet's expense. His critics, on closer examination, turn out to be well-meaning but misinformed, pedantic, and dogmatic. The Man of Law shows most of these characteristics, and the implication is strong that he, like the God of Love, is Chaucer's ironic portrait of critics who favored him with condescending praise and gratuitous advice.

The Man of Law's list of Chaucer's works and his grudging compliment to the poet for refusing to write about incest suggest that, although he professes not to care for Chaucer's style, he at least approves of his subject matter. All the works he mentions, it should be noted, are the unhappy affairs of noble lovers, and his enumeration of the misfortunes of Chaucer's heroines has the ring of lugubrious sentimentality. He is, indeed, an ill-informed and pretentious literary critic,[8] but in spite of his mistakes and pedantry he expresses a consistent and very common view of poetry. His use of the word "thrifty" and his reference to Chaucer's works as "sermons" are clues to this point of view. They indicate that the Man of Law regards the function of all poetry, including love poetry, as didactic. A story is worth telling only if it contains a lesson. Rhyme is a mere ornament, and the Man of Law, though he claims to know all about the Muses, declares with the air of someone not impressed by superficialities that he offers plain fare: he will speak in prose.

Even allowing for a certain amount of distortion, we can recognize in this passage Chaucer's reputation as it must have been known at about the time that he began the *Canterbury Tales*. His literary profile is sketched for us by one of the more distinguished of the pilgrims, a professional man with some pretensions to literary taste. It is a voice from Chaucer's audience. For the Man of Law, Chaucer is a follower of Ovid, especially the Ovid of the *Ars Amatoria* and the *Heroides*. Chaucer is the chronicler of the sufferings of noble lovers, of the wounds of Lucrece and Thisbe, the tears of Helen, and the woe of "Brixseyde." (Is he mistakenly putting Criseyde into the *Legend* under her original name?) Moreover, Chaucer has a reputation for respecting the canons of decency; he refuses to write about unnatural love.

Let us imagine what the first fragment of the *Canterbury Tales* would have done to increase that reputation among those who thought as the Man of Law did. There was the Knight's noble story, but that had been written some time ago. And then—three stories of "harlotrye" in succession! The final couplet of the unfinished Cook's Tale may stand to indicate the depth to which the onetime servant of the servants of the God of Love had sunk:

> And hadde a wyf that heeld for contenance
> A shoppe, and swyved for hir sustenance.   (4421–22)

If the story of Criseyde had been anathema to the God of Love, what would he have said of this? Chaucer must have been well aware that he was compounding his poetic felonies if indeed someone did not actually tell him so.

As a matter of fact, it is quite likely that someone did. In his biography of John Gower, John H. Fisher suggests that Chaucer's friend took it upon himself to ask the question that I have been formulating: *quo vadis?*[9] The suggestion that the Man of Law speaks for Gower is supported by a number of resemblances between them—the legal training, the sententious manner, and, most important, the didactic aesthetic, which actually fits the *Confessio Amantis* much more closely than it does Chaucer's love poetry.[10] Moreover, if anyone deserves the reproach of having told all the thrifty stories "in swich Englissh as he kan," it is John Gower.

Of course to argue that the Man of Law speaks for Gower is not to say that he is Gower. Obviously he ceases to speak for Gower when in condemning stories about incest he mentions two of the tales that Gower had used in the *Confessio.* Practically everyone is willing to accept this as a good-natured joke by Chaucer at Gower's expense, but actually the joke takes the edge off the satire leading up to it, which touches Gower much more closely. The implication that the author of the *Confessio* was, like the Man of Law, humorless and pedantic hits close to home. To suggest that he told immoral stories, however, amounts to a patently false jest that could hardly give offense. The joke is really on the Man of Law, who only makes himself seem ridiculously prudish in professing to be more moral than the moral Gower.

Up to a point, though, the didactic view of poetry held by the Man of Law represents a genteel literary taste common enough among Chaucer's audience, a taste shared by Gower and one to which he catered in his works. Moreover, the taste might easily have been attributed to Chaucer himself by those who read his courtly poems without seeing either their humor or their philosophical depth. In that case one can understand why they should feel that Chaucer was letting them down badly in the *Canterbury Tales.*

If the passage is Chaucer's amused response to some such unfavorable reaction, there is good reason why he chose a wealthy lawyer to speak about poetry rather than, say, a poor clerk. By letting the Man of Law state the case, Chaucer exposes its essential shallowness. The Sergeant of the Law is portrayed as the type of the wealthy bourgeois who condescends to dictate his taste to the artist. He insists that art be serious, dignified, and moral. But what he actually appreciates in art is not morality but respectability, which is the appearance that morality confers. The Sergeant of the Law, as the emphasis on the word *semed* in his portrait suggests, is a man of appearances. In his own life, we are led to suspect, he is perhaps neither so dignified nor so moral as he would like to appear, and therefore he likes to appropriate a high moral tone from the literature that meets his approval. He seems to appreciate thrifty stories, but does he in fact?

It is the function of his Prologue, I think, to show that he really does not. It begins with twenty-two lines eloquently describing the wretchedness of poverty, which are for the most part a paraphrase from the *De contemptu mundi* of Innocent III.[11] They are perfectly sound doctrine, but they are divorced completely from their context, which shows poverty to be only one example of the misery of the human condition. There is nothing in Innocent that corresponds to the surprising corollary that the Man of Law draws:

> O riche marchauntz, ful of wele been yee,
> O noble, o prudent folk, as in this cas!
> Youre bagges been nat fild with ambes as,
> But with sys cynk, that renneth for youre chaunce;
> At Cristemasse myrie may ye daunce!   (122–126)

The passage in *De contemptu mundi* turns directly from the misery of the poor to the misery of the rich:

> The rich man, however, is undone by abundance and dissipated by ostentation; he flies into folly and sinks into sin; and what had been venal pleasures turn into penal measures. Toil in the getting, fear in the possessing, sorrow in the losing constantly vex, worry, and torment his mind: "For where your treasure is, there will your heart be also."[12]

The Prologue departs not only from the dignified doctrine but also from the dignified diction of the Latin tract. The allusions to hazard and dancing take us out of the realm of morality straight back to the milieu of Perkyn Revelour in the Cook's Tale. The Man of Law's pronouncements on poverty and wealth, like the Wife of Bath's on chastity and marriage, reflect the bias of his experience, and the blunt materialism shows up his sententiousness as affectation.

The connection between prologue and tale (the tale begins with a reference to merchants) seems strained, but actually prologue and tale have a common theme but come to directly opposite conclusions, the former praising material wealth, and the latter exalting genuine spiritual poverty. The contradiction is our clue to the real intent of the passage: those who insist most loudly on morality in art are often morally insensitive.

The fact that Chaucer planned at one time to let the Man of Law tell a prose tale like the Melibee does not change matters. A homily would have served the purpose just as well as the Tale of Constance. In some respects, a prose tale would be the most literal application of a purely didactic theory of literature, implying that poetic craft is not essential to the ultimate end of poetry. Chaucer, however, had the better inspiration of adapting a story Gower had already told in the *Confessio* as an illustration of what he could do applying Gower's poetics to the same material. The tale chosen was especially appropriate to Chaucer's purpose if his purpose was to prove, like the Pardoner, that "A moral tale yet I yow tellen kan." It is a return to the abandoned theme of the *Legend,* the praise of constant women, only this time he is praising a servant of the true God instead of Cupid's saints, who are for the most part women of somewhat uncertain virtue. Constance thus makes amends for the sins of Alisoun and Malyne far more effectively than Cleopatra and Dido atone for the faithlessness of Criseyde.

The tale is well enough suited to the Man of Law's genteel, sentimental, and moralistic tastes, although it would be difficult to maintain that it is one that dramatically develops the character of its narrator as the Reeve's Tale does.[13] There are occasional passages, for example the one on Constance's wedding night (708–714), that tempt one to interpret them humorously as though they were lapses in taste of a man not quite equal to keeping up the high level of dignity he is aiming at.[14] But, whatever faults we may find in the tale or its teller, it must have seemed to Chaucer's audience a serious, straightforward, and occasionally moving account not so much of a good woman as of the womanly virtue she personifies.[15]

A comparison of the tale to its source shows that the effect of Chaucer's changes and additions was to heighten the religious tone of the story and to make it as dignified and moral as possible.[16] The morality is not merely a sop to his audience. In the Man of Law's Tale Chaucer returns to a philosophical theme that he had treated in the Knight's Tale and that recurs in the tales of several of the other pilgrims. Specifically, Chaucer is concerned in the Man of Law's Tale, as he was in the Knight's, with the problem of reconciling destiny and divine justice. How does one account for a world in which men grope blindly toward some ineluctable fate and in which the innocent suffer? Both tales contain long and complicated allusions to astrological influences on human affairs. However, in both tales the role of the stars is finally understood as subordinate to a divine providence that we are bound to accept even though we cannot fully understand it. In the pagan context of the Knight's Tale, providence is expressed in Boethian terms as the disposition of a "prime mover" who has established a "faire cheyne of love," a perfect whole composed of a series of imperfect parts (2987–3016). Man must have faith in the existence of this order and must make "vertu of necessitee" (3042). Theseus's outlook might be called a stoic equivalent of the ideal of constancy.

In the Man of Law's Tale the remote and impersonal order of the Prime Mover becomes the providence of the Christian God who directly and mysteriously dispenses justice and grace:

> God liste to shewe his wonderful myracle
> In hire, for we sholde seen his myghty werkis;
> Crist, which that is to every harm triacle,
> By certeine meenes ofte, as knowen clerkis,
> Dooth thyng for certein ende that ful derk is
> To mannes wit, that for oure ignorance
> Ne konne noght knowe his prudent purveiance.
>
> (477–483)[17]

The masculine and chivalric virtue represented by Theseus gives way to the feminine and passive virtue of Constance; she stands in relationship to him somewhat as the Alceste of the *Legend* does to Troilus. In all four of these figures, one feels Chaucer trying to establish some ideal of human faith and permanence in a universe of change.

But there is a current of pessimism about the human condition in the Knight's Tale that neither Theseus's rationalization of fate nor the happy ending can quite remove. "What is this world? what asketh men to have?" (2775), the dying Arcite asks, and the answer is given to us by Egeus, "This world nys but a thurghfare ful of wo" (2847). There is "Joye after wo" but also "wo after gladnesse" (2841).[18] The same pattern repeats itself in the Man of Law's Tale, but in spite of the Christian context, the gloomy impression of mutability is even stronger. This comes in part from the absence of romantic coloring, such as we find in the Knight's Tale, to relieve the repetitious chronicle of Constance's sufferings, but it also results from the fact that the dominant philosophical influence here is not *De consolatione philosophiae* but *De contemptu mundi.* Only one brief passage (813–816) is based on Boethius, but there are four from Innocent, not counting the stanzas on poverty in the Prologue. Two of these deal with the transience of earthly happiness (421–427, 1135–41), two with the castigation of drunkenness (771–777) and lechery (925–931). They total only thirty lines, yet not merely these passages but the bulk of the tale seems to breathe the somber spirit of *De contemptu mundi* or, to use Innocent's own title, *De miseria humane conditionis,* surely one of the most depressing books ever written. The reconciliation of Constance with Alla and with her father at the end are brief glimpses of light that serve only to contrast with the darkness of death that terminates them. There is "joye after wo," but it is of short duration.

Chaucer has thus kept his promise by providing a tale of "moralitee and hoolynesse" to which the scrupulous reader may turn. But that is not the last word in this fragment. When the Man of Law has finished, the Host, stretching in his stirrups, acknowledges, "This was a thrifty tale for the nones!" He calls on the Parson next because

> I se wel that ye lerned men in lore
> Can moche good, by Goddes dignitee!   (1168–69)

It would seem that we may expect another thrifty offering. However, the Parson sharply rebukes the Host for swearing, and the Host replies with indignation:

> "O Jankin, be ye there?
> I smelle a Lollere in the wynd," quod he.

"Now! goode men," quod oure Hoste, "herkeneth me;
Abydeth, for Goddes digne passioun,
For we schal han a predicacioun;
This Lollere heer wil prechen us somwhat."

(1172–77)

But before the Parson has a chance to reply, another pilgrim breaks
in: " 'Nay, by my fader soule, that schal he nat!' / . . . 'heer schal
he nat preche.' " Ostensibly the objection is to heretical doctrine
that a Lollard might preach: " 'He wolde sowen som difficulte, /
Or springen cokkel in our clene corn.' " But the more probable
motive is the desire to restore the gay mood of the company:

My joly body schal a tale telle,
And I schal clynken you so mery a belle,
That I schal waken al this compaignie.
But it schal not ben of philosophie,
Ne phislyas, ne termes queinte of lawe.   (1185–89)

The Man of Law's discussion of poetry and his tale have made
it appear, for a time, as though after the rebellion begun by the
Miller and carried on by the Reeve and the Cook, the *Canterbury
Tales* were to return to high seriousness and perhaps take the direction of prose. When the Host calls upon the Parson, we feel
that order and decorum have been inexorably restored. But the
holiday humor has only been suppressed, and at the first oppor-
tunity it breaks out again. Chaucer's critics are not to have their
way after all.

The Miller's magnificent coarseness amounted to Chaucer's
dramatic assertion of the poet's right to see life steadily and see
it *whole*. No character and no story, no matter how seemingly
churlish or indecent, will be denied a place in the human comedy.
The new interruption serves the same function and reassures us,
as it does the pilgrim audience, that the *Canterbury Tales* will also
continue to make us laugh. The tales will go on wavering between
the poles of "sentence" and "solaas," many of them successfully
steering a middle course between the two.

But the sermon has only been postponed, and when the moralists were put in their place in the Epilogue of the Man of Law's

Tale, Chaucer probably realized that he was only delaying the hour of their ultimate victory. The Parson will have the last word, and Chaucer must know that in the end he will turn to him. Worldly poetry can defend itself against worldly men and specious critics like the Man of Law. The Parson's Prologue, however, contains an attack on poetry for which the poet, the medieval poet at least, does not have a good answer.

If I may anticipate the end for a moment, the Parson's Prologue significantly resembles the Man of Law's Introduction in the way it is constructed.[19] Both links open with an involved calculation of the hour, based on the elevation of the sun and the length of the shadows. In the Man of Law's Introduction the sun has risen forty-five degrees and the shadows are equal in length to the objects that cast them. It is ten o'clock in the morning. In the Parson's Prologue the sun is rapidly setting, and the shadows extend to more than double the length of a human body. It is now four o'clock in the afternoon. We do not know how many days the pilgrims have been travelling or whether they are still on the way to Canterbury or on the way home, and we do not need to know. Placing the two passages side by side, we get the feeling of having lived through a long and satisfying day.

In the morning the Host had turned to the pilgrims and with rare solemnity lectured them on the value of time:

> Lordynges, the tyme wasteth nyght and day,
> And steleth from us, what pryvely slepynge,
> And what thurgh necligence in oure wakynge,
> As dooth the streem that turneth nevere agayn,
> Descendynge fro the montaigne into playn. . . .
> Lat us nat mowlen thus in ydelnesse.   (20–24, 32)

Like Pandarus, Harry Bailly waxes tedious in counseling 'bisinesse," and of course he is getting ready to address that seemingly busiest of men, the Man of Law.

In the evening he turns to the most genuinely busy man among the pilgrims, the good shepherd, who is not a justice but a just man. Once again in a portentous mood, the Host calls upon the Parson to tell the last tale and "knytte up wel a greet mateere" (X.

20–28). The Host wants to hear one last fable, but it is evening now and time for prayer. Like the Man of Law, the Parson gives the company *his* views on poetry:

> Thou getest fable noon ytoold for me;
> For Paul, that writeth unto Thymothee,
> Repreveth hem that weyven soothfastnesse,
> And tellen fables and swich wrecchednesse.
> Why sholde I sowen draf out of my fest,
> Whan I may sowen whete, if that me lest?   (31–36)

The Parson's image of sowing may remind us of the jolly pilgrim's objection to the "cokkel" in the "clene corn," but here the reference is not to the impure tares of heresy but to the fruitless chaff of fiction. Unlike the Man of Law, the Parson does not profess to be a critic of aesthetic niceties. Whether it is rhyme or the "rum, ram, ruf" of alliterative verse, it is all "draf" and "wrecchednesse." He offers to tell a tale in prose without apologizing for it as the Man of Law does, and he courteously asks the assent of the company and tells them that he speaks under the correction of more learned men than he. He is the only teller of a tale who seeks the general agreement of the pilgrims, and they have caught his spirit just as earlier at the Tabard they caught the spirit of the Host when they agreed to the plan of telling stories along the way:

> Upon this word we han assented soone,
> For, as it seemed, it was for to doone,
> To enden in som vertuous sentence.   (61–63)

This time the prose tale does follow.

As in the Man of Law's Introduction, one senses that in the Parson's Prologue Chaucer had reached a turning point but that this time he did not hope to turn again. For the last time he discusses poetry through the mouth of one of his characters; when he turns back to the subject at the end of the sermon, he is making his Retraction in his own person. There he provides another list of his works, this time complete, and repents of having written the majority of them, not before literary critics but before the only judge whose verdict ultimately matters.

Like the second fragment, I believe the final fragment of the

Canterbury Tales forms a sequence in which a view of poetry is stated, applied, and followed by an epilogue expressing Chaucer's intention. Both fragments may be seen as products of Chaucer's struggle with his conscience as an artist and with the problem of what constitutes the proper concern of the poet. The Man of Law's fragment is a half-humorous concession to the poet's responsibility for creating works of morality, but it ends by asserting his responsibility to his own vision. It is a kind of palinode *manqué*. An understanding of this sophisticated and worldly handling of the problem of artistic conscience gives us a perspective upon Chaucer's final uncompromising renunciation of poetry.

In Fragment II the issue is primarily one of good taste. The Man of Law professes to admire good poetry but implies that the poet should limit his range to proper subjects and treat them with becoming decorum. The tale shows that there is certainly a place for decorous art, but to make the standard of tales like that of Constance the criterion for all art is a position that Chaucer was too honest a writer to accept. Where the world alone is to be considered, art may take all of life for its province.

In Fragment X the issue is not the superiority of some artistic standards over others but the place of art within the total scheme of salvation. The position taken is that poetry cannot help save one's soul unless it is specifically directed toward that end. But in that case art becomes a mere adjunct of religion. There are times when the aims of the conscientious artist and the conscientious Christian coincide, but their goals remain fundamentally different. The artist is a humanist by profession, and we judge his work by human standards. Divine standards fall into a completely different category. By them, even a mediocre sermon may be better than some great poems. The difference between the Man of Law and the Parson on poetry is that the former would make morality an aesthetic quality while the latter has no such illusions. He recognizes the human limitations of poetry. Where there is a choice to be made between the highest aesthetic and the highest moral standards, the choice is clear. Art is not compromised by making it genteel; it is rejected insofar as it serves any purpose other than the salvation of man.

I have looked ahead because I feel that the end helps us to

understand Chaucer's problems in writing not only the Man of Law's Tale but all the rest. At this particular turn on the road to Canterbury, Chaucer chose to ignore both the Lawyer and the Parson and to follow the "joly body" who promises to tell the next tale. About the identity of that body, the manuscripts and modern editors are in disagreement.[20] Chaucer may well have changed his mind more than once about how to follow up the Man of Law's Tale, or he may never have come to a final decision. In any event, in Ellesmere and many of the best manuscripts, which lack the end-link to the Man of Law's Tale, the tale itself is directly succeeded by the pilgrim who is perhaps closer in spirit to her creator than any other—the good Wife of Bath.

CHAPTER IX

Experience and Authority in the Wife of Bath's Prologue and Tale

IN THE Wife of Bath's Prologue and Tale Chaucer perfects the technique with which he experimented in the Reeve's Prologue and Tale. He gets so deeply inside a character that not simply the point of view, the social attitudes and values, but the very language, imagery, and speech rhythms seem right for *this* pilgrim and no other and endow the character with the semblance of a life independent of the work. The Wife of Bath seems so solidly real that she can be quoted as an authority by a character in the Merchant's Tale (IV.1685–86) and by Chaucer himself in his "Epistle to Bukton": "The Wyf of Bathe I pray yow that ye rede." She is the greatest of Chaucer's personae, but not just in Kittredge's sense that all the Canterbury pilgrims are *dramatis personae*. The Wife of Bath is in a profound sense a persona of Chaucer the artist. She is completely herself; yet, she also embodies an energy and *Lebenslust* that readers like to attribute to Chaucer; and, more than that, she confronts at its deepest level a problem central to Chaucer's art.

> Experience, though noon auctoritee
> Were in this world, is right ynogh for me
> To speke of wo that is in mariage.

So begins the Wife of Bath. If we cut off her specific subject, the "wo that is in mariage," we can identify the issue as one that Chaucer himself is confronting as he develops and defends his new art of fiction. The clash between experience and authority became evident in *Troilus*. The Prologue to the *Legend of Good Women* attempted a rather abstract and intellectual reconciliation between the books in the poet's chest and his experience in the meadow. The General Prologue implies exactly what the Wife of Bath here boldly asserts: "Experience . . . is right ynogh for me/To speke." In her Prologue and Tale the Wife tries to establish that proposition. In the end she fails, of course (as she well knows), but her argument is the most persuasive case that can be made for "This world, that passeth soone as floures faire," the world of our human experience.

The case is ultimately grounded on the Wife's experience, but paradoxically she is also one of the great users of authority in Chaucer's poetry. Along with a great body of anonymous wisdom, she specifically cites Jesus, Solomon, St. Paul, St. Mark, Ptolemy, Simplicius Gallus, Valerius Maximus, Theophrastus, St. Jerome, Chrysippus, Eloise, and Ovid.[1] Indeed, her assault proceeds so vigorously and on so many different fronts that the reader and critic may fail to see the underlying strategy. There is direction to the flow of her discourse, the longest prologue allotted to any of the pilgrims, although the Wife herself may not be aware of it; and it will be helpful at the begining to break it down into its three component parts.[2]

In the first of these parts the Wife is defending her right to remarry as often as she pleases and comparing the relative merits of marriage and virginity. Here she addresses theological issues and bases her arguments upon biblical texts exactly like a medieval preacher. This section constitutes a pseudo-sermon, a fact brought out by the Pardoner, another master of the art of the pulpit, when he interrupts her with a tongue-in-cheek compliment: "Ye been a noble prechour in this cas" (165). She puts him in his place and proceeds to tell the story of her first three marriages. Here she is talking about marriage from a practical point of view—the day-to-day struggle between husband and wife. In this part she addresses herself to other women (ignoring the fact that the only other women in her audience are nuns) and dispenses advice on how to run a successful marriage. It is an *Ars Matrimonia* based on the Wife's own rich experience though heavily influenced, as we shall see, by "auctorite." The final part tells of the Wife's last two marriages in much greater detail. This section is in the manner of personal reminiscences or confessions. It is only in this section that we come to share the Wife of Bath's "experience" and in doing so to understand her better. The Prologue thus moves from authority to experience, from theological arguments toward an intimate domestic scene, and our views of the Wife change as we get deeper and deeper into her personality and into her past.

In commenting on the Wife's sermon on marriage, which it must be remembered is only the first part of her performance, the critic would do well to bear in mind her later appeal to the pilgrim audience, which sounds remarkably like the narrator's in the Miller's Prologue that "men shal nat maken ernest of game":

> But that I praye to al this compaignye,
> If that I speke after my fantasye,
> As taketh not agrief of that I seye;
> For myn entente is nat but for to pleye.   (189–192)

The Wife, like Chaucer, sees herself as an entertainer. Like the Miller she may claim the privilege of the holiday season to upset the normal order of things in the spirit of play. One way to do this is to preach a sermon. "A woman preaching," said Dr. Johnson, "is like a dog's walking on his hinder legs. It is not done well; but you are surprized to find it done at all." The Wife of Bath is well aware that she is playing a man's game; moreover, in her case, it *is* done remarkably well. The satire cuts two ways. It is satire of a woman preaching; at the same time it is a satire of preachers and their art.

Two bits of scriptural authority have been facetiously cited against her multiple marriages—the Wedding at Cana and the Samaritan woman. I say facetiously because according to the letter of the law, certainly as it was practiced in Chaucer's day, a widow was, as the Wife maintains, citing St. Paul (I Cor. vii, 39), "free/ To wedde" (49–50). I doubt that anyone would have thrown up the Samaritan to John of Gaunt in order to prove that his third duchess, Katherine Swynford, was not legally his wife. Such scriptural exegesis is what the Wife of Bath calls "glosyng." To gloss or explain the meaning of a text was, of course, the object of preaching, but abuse of this technique in Chaucer's day, the practice of finding ingenious and self-serving interpretations, had proceeded so far as to make "glosyng" practically synonymous with distortion of the text. The fact is that a clever preacher could make out scripture to mean whatever he wanted it to mean, and the Wife of Bath's "sermon" is a masterful demonstration of that technique. If men can "glosen, up and doun," so can a woman.[3]

It is a fact that practically every reference the Wife makes to Holy Writ twists around its meaning and violates if not the letter, then the spirit of the law. Tracking down the Wife's authorities is an amusing business. For example, we read in the epistle she cites to prove that she is free to remarry: "A wife is bound by the law as long as her husband liveth; but if her husband be dead, she is at liberty to be married to whom she will . . . . But she is happier if she so abide, after my judgment: and I think also that I have the Spirit of God" (I Cor. vii, 39–40). It is the same with all the other references to chapter seven of First Corinthians. What Paul tolerates as a necessary evil, the Wife of Bath celebrates as a positive good.

The fact that the Wife of Bath's sermon is a travesty of the Pauline teachings on marriage and celibacy has been used by D. W. Robertson, Jr., as *prima facie* evidence that the arguments of the Wife of Bath would have been rejected by the medieval reader with derisive laughter. Robertson calls attention to the fact that Chaucer's immediate source for these passages is not St. Paul directly but the Epistle of St. Jerome Against Jovinian, a major source of medieval antifeminist satire.[4] Jerome's letter is a polemic against the doctrines of the monk Jovinian, who was condemned as a heretic in 390. Jovinian's writings have not survived, but Jerome's letter makes it clear that he supported his arguments against celibacy of the clergy with many of the same passages cited by the Wife of Bath. What she is doing, in brief, is to present Jovinian's case, which Jerome had set forth only in order to demolish it. For Robertson the Wife of Bath is a neo-Jovinian heretic, a symbolic figure personifying carnality and carnal knowledge. She is the Synagogue deaf to the teaching of the New Law, one of those who hear but understand not. "Alisoun of Bath is not a 'character' in the modern sense at all, but an elaborate iconographic figure designed to show the manifold implications of an attitude."[5] Any sympathy we feel for the Wife, according to Robertson, is sheer sentimentality.

Robertson's case against the Wife of Bath cannot be lightly dismissed since it bears the stamp of authority, the orthodoxy of the very church that the Wife is defying. He does not allow enough for her playful intent, but notwithstanding her desire to amuse the pilgrims, her opinions ought to be taken seriously. If she plays a game, there is earnest in it, too, for the unorthodoxies she advocates in play are really the convictions she has lived by. The true limitation of Robertson's criticism of the Wife, and of his criticism in general, is that it relies too exclusively on authority. He cannot conceive that any real person in the Middle Ages, believing what Chaucer's good Parson believed, could have entertained the slightest sympathy for the Wife's arguments, much less that a "real" character could preach such views in a work of medieval fiction. Therefore, "Alisoun of Bath is not a 'character' in the modern sense at all."

Against such a position, with deference to all the learning that lies behind it, one may object with the Wife: "The experience woot wel it is noght so." It is not simply the fact that modern readers experience the Wife of Bath as a real "character," a fact to which Robertson would attribute little value. It is the fact that men and women at all times, and particularly in the late Middle Ages, often do not abide by what they may nevertheless sincerely believe. The domination of men's minds by the medieval Church, the sanctity and solemnity of its truth, is a hard fact that cannot be ignored. But if the modern reader turns from sermons and theology to the lives actually led by many laymen and clerics in the declining Middle Ages, he may well be shocked, or perhaps titillated, by the discrepancy between doctrine and practice. A great modern historian of the period writes: "The specific forms of the thought of an epoch should not only be studied as they reveal themselves in theological and philosophic speculations, or in the conceptions of creeds, but also as they appear in practical wisdom and everyday life."[6] Huizinga's study documents on page after page the gap between the idealistic conceptions of the time, be they religious or chivalric, and the actual behavior of medieval people. In spite of "courtly love," for example, the sexual lives of the aristocracy "remained surprisingly rude."

> In the erotic conceptions of the Middle Ages two diverging currents are to be distinguished. Extreme indecency showing itself freely in customs, as in literature, contrasts with an excessive formalism, bordering on prudery. Chastellain mentions frankly how the duke of Burgundy, awaiting an English embassy at Valenciennes, reserves the baths of the town "for them and for all their retinue, baths provided with everything required for the calling of Venus, to take by choice and by election what they liked best, and all at the expense of the duke." Charles the Bold was reproached with his continence, which was thought unbecoming in a prince. At the royal or princely courts of the fifteenth century, marriage feasts were accompanied by all sorts of licentious pleasantries—a usage which had not disappeared two centuries later. In Froissart's narrative of the marriage of Charles VI with Isabella of Bavaria we hear the obscene grinning of the court. Deschamps dedicates to Antoine de Bourgogne an epithalamium of extreme indecency. A certain rhymer makes a lascivious ballad at the request of the lady of Burgundy and of all the ladies.[7]

The fact that these very people also professed to venerate the ideals of love we find in romance is not a sign of hypocrisy: "We should rather picture to ourselves two layers of civilization superimposed, coexisting though contradictory. Side by side with the courtly style, of literary and rather recent origin, the primitive forms of erotic life kept all their force; for a complicated civilization like that of the closing Middle Ages could not but be heir to a crowd of conceptions, motives, erotic forms, which now collided and now blended."[8] The same observations could be made about the religious ideals supposedly governing love and marriage. In spite of St. Paul and St. Jerome, the predominant impression of medieval love and marriage is one of sensuality and of the overriding importance of political and material interests.

The most faithful mirror we have of this reality is literature such as Chaucer's that portrays the different layers of a civilization as "superimposed, coexisting though contradictory." Nowhere has Chaucer drawn this picture with greater complexity than in the figure of the Wife of Bath whose experience is at odds with the "auctorite" of her age. I have argued that the Miller's Tale presents us "the people's unofficial truth" as a holiday game. The Wife of Bath's Prologue shows us that this truth is not entertained for holiday alone but underlies the very substance of daily life, the couplings and quarrels of ordinary men and women. This is not to deny the higher truth its primacy. Ultimately both the Wife of Bath and Chaucer bow to that primacy, but they also testify how very profoundly experience may contradict authority.

The Wife of Bath's authorities may easily be turned against her, but her very citation of those authorities reveals a knowledge of life that challenges the theoretical moralist in a much more profound way. The Wife is willing to concede the superiority of virginity on principle:

> I graunte it wel, I have noon envie,
> Thogh maydenhede preferre bigamye.
> It liketh hem to be clene, body and goost;
> Of myn estaat I nyl nat make no boost.
> For wel ye knowe, a lord in his houshold,
> He nath nat every vessel al of gold;
> Somme been of tree, and doon hir lord servyse.
>
> (95–101)

She is echoing II Tim., ii, 20: "In a great house there are not only vessels of gold and of silver but also of wood and of earth; and some to honor and some to dishonor." Paul regards the wooden vessels as dishonorable, but not so the Wife. In her rendering, the golden vessels, the virgins, are for show but perform no useful function. It is the sturdy, everyday, wooden vessels that "doon hir lord servyse." She believes that she is serving her lord by using her special talent:

> God clepeth folk to hym in sondry wyse,
> And everich hath of God a propre yifte.   (102–103)

She is echoing Paul's patronizing concession to human frailty: "But I speak this by permission, and not of commandment. For I would that all men were even as I myself. But every man has his proper gift of God, one after this manner, and another after that. I say therefore to the unmarried and widows, It is good for them if they abide even as I" (I Cor., vii, 6–8). But the Wife turns grudging concession into a glorious mandate. Her deepest conviction is that everything that has been created is good and meant to be used. Celibacy, though she does not say it openly, seems to her a form of hoarding, a miserly clinging to the most precious of God's gifts. Elsewhere in the New Testament, man is enjoined to use his God-given talent as generously as God has given it. He must not bury his talent in the ground, or hide his light under a bushel. The Wife has no doubt about what her "propre yifte" may be. She may not be the "breed of pured whete-seed" but the good nourishing "barly-breed" with which "Oure Lord Jhesu refresshed many a man" (143–146). "Fressh" and "refresshed" are among her favorite words,[9] and she will bring refreshment to man in her own way:

> In wyfhod I wol use myn instrument
> As frely as my Makere hath it sent.
> If I be daungerous, God yeve me sorwe!   (149–151)

As we shall see there are some strings attached to her generosity, but she has real generosity for all that, as well as gratitude for God's handiwork.[10] However misdirected, generosity and gratitude are genuine virtues, and even in twisting the words of St. Paul, the Wife of Bath is displaying a love of life that strikes many of us as a virtue more compelling than the Pauline virtue of celibacy.

What the Wife is truly challenging is a statement of Paul's much used by Jerome against Jovinian: "It is good for a man not to touch a woman" (I Cor., vii, 1; cf. WBProl 87). The bulk of her "sermon" is a defense of the flesh, but in her peroration she ventures upon a further heresy that would overturn not only the authority of Paul but the very principle of hierarchy on which the social order is based:

An housbonde I wol have, I wol nat lette,
Which shal be bothe my dettour and my thral,
And have his tribulacion withal
Upon his flessh, whil that I am his wyf.
I have the power durynge al my lyf
Upon his propre body, and noght he.
Right thus the Apostel tolde it unto me.   (154–160)

What Paul really said is: "The wife hath not power of her own body, but the husband: and likewise also the husband hath not power of his own body, but the wife" (I Cor., vii, 4). Elsewhere he says: "Wives, submit yourselves unto your own husbands, as unto the Lord" (Eph., v, 22). That woman stands below man in the chain of being is as axiomatic as that man is subject to his lord, and that all men are subject to God. In the next part of her Prologue, therefore, the Wife shakes something even more fundamental than the notion that the flesh is inherently wicked: she advocates not just equality of the sexes but female supremacy. She draws an awe-inspiring picture of herself as a shrew. Again, however, the satire cuts two ways. Her advice to women on how to achieve and maintain marital sovereignty also tells us a good deal about what is wrong with medieval marriage and the medieval image of woman.

The Wife's criteria for selecting a mate are the sound economic ones of her time:

I shal seye sooth, tho housbondes that I hadde,
As thre of hem were goode, and two were badde.
The thre were goode men, and riche, and olde;
Unnethe myghte they the statut holde
In which that they were bounden unto me.   (195–199)

Right away the reader may spot a contradiction of which the Wife of Bath seems oblivious. The "statut" to which she refers is, of course, the "marriage debt" (I Cor., vii, 3–4) to which the Wife has already alluded (155). The rich men, therefore, were too poor to pay their debts. The contradiction shows that the Wife of Bath wants two things that are rarely if ever compatible in a medieval marriage. First, she wants money and independence. Although she marries the old men for their money, she is less interested in money itself than in the things money can buy, the most important of which is power. Instinctively, the Wife realizes that the inferior position of women in society is due to their economic dependence. Her marriage terms, therefore, are legal control of her husband's property. Thus the bond of matrimony is for her a means of purchasing her freedom. However, secondly, she also craves love, and this is something her old husbands cannot give her, or, as she sees it, something they have already given her:

> A wys womman wol bisye hire evere in oon
> To gete hire love, ye, ther as she hath noon.
> But sith I hadde hem hoolly in myn hond,
> And sith they hadde me yeven al hir lond,
> What sholde I taken keep hem for to plese,
> But it were for my profit and myn ese?   (209–214)

The Wife regards "love" like any other commodity to be bought and sold in the world's marketplace. "Wys" is a key word in her Prologue as it was in the General Prologue, and the wisdom she talks about is the shrewd prudential wisdom of the Merchant and the Sergeant of the Law. By such wisdom she succeeds in obtaining the upper hand in the business of marriage.

The example she gives of such wisdom is an elaborate trick that she employed against her first three husbands. These she does not bother to differentiate in any way. All three are essentially the same unpleasant old man: lecherous though sexually feeble, rich and miserly, jealous and cowardly. We are constantly reminded of him through the insults the Wife of Bath hurls at him, nearly all of which rub in his age: "Sire olde kaynard," "Sire olde lechour," "Moote thy welked nekke be tobroke!", "olde dotard shrewe," "olde barel-ful of lyes." Her strategy is to wait for a morning after her husband has come home so drunk that he can remember nothing of the night before. At such a moment, when he is defenseless, she unleashes her fury. The brunt of her attack is to accuse him of having made a series of outrageous and humiliating charges against women, which she rehearses indignantly in the most lurid terms. This diatribe is a compendium of antifeminist literature, drawn by Chaucer from a variety of sources. Most of these charges were no doubt ancient in St. Jerome's day: women are by nature unchaste, they waste their husbands' property, they are born liars, they expect a man to remember their birthdays and put up with their relatives.

The following passage, lifted directly from the Theophrastus portion of *Jerome Against Jovinian,* is typical:

> Thou seist that oxen, asses, hors, and houndes,
> They been assayed at diverse stoundes;
> Bacyns, lavours, er that men hem bye,
> Spoones and stooles, and al swich housbondrye,
> And so been pottes, clothes, and array;
> But folk of wyves maken noon assay,
> Til they be wedded; olde dotard shrewe!
> And thanne, seistow, we wol oure vices shewe.
>
> (285–292)

The statement assumes that a woman is exactly like any other piece of property—an ox, an ass, a stool, a pot—an assumption that goes unquestioned by Theophrastus or St. Jerome. The Wife of Bath does not question it either; the only insult she sees is that women conceal their defects like any shrewd horse trader, not that a woman is like a horse. We begin to see that her own ideas about marriage are derived from the antifeminist tradition, only the Wife is determined to use them to her own advantage. If marriage is a business deal, she is the one who means to come out ahead.

The old husband is obsessed with the idea of preserving his property, which includes what the Wife likes to call her *bele chose.* His jealousy is, therefore, another form of miserliness. If he allows her any freedom, it is like leaving his treasure unguarded in the street. The Wife complains that he hides the keys to his money chest and accuses him of wanting to lock her up in his chest too. Chaucer does not need Freud or Norman O. Brown to tell him that money is both an erotic symbol and substitute. The Wife's love of spending and of dressing up in her flamboyant scarlet gowns satisfies sexual needs. The husband's miserly possessiveness is a sign of his impotence. He keeps the key to his money chest hidden because he cannot use the treasure himself, and so he wants to make sure that no one else does. The Wife is all for spending both the money and the other treasure.

To remain at liberty to do as she pleases she thus engages in a preemptive strike, forcing the enemy to recant accusations that he never made. "And al was fals" (382), she tells the pilgrims, but actually it was all true. She freely admits her own guilt but pleads the law of self-defense. She herself does not realize to what extent her philosophy of marriage has been forced upon her. She knows that her body has a market value. If she wanted to sell her *bele chose,* she tells her husband, she could dress as freshly as a rose, but she will keep it for his own tooth. Nevertheless, she does not scruple to sell to her husbands what she gives away freely to her lovers:

> I wolde no lenger in the bed abyde,
> If that I felte his arm over my syde,
> Til he had maad his raunson unto me;
> Thanne wolde I suffre hym do his nycetee.
> And therfore every man this tale I telle,
> Wynne whoso may, for al is for to selle.   (409–414)

The last statement, her guiding principle, would be cynical if the Wife of Bath's image of herself as a domestic tyrant and hard-boiled business woman were actually true. But we must not take the Wife completely at her own estimate. Her picture of herself contains a large element of fantasy in which she sees herself as the heroic daughter of Venus and Mars, marching through life and winning all of her battles. Her hunger for power in all of her relationships with men is an inversion of her craving for love and security, which the medieval institution of marriage denies to her. Thus she adopts the stereotype of the virago that authority has created. She seems to be the monster of the anti-feminist myth incarnate, but if she is a monster, she is a Frankenstein monster. It is men who have made her so aggressively masculine. The humor as well as the pathos of her situation is that the masculine role she sees herself as playing is at odds with her feminine nature.

Chaucer satirizes the Wife, but at the same time he exposes the shallowness and cynicism of the antifeminist point of view. It is the senile, self-pitying wisdom of old age, and, even though they have not actually had the courage to take this stand, the Wife's old husbands would be fit spokesmen for it. "What eyleth swich an old man for to chide?" (281), the Wife asks contemptuously, and the reader may well ask the same question. Antifeminist satire is the refuge of the frustrated male ego, taking perverse pleasure in contemplating a scapegoat of its own invention. The Wife deserves some credit for having the wit to fling all the taunts back in the teeth of the enemy and to fight him with weapons forged against her. Out of cautionary tales for husbands she makes a school for wives.

She herself is saved from the cynicism of the authorities by her pleasure in life and her humor. She obviously has a glorious time tormenting her husbands and bears them no real malice. Her ferocity is mostly an act, a part of the game she enjoys playing as she enjoys everything. Behind her termagant's mask, she can laugh at the old men and even feel a little sorry for them:

> As help me God, I laughe whan I thynke
> How pitously a-nyght I made hem swynke!   (201–202)

She gave the old men what they paid for.

With her last two husbands the Wife of Bath's troubles begin. It is in this section that she digresses most freely. Memories come flooding in and create a powerful impression of experience that has been lived through. We have a vivid sense of a woman getting on in years as she looks back at her youth and remembers some of the people in her life who are now dead and gone. A note of solemnity creeps in as she refers to one or another of them. Her fourth husband: "God yeve his soul reste!/He is now in his grave and in his cheste" (501–502). The fifth: "God lete his soule nevere come in helle!" (504). Her closest friend and namesake: "God have hir soule! hir name was Alisoun" (530). She recalls how her mother taught her how to catch a man, giving the reader, as though in a series of mirrors, the picture of a chain of Wives stretching all the way back to Eve, each one learning about men at her mother's knee. At moments one feels a mood of *ubi sunt*, the years, the pleasures, the youths and maidens. The Wife of Bath looks back with nostalgia on her good times:

> How koude I daunce to an harpe smale,
> And synge, ywis, as any nyghtyngale,
> Whan I had dronke a draughte of sweete wyn!
> (457–459)

A wistful note of self-awareness creeps into these reminiscences
that belies the belligerent tone of the rest:

> But, Lord Crist! whan that it remembreth me
> Upon my yowthe, and on my jolitee,
> It tikleth me aboute myn herte roote.
> Unto this day it dooth myn herte boote
> That I have had my world as in my tyme.
> But age, allas! that al wole envenyme,
> Hath me biraft my beautee and my pith.
> Lat go, farewel! the devel go therwith!
> The flour is goon, ther is namoore to telle;
> The bren, as I best kan, now moste I selle;
> But yet to be right myrie wol I fonde.   (469–479)

In this famous passage the Wife of Bath has almost forgotten her
audience and is talking to herself somewhat like the Reeve in his
Prologue. However, unlike the Reeve who speaks of the past as so
much "wrecchednesse," the Wife is neither bitter nor spiteful.
She believes that she has made the most of her life and speaks with
a magnificent sense of propriety of "*my* world" and "*my* tyme."
Yet the spirit of these lines is also tinged with a melancholy awareness that time and the world are no man's possession; they move
on. The best is not to be: "The flour is goon." But the Wife is by
no means ready to give up: "The bren, as I best kan, now moste
I selle." She is on the lookout for her sixth husband, and she is
being merry at this very moment, preaching, lecturing, and con-
fessing to her fellow-pilgrims.

The pattern of the Wife of Bath's life is epitomized in two
closely related episodes: the wooing of her fifth husband and the
funeral of the fourth. Significantly, the courtship comes first. The
Wife starts flirting with Jankyn one spring while her husband is
in London on business:

> And so bifel that ones in a Lente—
> So often tymes I to my gossyb wente,
> For evere yet I loved to be gay,
> And for to walke in March, Averill, and May,
> Fro hous to hous, to heere sondry talys—
> That Jankyn clerk, and my gossyb dame Alys,
> And I myself, into the feeldes wente.   (543–549)

Here is Chaucer's finest adaptation of the reverdie as the Wife of Bath remembers another April that brought other stories, other pilgrimages, other marriages. We see the Wife of Bath in the same situation, past and present. Nature is undergoing its annual renewal, and the Wife, too, blooms again as she strolls through the meadows with the young student she has decided to marry if she gets the chance. And she revives again with the pleasure of the memory as she tells the pilgrims about it.

It is consistent with her image of herself that she gives a good practical reason for spreading her nets for Jankyn. She believes in always having a prospective husband in reserve—just in case—because a mouse that has only one hole to run to isn't worth a leek. But her self-deception should not fool us. It should be perfectly obvious to everyone except the Wife herself that she was already head over heels in love with Jankyn. So there is dramatic irony when she congratulates herself on how she practiced her wiles on the young man:

> I bar hym on honde he hadde enchanted me,—
> My dame taughte me that soutiltee.   (575–576)

He has in fact bewitched her.

> And eek I seyde I mette of hym al nyght,
> He wolde han slayn me as I lay upright,
> And al my bed was ful of verray blood;
> But yet I hope that he shal do me good,
> For blood bitokeneth gold, as me was taught.
> And al was fals; I dremed of it right naught.
> (577–582)

But it was all true even though she made up the dream. She is capable of inventing her own Freudian symbols, and the dream does betoken gold—for Jankyn, who will marry her for her fortune.

She has lost her thread for a moment:

> But now, sire, lat me se, what I shal seyn?
> A ha! by God, I have my tale ageyn.   (585–586)

So absorbed has she become in her courtship of Jankyn that the Wife has forgotten to tell the pilgrims about the death of her fourth. She describes how she walked behind his coffin on the way to church, pretending to weep into her handkerchief—"As wyves mooten, for it is usage." But as her head is discreetly bowed, her eyes are fixed in another place. Jankyn is walking directly in front of her as one of the pallbearers:

> As help me God! whan that I saugh hym go
> After the beere, me thoughte he hadde a paire
> Of legges and of feet so clene and faire
> That al myn herte I yaf unto his hoold.   (596–599)

The coffin and the mourners are forgotten before the vision of life, symbolized eloquently by Jankyn's legs. The entire story of her life is compressed into this one image of the old husband being carried out horizontally, intersected by the new one coming in vertically. It is the eternal cycle of weddings and funerals, death and renewal in which she is caught up. That she at the age of forty responds to the call of Nature like a girl of sixteen adds to the humor but also conveys a depth of feeling that is achieved by none of Chaucer's younger lovers. There is more passion in her reaction to Jankyn's legs than in all the complaints of Palamon and Arcite. As she bids an unsentimental farewell to the past, her heart is already in tune with the new season of "yowthe" and "jolitee."

Ironically the Wife of Bath regards the great love of her life as her worst mistake. By marrying Jankyn, she violates all of her principles. For the first time, she marries for love instead of for money, and this time she is the wealthy widow who makes over her property to him. Of all her husbands he was "the mooste shrewe," for he beat her, insulted her, and played hard-to-get; and yet, "I trowe I loved hym best." He is really the kind of man she has wanted all along. However, she cannot understand their relationship except in the terms she has always used, the law of supply and demand.

> Greet prees at market maketh deere ware,
> And to greet cheep is holde at litel prys:
> This knoweth every womman that is wys.   (522–524)

The fifth marriage reverses the pattern of the first three. Now she is "riche and olde" though still very much capable of rendering the marriage debt. No doubt she remains attractive, but there can be little doubt about Jankyn's motives in marrying a woman twice his age. Moreover, the tables are now turned in another respect. Jankyn torments her by reading aloud from his "book of wikked wyves," an anthology of antifeminist literature treasured up from his student days at Oxford. She is forced now to swallow her own medicine. Her indignant summary of the book provides us with another picture of antifeminism seen from the woman's point of view. The volume is a long record of human history that goes back, as many medieval histories do, to the fall of man. According to Jankyn's book, history from that time has followed one simple pattern: it is the chronicle of a world made wretched by the depravity of women. The list of wicked wives is a typical medieval catalogue that tries to prove a point by piling up examples, the more the better. But this chain of examples comes right down to the present. Adam and Eve, Samson and Delilah, Agamemnon and Clytemnestra—all lead up to Jankyn and Alisoun acting out the same old comedy.

The list of disasters becomes comic through the dramatic context, and especially through the way in which the famous stories and anecdotes are brought down to the Wife of Bath's own level of comprehension. Delilah is Samson's "lemman"; Xanthippe "caste pisse" upon the head of "sely" Socrates; the unnatural love of Pasiphae is so revolting to the Wife that she refuses to talk about it—"Fy! spek namoore—it is a grisly thyng."

One day when she can stand it no longer, the Wife of Bath sneaks up behind Jankyn's chair, rips three pages out of his book, and knocks him into the fireplace. Charles Muscatine has aptly characterized the symbolism in this climactic action: "In the context of the *Prologue's* doctrinal material, we behold not only a magnificently natural creature in domestic squabble; she is also the embodiment of experience ripping the pages of the book of authority, and of miltant feminism fetching traditional masculine domination a healthy blow on the cheek."[11] Not only in this instance but in every respect the Wife's fifth marriage dramatizes in human terms her lifelong struggle against authority. Jankyn represents authority in all three of its aspects: he is a man, a husband, and a clerk. Moreover, he is a worthy antagonist. He hits her back so hard that he believes he has killed her:

> And whan he saugh how stille that I lay,
> He was agast, and wolde han fled his way,
> Til atte laste out of my swogh I breyde.
> 'O! hastow slayn me, false theef?' I seyde,
> 'And for my land thus hastow mordred me?
> Er I be deed, yet wol I kisse thee.'   (797–802)

It is hard to tell whether she really thinks she is dying or whether she is acting. In her melodramatic imagination, it would be a highly romantic finish to be murdered by the man she loves, and she will die upon a kiss.

But ironically it is she who will be the death of him. At last he, too, capitulates likes the old husbands and is subjected to the ultimate humiliation. She makes him burn his book, but it is a hollow victory. The Wife of Bath does not understand that she has broken his spirit and that the book is the symbol of his manhood and self-esteem. She says that they were happy, and perhaps she thought they were:

> After that day we hadden never debaat.
> God helpe me so, I was to hym as kynde
> As any wyf from Denmark unto Ynde,
> And also trewe, and so was he to me.   (822–825)

But her professions of peace and fidelity have a pathetic ring. We are not surprised that Jankyn is dead, and while it would be going too far to say she killed him, the final episode shows us that the Wife's battle for mastery is too destructive to allow us to laugh at the end with the Friar as we might laugh at the end of a fabliau.

The joy of the Miller's Tale lies in its fantasy and innocence. We are not permitted to think that its Alisoun may survive her sely John by many years, perhaps to marry at the age of forty a young clerk who reminds her of her first love hende Nicholas. The Wife of Bath's Prologue is comedy of a higher order. We understand by the end that she is fighting a losing battle, the outcome of which is predetermined.

The Wife of Bath is not really a free agent. Though she refuses to accept her lot as a medieval wife, her only recourse is to adopt the psychology and tactics of a medieval husband. Her life is grounded on the premises of antifeminism because the world teaches her no others, and the Church teaches only abject submission. She is, in the last analysis, the creature of authority, and in her most candid utterance does obeisance to it in her own way:

> Allas! allas! that evere love was synne!
> I folwed ay myn inclinacioun
> By vertu of my constellacioun;
> That made me I koude noght withdrawe
> My chambre of Venus from a good felawe.   (614–618)

No matter what the Wife of Bath maintains in her opening "sermon," these lines contain her confession that she is wrong although she does not fully understand why. Her sense that her entire life has been determined is profoundly true although the only terms she knows to express it are those of the astrologers. Into the planetary opposition of Venus and Mars men read the feminine and masculine principles that conflict in society and in the human mind. The ancient myth of the love of Venus and Mars expresses a deep psychological wish for unity; Vulcan's net is the reality principle. The old husband has his revenge after all. The Wife of Bath struggles inside the net as we do, too. One would like to have had Alisoun and Jankyn live happily ever after, but that is not life. It happens only in fairy tales. And so Chaucer has the Wife of Bath tell a fairy tale in which she and Jankyn do live happily ever after. In fiction all the contradictions that she cannot work out in her life are resolved.

The story is set back in the "olde dayes" of King Arthur, many hundreds of years ago when chivalry and fairies still existed. That they no longer exist is the point of the Wife's good-natured joke to pay back the Friar for laughing at her. She is right of course: chivalry and fairies have no place in an imperfect world overrun by friars. It is the Wife's way of saying that she knows her tale is only make-believe, and yet it contains more truth about herself than she knows.

The Wife's purpose in telling the tale is a combination of

sentence and *solaas*. It is a version of the ancient motif of the fairy bride who takes a mortal lover, and the Wife uses it as an exemplum of her belief that all will turn out for the best in a world where men give sovereignty to women. The tale begins with a typical act of male aggression—rape—which is a capital offense in the chivalric times of King Arthur. But male justice is tempered by female mercy. In an act reminiscent of the intercession of Ypolita and Emelye with Theseus for the lives of Palamon and Arcite, the Queen and other ladies of the court ask for the life of the young rapist. He may save himself if he can find out the answer to the question: "What thyng is it that wommen moost desiren." The Wife is giving her version of Arcite's despairing question: "What is this world? what asketh men to have?" At the same time, the question is one about herself that may have occurred to the reader of her Prologue. What does the Wife of Bath really want? The hero of the story conducts an opinion poll among women, and the answers he gets are as various as the character of the Wife:

> Somme seyde wommen loven best richesse,
> Somme seyde honour, somme seyde jolynesse,
> Somme riche array, somme seyden lust abedde,
> And oftetyme to be wydwe and wedde.
> Somme seyde that oure hertes been moost esed
> Whan that we been yflatered and yplesed.   (925–930)

The list continues and contains all the things that mean a lot to the Wife of Bath. None of them, however, is the key to her character.

The right answer is known only to the old hag the knight encounters at the forest's edge, the borderline between this world and another that contains a wisdom imparted to few mortals. It is the wisdom possessed by the old crone whose wrinkles hint at knowledge and experience beyond time and age. We may guess that she is really the elf-queen, but it does not occur to the hapless knight who is desperate enough by now to promise anything for the secret.

The secret is sovereignty both in love and in marriage, an answer that satisfies the Queen and her court and is obviously the

answer that the Wife of Bath's experience has taught her. Yet
there is more to the tale than this. The Wife not only intends to
show that this is what women truly desire but that it is a reasonable
wish, one that, if only men were sensible enough to grant, would
be the solution to all our problems.

The knight has saved his neck, but he has not changed. When
the hag demands that he fulfill his promise by making her his
wife and his love, he is filled with shame and loathing. On their
wedding night he tells her,

> Thou art so loothly, and so oold also,
> And therto comen of so lough a kynde,
> That litel wonder is thogh I walwe and wynde.
> So wolde God myn herte wolde breste!   (1100–1103)

The miracle the tale must perform is to change his character, and
the loathly lady attempts to do so by giving him a sermon on
"gentilesse," the true nobility that resides in a man's character,
not in wealth or family. The lesson is full of high sentence supported by such authorities as Dante, Valerius Maximus, Seneca, and
Boethius. The young man has despised the old woman for her age
and ugliness, her poverty and low condition, and she shows him
that youth, wealth, and rank are false values.

The long sententious passage may seem a digression out of
character for the Wife of Bath. Yet the speech is essential to the
tale, and its digressive, sententious character really is the Wife's
style. What is perhaps surprising is the morality, and the reader
will be quick to see how little the Wife of Bath has practiced in her
own life what the old hag of her story preaches to the young man.
She has valued the things that he has valued—wealth, youth, and
position—the things that this world values. But in the world of
fiction we are free to cherish the true values that most of us may
ignore in the everyday world. And even though the story is set in
the world of the imagination, the grace of such a world is to show
us a better truth about ourselves. The loathly lady is the Wife's
fictional spokesman and shows us, I think, that Alisoun of Bath is
really a woman of principle.

At the end of her lecture, the loathly lady presents her knight
with another riddle: would he prefer to have her as she is and to

be a true and faithful wife, or would he have her young and beautiful without being able to trust her? Chaucer has significantly altered the question that is asked in all the analogues where the hero is given a choice of having his wife fair by night and foul by day or the other way around. In the analogues the knight must choose between his pleasure and his pride. Chaucer has made the question much more challenging by making it a choice between pleasure and pride, on the one hand, and faithfulness and humble submission on the other.[12] The form the question takes in the tale also expresses the choice that the Wife of Bath has been making all of her life, only she has always chosen pleasure and pride.

However, both the loathly lady's question and her lecture on "gentilesse" show another side of the Wife of Bath. Chastity and humility, in fact, do have a great importance for her, but her worldly values have never allowed her to practice these virtues. She deceived her first three husbands because they were unable to satisfy her, but, as she tells us, she remained faithful to the last two. However, her pride has never permitted her to yield fully to any man. Since the society in which she lives does not allow an intelligent woman any self-respect unless she is a saint or martyr, she has cultivated a masculine pride by humbling men like one of the legendary amazons.

The knight in her tale deliberates long and hard and finally comes up with the right answer—not simply to the second riddle but to the first as well. His answer is to allow his wife to choose for herself, and in allowing her to choose, he is of course giving her sovereignty. It is not sovereignty over *him,* however, although the Wife of Bath may think so. It is sovereignty over herself—the right to exercise her own free moral choice as a human being and as a woman. This is what women truly desire most, not sovereignty over men but over themselves.

As soon as the riddle is answered, just as in a fairy tale, the spell is broken and all wishes come true. "Kys me," cries the lady, and the knight finds that she has been transformed into a ravishing young woman. She rewards him not only with pleasure and pride but with faith and obedience. "And thus they lyve unto hir lyves ende/In parfit joye." The fairy tale ending is not without its poignancy, however. The Wife of Bath of course identifies herself with the old hag throughout the tale, but the Wife can become young and beautiful again only through the power of the imagination. In the story of the blackguard knight reformed we can see the transformation of Jankyn who in the fairy tale, besides being young, handsome, and "fressh abedde," turns into a gentleman and ideal husband. But the Wife of Bath and Jankyn did not live happily ever after. They are victims of human ignorance and pride and of the world and time. Lest we grow sentimental over such an ending, the Wife's conclusion returns us to reality:

> and Jhesu Crist us sende
> Housbondes meeke, yonge, and fressh abedde,
> And grace t'overbyde hem that we wedde;
> And eek I praye Jhesu shorte hir lyves
> That wol nat be governed by hir wyves;
> And olde and angry nygardes of dispence,
> God sende hem soone verray pestilence!   (1258–64)

Nothing has changed as a result of the story.

In the Wife of Bath's Tale Chaucer creates not only the point of view, favorite opinions, and characteristic speech mannerisms of one of his characters but that character's innermost fantasies. In showing us the relationship between those fantasies and the Wife's actual life, as she has described it to us in the Prologue, Chaucer also says something profound about the *sentence* and *solaas* of fiction. "Solaas" is something more meaningful than entertainment; fiction may be exactly what we mean by the word solace today: consolation. Fiction may give us the dreams denied to us in our lives. Fiction also gives us *sentence,* not the morality by which most of us live but a better morality by which we ought to live. In brief, fiction can transcend the limitations of our experience. The Wife of Bath's experience tells her about "the wo that is in mariage." Her tale goes beyond such limited experience.

Just as the Wife of Bath closely identifies with the old hag of her story, so Chaucer, I believe, identifies with the Wife. It is not simply that he has projected into her character much of his own gusto and humor. In a way, the Wife of Bath's marriages reflect upon the growth of his poetry although of course I do not mean to suggest that Chaucer intended any such interpretation or was even aware of it. The young Chaucer was wedded to old forms and old authorities with which he never lived entirely at ease; in the world, he strove to rise by serving the court. As he grew older, he gradually emancipated his poetry. As an artist, more and more, he drew upon his own experience and followed the dictates of his heart. As a courtier, so the documents show, he continued to serve the world although the General Prologue suggests that it was with a sharpening sense of irony. In *Troilus* and the *Legend of Good Women,* Chaucer is still trying to reconcile the truths of experience and authority. In the *Canterbury Tales,* he expresses their conflict more and more explicitly and deals honestly with the limitations of each. The frame story purports to relate the actual experience of a number of people as the narrator observed them on the road to Canterbury. In several instances they give us intimate revelations of their private lives; the tales they tell often make an ironic contrast with those lives. Yet the pilgrims' stories also show us he limitations of a vision based on experience alone. Through the medium of fiction even the most abandoned of them show an inner worth that is not revealed to the eye of experience. It is so with Chaucer as well. He is the most reticent of poets, but like any creator, he reveals something of himself in his creatures. All of the Canterbury pilgrims are in some measure *personae* of Chaucer, their worth is his worth and their failings, his failings. None is closer to him than the good Wife of Bath. Flaubert is supposed to have said of his greatest character, "Madame Bovary? C'est moi!" Chaucer could have said, "The Wyf of Bathe? It am I!"

CHAPTER X

The Moral Question
in the Clerk's Tale

*t*HE CLERK'S TALE is the best of the stories of "moralitee and hoolynesse" that Chaucer promised the reader in the Miller's Prologue. The plot and characters have inspired responses ranging from strong sympathy to violent antipathy, and even those readers who find Griselda's meek surrender of her children perverse, revolting, or absurd testify to the emotional appeal of the story however much they may feel compelled to reject that appeal. The moral of the tale, if rightly understood, is more than a conventional bit of piety. The Clerk teaches that the noblest way to combat and overcome the inequality and injustice to which all men are subject is not to fight against them tooth and nail like the Wife of Bath but to endure them with patience and humility like Griselda. However, precisely because it is the most successful of the moral tales, the story of patient Griselda brings most sharply into focus a problem inherent in all of them: to what extent is the stuff of fiction an adequate vehicle for Christian teaching? If there is an example in the *Canterbury Tales* of fable being turned into genuinely Christian parable, the Clerk's Tale must be it. If it is flawed, we must ask why this is so.

The question was well put in James Sledd's excellent essay, *"The Clerk's Tale:* The Monsters and the Critics." "The moral question is," Sledd wrote, "whether the *Clerk's Tale* offers us *sen-*

tence or *solas,* whether it is a sermon or a story or both together."[1] Sledd was defending the tale against a naive kind of criticism that, measuring the story by our notions of credible behavior, is appalled at Walter's monstrous cruelty and Griselda's even more monstrous stupidity in putting up with it. By phrasing the question as he did, Sledd implied, and then proceeded to demonstrate, how grossly unfair it was to read the tale as if it dealt with real people and situations instead of reading it as an exemplary story illustrating certain Christian virtues by conventional signs comprehensible and acceptable to the medieval reader. Although he did not claim that Chaucer had solved all his problems, Sledd showed how the poet had skillfully set about his task of combining *sentence* and *solaas,* story and sermon, to produce a work that the critic could describe approvingly, if somewhat patronizingly, as "a fairly straightforward, middling kind of yarn."[2]

I have no doubt that Sledd's way is the right approach to the tale, but the "moral question" does not disappear or lose its relevance when we make allowance for the fact that the Clerk's Tale is both story and sermon. Even more insistently than in the other moral tales, I find a clash in the Clerk's between the demands of the story and those of the sermon. By catering sometimes to the one demand, sometimes to the other, Chaucer does not minimize or soften that clash, and at times, I feel, he deliberately accentuates it. In the more sermonlike Man of Law's tale, which is filled with preaching, there is less of a discord because characterization is sacrificed to the morality. Custance is hardly felt to be a woman so much as a personification of Constancy. Griselda is a personification of Patience, but she is also humanized enough to engage our sympathy for the woman, not merely for the virtue she represents. The result, I think, is a conflict that makes the Clerk's Tale perhaps more interesting than "a fairly straightforward, middling kind of yarn." One does not have to experience the characters as "monsters" in order to feel a split between the human and moral roles that they are made to play.[3]

The problem is expressed dramatically in the Clerk's Prologue where Chaucer has amusingly made the Host impose upon the Clerk the task of all medieval storytellers, which is of course also Chaucer's own in writing the Clerk's Tale. Harry Bailly both likes the Clerk and stands somewhat in awe of the young man's learning and scholarly reserve. In requesting a story from the Clerk, he tries to jolly him up a bit and to suggest respectfully that he share in the holiday spirit of the pilgrimage by entertaining the company:

> It is no tyme for to studien heere.
> Telle us some myrie tale, by youre fey!
> For what man that is entred in a pley,
> He nedes moot unto the pley assente.
> But precheth nat, as freres doon in Lente,
> To make us for oure olde synnes wepe,
> Ne that thy tale make us nat to slepe.
> Telle us some murie thyng of aventures.   (8–15)

The Host is obviously afraid of a boring sermon from the studious Clerk whose conversation was "sownynge in moral vertu," and asks him for "something with a plot." Moreover, he begs that the Clerk talk down to the level of the "lewed" company:

> Speketh so pleyn at this tyme, we yow preye,
> That we may understonde what ye seye.   (19–20)

The Clerk's response is a model of compliant obedience practicing the very virtue he is about to teach:

> "Hooste," quod he, "I am under youre yerde;
> Ye han of us as now the governance,
> And therfore wol I do yow obeisance,
> As fer as resoun axeth, hardily."   (22–25)

He will tell a tale of "aventures" to oblige the Host, but only to the extent that "resoun axeth," and reason demands that it not be an idle story but one that is, indeed, "sownyng in moral vertu." The story is taken from another "worthy clerk," the great Petrarch who "Enlumyned al Ytaille of poetrie,/As Lynyan dide of philosophie." Here is the Clerk's conception of poetry and philosophy. Their purpose is not, as the Host ignorantly supposes, to "studie aboute som sophyme" or to compose in "heigh style" that lesser men cannot understand, but to illuminate the lives of their fellow men with eloquence and wisdom. This is the purpose of the Clerk's own tale. In further compliance with the Host's wish, the style of the tale is notably chaste and free of the rhetorical ornament employed by some of the other pilgrims. In that sense it is a "straightforward" story, but one that is pregnant with meaning.

The plot of the Clerk's Tale is a version of one of the most popular of European folktales, which gives us the myth of Cupid and Psyche and the fairy tale "East of the Sun and West of the Moon."[4] In these stories a mortal girl is claimed by a supernatural lover, loses him, and then gets him back by passing a series of tests. The girl loses the lover through her own fault—he comes to her only at night and she is strictly forbidden to try to see him, but of course she cannot overcome her curiosity. She then regains him through patient suffering. One branch of this tale, designated by folklorists as the "Patience Group," turns the girl into a wife whose husband tests her obedience, and it is this version of the story that Boccaccio used for the final tale of the *Decameron*. Boccaccio's version was read in his old age by Petrarch, who admired it so much that he turned it into Latin prose and gave it a Christian and allegorical coloring.[5] The basic moral Petrarch found in the tale is straightforward and explicit enough. The Clerk gives quite a literal translation of Petrarch's conclusion:

> This storie is seyd, nat for that wyves sholde
> Folwen Grisilde as in humylitee,
> For it were inportable, though they wolde;
> But for that every wight, in his degree,
> Sholde be constant in adversitee
> As was Grisilde; therfore Petrak writeth
> This storie, which with heigh stile he enditeth.
>
> For, sith a womman was so pacient
> Unto a mortal man, wel moore us oghte
> Receyven al in gree that God us sent;
> For greet skile is, he preeve that he wroghte.
>   (1142–52)

Walter's testing of Griselda is only a figurative way of showing us how the Lord tests his creatures for their own good.

However, in the frame story of the *Canterbury Tales*, the Petrarchan moral takes on a specific application. The Clerk's Tale, in Kittredge's theory of the "Marriage Group," is a reply to the

Wife of Bath.⁶ The Wife had maintained: "it is an impossible/ That any clerk wol speke good of wyves" (688–689). The Clerk directly responds to that challenge:

> Men speke of Job, and moost for his humblesse,
> As clerkes, whan hem list, konne wel endite,
> Namely of men, but as in soothfastnesse,
> Though clerkes preise wommen but a lite,
> Ther kan no man in humblesse hym acquite
> As womman kan, ne kan been half so trewe
> As wommen been, but it be falle of newe.   (932–38)

Furthermore, according to Kittredge, the Clerk answers the Wife of Bath's exemplum of female sovereignty with a story in which the husband is absolute lord and master. However, both the Clerk and Kittredge recognize that if the issues are only the attitude of clerks toward women and of sovereignty in marriage, then the Clerk's Tale, far from refuting the Wife, is grist for her mill. She said it was impossible for a clerk to speak well of women, "But if it be of hooly seintes lyves" (690), and Griselda's patience is certainly that of a saint. The Clerk amusingly concedes that point in his Envoy by giving satiric advice to women to emulate not Griselda but the Wife of Bath:

> O noble wyves, ful of heigh prudence,
> Lat noon humylitee youre tonge naille,
> Ne lat no clerk have cause or diligence
> To write of yow a storie of swich mervaille
> As of Grisildis pacient and kynde,
> Lest Chichevache you swelwe in hire entraille!
>   (1183–88)

The Clerk's Tale is only the opposite face of the coin of anti-feminism, praising woman for superhuman virtue where the anti-feminist tracts accuse her of inhuman vice. The issue of sovereignty in marriage is also a red herring. The tale does answer the Wife of Bath, but on a more sophisticated level than the plain advice: "Wives, submit yourselves unto your husbands, as unto the Lord."⁷

The Clerk's Tale sets out to demonstrate in a more subtle way and in a more serious context the theme of the loathly lady's sermon to her knight: "Crist wole we clayme of hym oure gentillesse" (1117).[8] It teaches that empty values like status and wealth and even real values like the love we bear our children are secondary to the virtues of Christian humility and obedience. Man or woman becomes truly noble only in humbling himself to a higher will. He must recognize that the adversities of this world are not really inflicted on us by husbands and other earthly lords but that these latter are only God's instruments to try us.

The story shows that Griselda has nobility in this true sense. Her father is not just poor; among Walter's subjects he is the "povrest of hem alle" (205). Walter elevates Griselda to the rank of marchioness, and we see what this means in the eyes of the world when the ladies of the court are ordered to remove her rags:

> And for that no thyng of hir olde geere
> She sholde brynge into his hous, he bad
> That wommen sholde dispoillen hire right theere;
> Of which thise ladyes were nat right glad
> To handle hir clothes, wherinne she was clad.
> But nathelees, this mayde bright of hewe
> Fro foot to heed they clothed han al newe.   (372–378)

What we are meant to see is that Griselda stands royally dressed in her humility, and that is made plainest the moment when she once again removes the worldly finery Walter gave to her:

> "My lord, ye woot that in my fadres place
> Ye dide me streepe out of my povre weede,
> And richely me cladden, of youre grace.
> To yow broghte I noght elles, out of drede,
> But feith, and nakednesse, and maydenhede;
> And heere agayn your clothyng I restoore,
> And eek your weddyng ryng, for everemore.
>
> "The remenant of youre jueles redy be
> Inwith youre chambre, dar I saufly sayn.
> Naked out of my fadres hous," quod she,
> "I cam, and naked moot I turne agayn."   (862–872)

In the last lines, she is echoing Job, the proverbial type of patience: "Naked came I out of my mother's womb, and naked shall I return thither: the Lord gave and the Lord hath taken away, blessed be the name of the Lord" (Job i, 21). By bowing to her earthly lord's bidding, Griselda raises herself above the Marquis Walter and above all men, save one, and she thereby exemplifies the Clerk's statement that woman's superiority lies in her greater humility—if she will only accept the role that has been assigned to her by Providence.

Job is only one of the biblical types whom Griselda resembles. She sets down her water pot like Rebecca at the well (Gen., xxiv, 13–18) and kneels "Biside the thresshfold in an oxes stalle" (291), a reminder of the humble birthplace Christ chose for His Nativity. Her acceptance of Walter's proposal echoes Christ's words in the Garden of Gethsemane:

> "Lord, undigne and unworthy
> Am I to thilke honour that ye me beede,
> But as ye wole youreself, right so wol I.
> And heere I swere that nevere willyngly,
> In werk ne thought, I nyl yow disobeye,
> For to be deed, though me were looth to deye."
>
> (359–364)

It is part of Griselda's appeal as a character that she, too, would have preferred to let this cup pass from her lips. The seemingly cruel sergeant who takes away her children is like one of Herod's soldiers, and Griselda herself becomes a Rachel who does not even dare to mourn.

If we can keep our attention firmly fixed on the *sentence* of the Clerk's Tale, it contains an eloquent lesson, but the Clerk has also contracted to tell a tale with human interest, and I am afraid that his concessions to the human love for stories seriously undermine his "hy sentence." The tale also contains an element of pathos, constantly verging on sentimentality. This effect results partly from emphasizing Griselda's innocence by blackening the character of Walter. Chaucer has added passages in which the narrator deplores the needlessness of Walter's persistent testing.[9] But, if in the end we are to understand that these tests by a mortal man are supposed to reconcile us to whatever tests divine providence sets for us, these complaints against Walter sorely try the reader's patience. If it isn't necessary, then why does he do it, and why does Griselda put up with it? These small additions, far from coating the moral pill, tend to make us want to vomit it up.

More deadly yet to the moral interpretation are a few passages in which pathos is pushed beyond the point of sentimentality to the edge of comedy.[10] Griselda's speech on leaving Walter's palace is a noble statement. The rhetorical style and the allusion to Job prevent us from visualizing too concretely the image of Griselda returning to Janicula's house in her old smock. But that is not the case when Griselda returns to the palace to get it ready for Walter's new bride:

> And with that word she gan the hous to dighte,
> And tables for to sette, and beddes make;
> And peyned hire to doon al that she myghte,
> Preyynge the chambereres, for Goddes sake,
> To hasten hem, and faste swepe and shake.   (974–978)

It is difficult to take seriously most of the sixth and last part of the Clerk's Tale, or to believe that Chaucer took it entirely seriously. One stanza in particular makes such outrageous demands on the reader that he may certainly be forgiven if he rebels:

> "O tendre, o deere, o yonge children myne!
> Youre woful mooder wende stedfastly
> That crueel houndes or som foul vermyne
> Hadde eten yow; but God, of his mercy,
> And youre benyngne fader tendrely
> Hath doon yow kept,"—and in that same stounde
> Al sodeynly she swapte adoun to grounde.   (1093–99)

On the surface the passage is meant to show us the extent of Griselda's suffering, the grief that she has had to repress all those years. But when we read that "God of his mercy,/And youre benyngne fader tendrely" has preserved the children, the patience and credulity of this reader at least are stretched to the breaking point. We may perhaps constrain ourselves to accept Griselda as a type of the Lord's suffering servant, but the linking of God's mercy and Walter's tender benignity drives us to reject the other half of that equation. The mention of "crueel houndes" and "foul vermyne" provides us with more appropriate images for Walter. Nor is the image of Griselda—"Al sodeynly she swapte adoun to grounde"—calculated to move many readers to tears, especially if they recall that she had already swooned once only twenty lines before. As she lies there, the attendants have difficulty prying the children out of her embrace. Everyone is weeping:

> O many a teere on many a pitous face
> Doun ran of hem that stooden hire bisyde;
> Unnethe abouten hire myghte they abyde.   (1104–6)

The reader, too, may find that he can no longer "abide about Griselda," although for a different reason.[11]

As in the Knight's Tale such passages are too few and far between to oblige us to reject the *sentence* of the story or to read in irony at the Clerk's expense. They do have the effect of making one extremely uneasy. The Clerk's Tale, though the best of the moral tales, nevertheless dramatizes the difficulties of wedding *sentence* and *solaas* and of reconciling the "truth" of Christian doctrine with the "truth" of fiction. The Clerk is not among those pilgrims whose characters are highly developed in their tales, and it would be wrong to argue that the purpose of the tale is to show his "unworldliness." Nevertheless, the Clerk does represent a class of well-meaning moral teachers whose knowledge of books far exceeds their experience of life. (Petrarch is one of them.) The story of patient Griselda is a classic example of the efforts of medieval clerks to use seemingly naive tales as vehicles for moral instruction. Indeed, intellectuals of all ages have been charmed by the simplicity of fairy stories and have adapted them to their own ends.

Fairy tales, however, have their own conventions and their own inner "truth," which is easily falsified by the literary art of the learned author who seeks to impose his moral upon them. Among the conventions of fairy stories is the acceptance by the audience of a world of make-believe; we understand that the magic, the cruelty, the good and wicked characters do not really exist, but we willingly suspend our disbelief. The signal that we are entering such a world is the formula "Once upon a time." The Wife of Bath perfectly understands this convention and sets her fairy tale "In th'olde dayes of the Kyng Arthour" (857). For all its comedy and moral *sentence,* the tale itself remains one of riddles and magic; the loathly lady and her knight remain stock figures of the fairy tale whom we can accept without puzzling over their motives and behavior. In contrast the Clerk's Tale attempts to lend to the fairy tale material an air of pseudo-reality. The Clerk tells us that Petrarch's Proem with its elaborate description of Piedmont, Saluzzo, and the sources of the River Po is "a thyng impertinent," that is to say, irrelevant, to the tale itself. He will eschew Petrarch's "heigh stile" and does eliminate much of the Petrarchan ornament. Still, he too begins his story by giving it a firm local habitation:

> Ther is, right at the west syde of Ytaille,
> Doun at the roote of Vesulus the colde,
> A lusty playn habundant of vitaille. . . .   (57–59)

The Clerk certainly does not expect us to accept the tale as historically true; nevertheless, he rationalizes it as much as possible. Thus he attempts to motivate Walter's irrational testing, suggesting that it is a kind of monomania. The stock characters of the fairy tale are given a psychological dimension, rudimentary but sufficient to disconcert us with their fairy tale behavior.

The fantasy world of the fairy tale powerfully expresses and fulfills the universal wish for justice and a happy ending. The "moral" of fairy tales is that the innocent will finally be rewarded and the wicked punished. To be sure, Griselda gets back all that Walter has taken away, but that is almost beside the point in a tale meant to show us that virtue is its own reward and that our miseries on earth serve to exercise that virtue. The ending of the Wife of Bath's Tale is one of "parfit joye" (1258). The ending of the Clerk's Tale is one of "pitous joye" (1080). The words "pitous" and "pitously' occur five times in the conclusion. The happy ending is thus amply qualified by tears.

Sophisticated men like the Clerk know that the rewards and punishments of this world are not distributed with the even-handed justice of the fairy tale. Yet the stories they tell often display another kind of naiveté: the belief that the literal level of a tale does not much matter if we can grasp its inner meaning. The Clerk's Tale actually takes some pains with the literal level by introducing elements of naturalism into the background and characterization. However, these elements make the violations of human nature seem all the more perverse. If we did not in some measure believe in Griselda, her unnatural patience would be easier to bear. Of course, the response to the Clerk's Tale that sees the characters as "monsters" is also naive. It assumes that the tale is trying to persuade us that the story has a "reality" independent of its meaning. Such criticism misses the point. But moralists like the Clerk may be missing an important point about some kinds of fiction. They want us to see a real "truth" in the imaginary tale. But the "lewed" reader often cares little for such a truth and asks only to be persuaded that the tale itself is "true," so that his imagination may rest, if only for a time, on the unstable illusion of fiction.

CHAPTER XI

The Bourgeois
Misanthrope

T HE MERCHANT'S is the only one among the tales of the Canterbury pilgrims that contains real obscenity; yet, as a literary performance it may be the most cultivated of them all, extreme both in its coarseness and its sophistication. The erotic scenes might cause the Wife of Bath to blush, but for the sheer range of style and allusion within a single work one must go back to *Troilus and Criseyde* to find comparable variety in Chaucer's poetry.[1]

Imagery and language throughout the tale are full of innuendo, sometimes subtly suggestive:

> But certeynly, a yong thyng may men gye,
> Right as men may warm wex with handes plye,
>   (1429–30)

at times openly lewd, as in January's leering apology to May on their wedding night:

>   "Allas! I moot trespace
> To yow, my spouse, and yow greetly offende,
> Er tyme come that I wil doun descende."   (1828–30)

Descriptions of sex are more explicit than anything in the Reeve's Tale; they are brilliantly satiric but cold, lacking any trace of lustiness or gaiety. What is missing is a sense of pleasure; that much at least was supplied by a scribe who inserted eight lines of wretched but enthusiastic doggerel amplifying the narrator's laconic statement of what January saw in the pear tree.[2]

The narrator himself is capable of passion, but his dominant feelings, all the stronger for being tightly reined in, are hatred and revulsion. Elsewhere Chaucer is able to make us feel delight and wonder at the Miller's wart, the Cook's sore, or the Canon's Yeoman's sweat; nowhere but in the Merchant's Tale are we made to feel disgust for the body and horror at the act of love:

> He lulleth hire, he kisseth hire ful ofte;
> With thikke brustles of his berd unsofte,
> Lyk to the skyn of houndfyssh, sharp as brere.
>
> (1823–25)

The force of these lines depends not just on the sharpness of the old man's beard against May's "tendre face," but on the image implied in "lulleth," something mothers normally do to babies when they sing lullabies. The choice of words throughout the tale is very deliberate. January's later jealousy is pictured as a mother's anxious solicitude for her child. When he sees what is happening in the tree, he roars "As dooth the mooder whan the child shal dye" (2365), a line that prompted Tatlock to comment: "Nothing is sacred."[3]

The imagery associated with January—he is pictured as a mother, as a variety of animals and birds, as a blossoming pear tree—is one instance of the artistry of the Merchant's Tale. Much of that art is unobtrusive, but often it is put on display as in this outburst against Fortune:

> O sodeyn hap! o thou Fortune unstable!
> Lyk to the scorpion so deceyvable,
> That flaterest with thyn heed whan thou wolt stynge;
> Thy tayl is deeth, thurgh thyn envenymynge.
> O brotil joye! o sweete venym queynte!   (2057–61)

The passage sounds like some in *Troilus,* but the image of the scorpion's tail with its sweet venom is sexual[4] and relates Fortune

with Damyan, who has previously been addressed by exactly the
same kind of apostrophe:

> O perilous fyr, that in the bedstraw bredeth!
> O famulier foo, that his servyce bedeth!
> O servant traytour, false hoomly hewe,
> Lyk to the naddre in bosom sly untrewe,
> God shilde us alle from youre aqueyntaunce!
> (1783–87)

There is a wealth of literary allusion. The tale abounds in examples drawn from classical mythology and the Bible. Authorities
cited include Theophrastus, Dionysius Cato, Seneca, Martianus
Capella, Constantinus Afer ("the cursed monk daun Constantyn"),
Ovid, and Claudian. The treatment of the material is extremely
varied. The basic fabliau plot of the seduction in the tree has
undergone vast rhetorical amplification. It is no wonder, though
it may come as a surprise, that the Merchant's Tale is second in
length only to the Knight's, edging out the Clerk's by 54 lines.[5]

The coupling of obscenity with poetic art, the preparation of
the fabliau denouement with the high style of sermons and romance
is the object of the Merchant's Tale. The language normally employed for noble and elevated matter is systematically applied to
what is trivial, vulgar, and debased. The result goes beyond anything else in Chaucer's "mixed style." The cumulative effect of this
technique is to degrade the art of poetry and to make language
itself a principal object of the narrator's satire.

An example of how language is used throughout the tale is
the rendering of January's invitation to May to make love in the
garden in the words of the Song of Songs:

> "Rys up, my wyf, my love, my lady free!
> The turtles voys is herd, my dowve sweete;
> The wynter is goon with alle his reynes weete.
> Com forth now, with thyne eyen columbyn!
> How fairer been thy brestes than is wyn!
> The gardyn is enclosed al aboute;
> Com forth, my white spouse! out of doute
> Thou hast me wounded in myn herte, O wyf!"
> (2138–45)

The narrator's comment on the speech is, "Swiche olde lewed wordes used he" (2149).[6] January is, of course, "olde" and "lewed," and the passage satirizes his blind infatuation. It satirizes May whose intrigue with Damyan makes the image of her as a turtledove sharply ironic. But the narrator's contempt is aimed specifically at the *words* of the Song, and, by implication, at its traditional allegorical meaning that interprets the bride and bridegroom as Christ and His Church. What the narrator's comment on the words of the Song means is that he thinks them as "lewed" as January, as meretricious as May.

The passage makes explicit the narrator's obsession throughout the tale with what he considers to be sham language. His story is certainly a satire of marriage and women, but it is also an attack on the lies he believes have been propagated about marriage and women by clerks and poets—all the cant about purity, domestic happiness, and innocent love. The Clerk of Oxenford and his tale of Griselda furnish a convenient occasion for this satire, and there are a couple of echoes of the Clerk's Tale, just as there are some allusions to the Wife of Bath. But the attack extends far beyond the confines of the "Marriage Group." It aims at all forms of human idealism among which poetry and religion are prominent. By imitating and distorting the style of works that celebrate love and marriage, and by applying their language to the marriage of January and May, this storyteller means to strip away the illusion of beauty and sanctity with which the Christian and courtly traditions have, so he thinks, disguised the animal lust and economic interest that are the only basis he can conceive for intercourse between man and woman.

At the beginning of the tale January, the sixty-year-old bachelor exhausted by a life of lechery, prays to the Lord that he may be permitted to know the "hooly boond" of matrimony and declares "That in this world it is a paradys." At this point the narrator chimes in with an extraordinary 126-line speech in praise of marriage, which is one of the finest examples of sustained sarcasm in literature. Notable throughout the passage is the heavy stress laid on the sacramental and divinely-ordained character of marriage:

A wyf is Goddes yifte verraily.   (1311)

> Mariage is a ful greet sacrement.   (1319)

> O blisful ordre of wedlok precious,
> Thou art so murye, and eek so vertuous,
> And so commended and appreved eek
> That every man that halt hym worth a leek,
> Upon his bare knees oughte al his lyf
> Thanken his God that hym hath sent a wyf.   (1347–52)

> Love wel thy wyf, as Crist loved his chirche.   (1384)

"God" or the possessive "Goddes" occurs ten times in the 126-line passage, a density of that word per line exceeded only by the good Parson in his tale and the hypocrite friar in the Summoner's Tale.[7] There are numerous allusions to the Bible including a series of Old Testament exempla involving the biblical heroines Rebecca, Judith, and Abigail. The sarcasm of the entire passage makes every one of these references blasphemous. When the narrator begins,

> And certeinly, as sooth as God is kyng,
> To take a wyf it is a glorious thyng,   (1267–68)

he means exactly the opposite. It is hard to say whether the speaker really believes that it is "sooth" that God is king or whether the stories in the Bible are true, but if he does, he believes in a God with a malicious sense of humor:

> The hye God, whan he hadde Adam maked,
> And saugh him al allone, bely-naked,
> God of his grete goodnesse seyde than,
> "Lat us now make an helpe unto this man,
> Lyk to hymself"; and thanne he made him Eve.
>   (1325–29)

The women celebrated in Jewish and Christian tradition as heroines are in the narrator's eyes deceivers and destroyers of men.[8] The choice of Rebecca is especially apt in this tale since she deceived her blind old husband. In short, the underlying idea in the passage is to expose the religious ideal of woman and marriage as a huge fraud.

Later in the tale, an elaborate simile is used to describe January's erotic fancies:

> Heigh fantasye and curious bisynesse
> Fro day to day gan in the soule impresse
> Of Januarie aboute his mariage.
> Many fair shap and many a fair visage
> Ther passeth thurgh his herte nyght by nyght,
> As whoso tooke a mirour, polisshed bryght,
> And sette it in a commune market-place,
> Thanne sholde he se ful many a figure pace
> By his mirour.   (1577–85)

The simile of the mirror may be applied to the theme and the technique of the tale.[9] What the Merchant's Tale is saying, in effect, is that the human imagination is a distorting mirror that deceives by turning ugliness into beauty. Art is also a mirror that can hold up a false and flattering image to man. But the art of the Merchant's Tale is an art of disenchantment. It holds the mirror of art up to a reality so hideous that the most trusting beholder will be shocked into truth.[10]

Thus this poet celebrates the wedding of January and May by invoking the solemnity and splendor of Christian ceremony and pagan literature. The priest pronounces the words of the marriage service, makes the sign of the cross over the couple, and prays that God may bless them. The wedding banquet that follows is done in the style of an epithalamion. The gods themselves participate in the feast:

> Bacus the wyn hem shynketh al aboute,
> And Venus laugheth upon every wight,
> For Januarie was bicome hir knyght.   (1722–24)

May looks as meek as "Queene Ester" (1744), while January, plying himself with aphrodisiacs, contemplates pressing her in his arms "Harder than evere Parys dide Eleyne" (1754). Such is the Christian Humanism of the Merchant's Tale. Finally when the priest has blessed the marriage bed, and January is left alone with

May, the style drastically changes again. We are given close-up pictures of the old man's rough skin, scraggly beard, skinny neck, and shaking dewlap. In bed he is no longer Ahasuerus or Paris but "coltissh, ful of ragerye,/And ful of jargon as a flekked pye" (1847–48).

The sparks from Venus's wedding torch have set January's squire aflame, and the plot now moves into a stylistic mixture of fabliau and romance. Damyan feigns sickness like Troilus, and January, feeling sorry for him, as sely John feels sorry for Nicholas's supposed illness, sends May to his bedside. The intrigue between Damyan and May reads very much like a speeded-up version of the first two and one half books of *Troilus* with many fabliau touches. There is no Pandarus, of course, but there is always January. To get away from him long enough to read Damyan's love letter, May has to seek refuge "Ther as ye woot that every wight moot neede" (1951). Such euphemisms and feigned embarrassments are among the narrator's most effective ironic devices. He will tell us that January, having awakened with a fit of coughing, asks May to strip because her clothing gets in his way:

> But lest that precious folk be with me wrooth,
> How that he wroghte, I dar nat to yow telle.
>   (1962–63)

The fabliau heroine is often a "mal-mariée," a young woman married to an old husband, but the fabliau authors spare the audience the details of the sexual life between husband and wife. This narrator tells us enough to repel us, then affects a sudden fear that his refined audience may be offended.

It is in this context that the theme of the heroine's "pitee" is introduced. May's motive for promising her favors to Damyan is not disgust at her old husband but "pitee of this sike Damyan" (1979). The narrator's comment on May's courtly sentiments is "Lo, pitee renneth soone in gentil herte!" (1986), the very line Cupid applied to Alceste in the *Legend* and the narrator to Theseus in the Knight's Tale. It has been called Chaucer's "favorite line" (it occurs once more in the Squire's Tale), but its use at this point in the Merchant's Tale seems an odd way to show favor. The effect is to implicate Chaucer's courtly poetry in the cover-up of the true character of love, marriage, and the human condition. In the symbolism of the tale, such language renders men blind.

January's physical blindness is, of course, symbolic of his blindness all along: "For love is blynd alday, and may nat see" (1598). However, not just January but most men are blind. And like January they construct real or imaginary gardens. January's private pleasure garden is the central symbolic setting of the tale. With the very first mention of it, the garden is given all sorts of literary associations. The author of "the Romance of the Rose" could not describe its beauty, and we are reminded of the Garden of Mirth. Pluto and Proserpine "and al hire fayerye" (2039) frequent January's garden. The mention of this archetypal January and May couple recalls the fair vale of Enna where Proserpine was abducted by dusky Dis. However, in the Merchant's Tale, the classical god of the underworld and goddess of spring have become King and Queen of the fairies. We may think of the elf-queen and her jolly company in the Wife of Bath's tale, and Proserpine turns out to be a mythological Wife of Bath in her quarrel with Pluto. The passage imitated from the Song of Songs adds the closed garden of that great poem to the literary associations of January's garden. Finally, lurking behind all these associations and controlling them is the Garden of Eden, symbolizing man's lost innocence. Eden, too, was once a place where God and his angels liked to resort until it came to be closed around by a wall.

As one would expect in the Merchant's Tale, however, there is also an obscene symbolism at work. The garden is entered through a "smale wyket" to which January alone possesses the key. But May makes a wax impression and provides Damyan with a duplicate. "Fresshe May" and the garden are already identified on a common symbolic level with spring. In a literal sense May's private parts are January's garden (Villon's Belle Heaulmiere refers to her "jardinet"), which he enters by opening the gate with his key.

The significance of the imagery is that in marrying May for his pleasure and in constructing the garden for the same reason, January is trying to recapture his lost innocence. He has pretended all along that he is marrying primarily in order to save his soul. By marrying May he thinks he can make love as innocently with her in his garden as Adam and Eve did before the fall. To carry the image out to its most physical level, her chaste body allows him to satisfy his desire without fear of sin. Thus on his wedding night he embraces "His fresshe May, his paradys, his make" (1822).[11]

The final action in the garden, therefore, amounts to a second loss of innocence—a false innocence, needless to say, January's blind illusion of innocence. Within the garden stands the pear tree, which becomes the tree of knowledge. What knowledge means is suggested by the phallic shaped fruit. Damyan crouches in the shrubbery at first like a fertility god, then appears in the branches of the tree itself like the serpent. January enfolds the tree with his arms, the futile gesture of his blind jealousy but at the same time the symbol of his blind innocence, for ironically blind old January is at this point still innocent.

With the stage thus set, our genteel narrator once again apologizes:

> Ladyes, I prey yow that ye be nat wrooth;
> I kan nat glose, I am a rude man—   (2350–51)

He must show us the naked truth:

> And sodeynly anon this Damyan
> Gan pullen up the smok, and in he throng.   (2352–53)

The veil of poetry is lifted, and simultaneously Pluto restores January's sight, and he receives knowledge of good and evil. What that knowledge amounts to is the image of a man and a woman copulating in a tree, an image that Charles Darwin has perhaps sharpened for Chaucer's twentieth-century reader.

But January is not allowed the dignity of a tragic recognition. Proserpine has given May her answer, a brilliant bit of fiction. She persuades January not to trust the knowledge of his eyes but her lying words:

> "Beth war, I prey yow; for, by hevene kyng,
> Ful many a man weneth to seen a thyng,
> And it is al another than it semeth.
> He that mysconceyveth, he mysdemeth."   (2407–10)

January is only too willing to let the truth be decently hidden once more under the smock of language. He returns to his blind illusion, and we last see him softly stroking May's belly, which he thinks will produce the heir who will redeem his hopes. The narrator turns to the audience:

> Now, goode men, I pray yow to be glad.
> Thus endeth heere my tale of Januarie;
> God blesse us, and his mooder Seinte Marie![12]

May's statement—"He that mysconceyveth, he mysdemeth"—could be taken as the ironic thesis of the Merchant's Tale. Most men misconceive and misdeem, most men remain blind because they choose to believe the lies of women and the lies of poets. They do so in order to remain happy. The ending reminds one of Swift's definition of happiness as the state of being well deceived.

However, the ultimate effect of the Merchant's Tale is to make the reader reject such a moral and to turn him not against women or marriage, not against poetry, but against the narrator's warped vision. Although we may be amused at first, the tale becomes a chilling illustration of what happens to satire when it is divorced from humanity and employed as the weapon of misanthropy. The narrator's point of view is distorted by his inability to love. We see finally that he is blinder even than January; his brilliant use of language for destructive ends proves self-destructive. What the reader of the Merchant's Tale must finally do is to invert the sarcasm. In spite of the tale, in spite of the fact that old men marry young girls and young girls deceive them, marriage *is* a glorious thing, *is* divinely ordained, *is* a holy sacrament, or ought to be. We need not turn against our ideals simply because they rarely measure up to reality. The Wife of Bath knows this and so does the Clerk.

The reader has doubtless noticed that I have avoided calling the narrator of the tale the Merchant. I do not think that the tale was designed for some other pilgrim or, least of all, for the familiar Chaucerian persona. There are good reasons for identifying the teller as a bourgeois. His one spokesman in the tale is January's friend Justinus. Justinus is a cautious businessman. His approach to marriage is that of anyone investigating an important deal:

> I warne yow wel, it is no childes pley
> To take a wyf withouten avysement.

Men moste enquere, this is myn assent,
Wher she be wys, or sobre, or dronkelewe,
Or proud, or elles ootherweys a shrewe,
A chidestere, or wastour of thy good,
Or riche, or poore, or elles mannyssh wood.
Al be it so that no man fynden shal
Noon in this world that trotteth hool in al,
Ne man, ne beest, swich as men koude devyse.

(1530–39)

The passage is drawn from the same passage in *Jerome Against
Jovinian* as the one in the Wife of Bath's Prologue where a woman
is implicitly compared to "oxen, asses, hors, and houndes," etc.
Like every worldly purchase, a prospective wife must be put on
the scales, her debits and credits must be tallied on the ledger
sheet; and the buyer is lucky

With any wyf, if so were that she hadde
Mo goode thewes than hire vices badde.   (1541–42)

Is it any surprise that Justinus is himself unhappily married? He
does in fact sound like the Merchant:

For, God it woot, I have wept many a teere
Ful pryvely, syn I have had a wyf.   (1544–45)

It is the same whining note on which the Merchant begins his
Prologue:

Wepyng and waylyng, care and oother sorwe
I knowe ynogh, on even and a-morwe.   (1213–14)

Yet there is too much comfort in blaming the bitterness of the
tale on the Merchant's two-month adventure in marriage. It has
been said that the tale would not seem bitter at all were it not
for the Prologue. It seems to me rather that the Prologue takes
away some of that bitterness by letting us blame it on the comic
figure of the disillusioned Merchant. But neither the portrait of
the pompous businessman in the General Prologue nor the self-
pitying figure who pours his sorrow out to the Host account ade-
quately for what happens in the tale—for the controlled anger
and hard intellectual brilliance. We may call the narrator the

Merchant, but in doing so we ignore the more interesting persona that emerges from the story.

Like all the tales, the Merchant's expresses something not only of its pilgrim narrator but of Chaucer himself. The Merchant's Tale shows us a portrait of the artist as he might have become except for the saving grace of his affection for the objects of his satire. There is a danger for every satirist that his observation of mankind may sour his imagination, that his judgment of man will wear away the last drop of his charity, that he will come to despise his own kind. At the end of *Gulliver's Travels,* Gulliver withdraws to the stables because he cannot tolerate the smell of his family. E. T. Donaldson once pointed out the resemblance between the persona of Chaucer the Pilgrim and Lemuel Gulliver.[13] He meant, of course, the kindly ship's doctor who tries to help the Lilliputians, not the insane survivor of Houyhnhnmland. But the Gulliver of the final book grows out of the Gulliver of the first. Each is a dupe—the one of his natural goodness, the other of his overpowering sense of evil. The image of this last Gulliver seems to me to express Swift's horror at the streak of misanthropy in his own soul. The satire of Gulliver's madness in the last chapter of the *Travels* is a tragic vision in which one can detect Swift's own fear of going mad. It is like an art of exorcism. Chaucer's art is of a gentler nature, but his narrative persona, too, has a darker side, a vein of *saeva indignatio* that lies deeply buried in the dream visions, in *Troilus,* and in the General Prologue. In the Merchant's Tale this side of Chaucer's genius is for once given free rein only to be dismissed and banished like an evil spirit from the holiday journey of the Canterbury pilgrims.

CHAPTER XII

The Bourgeois
Sentimentalist

IF THE Merchant's Tale reveals the point of view of a misanthrope incapable of loving anyone, the Franklin's Tale, in refreshing contrast, shows the point of view of a man who loves everybody. The Merchant satirizes all ideals and values, including those of his fellow pilgrims. His tale aims specifically at the Wife of Bath and Clerk, of course, and it is hardly an accident that old January is introduced as "A worthy knyght" (1246) and that he is made a cuckold by his own squire. The Franklin's Tale not only holds a flattering mirror up to human nature but is meant as a personal compliment to three of the worthy pilgrims the Franklin especially admires: the Knight, the Squire, and the Clerk. I have argued that the Merchant's Tale shows us the dark side of Chaucer's genius, an argument with which I would expect some to disagree. There can be little disagreement, however, that the Franklin reflects the sunny side of Chaucer's personality and has much in common with the genial narrator of Chaucer's earlier poetry. In fact, the white-bearded Franklin resembles his creator in several points. Both Chaucer and the Franklin served as members of parliament and as justices of the peace. Chaucer's repeated jokes about his corpulence indicate that he shared the Franklin's love of a good table. But the most important thing they have in common is a general benevolence toward the world and its people.

The Franklin is so attractive a character, his tale radiates so much good sense and good humor, that it is tempting to accept Kittredge's theory that he speaks for Chaucer and happily resolves the debate on marriage. Dorigen and Arveragus mutually give up sovereignty over each other, an arrangement on which the Franklin comments:

> Heere may men seen an humble, wys accord;
> Thus hath she take hire servant and hir lord,—
> Servant in love, and lord in mariage.   (791–793)

Whether or not the Franklin is here speaking for Chaucer, Kittredge certainly speaks for the majority of Chaucer's modern readers. "We need not hesitate," he concludes, "to accept the solution which the Franklin offers as that which Geoffrey Chaucer the man accepted for his own part. Certainly it is a solution that does him infinite credit. A better has never been devised or imagined."[1]

The Franklin's ideal of marriage based on mutual love and forbearance naturally appeals to us because it is so very much our own, but for that very reason we should be cautious of accepting it uncritically. Perhaps a better solution never has been devised or imagined, but this is not the same thing as saying that it works. The Franklin's Tale, of course, is meant to show that it does. Dorigen and Arveragus talk about their problem like a sensible modern couple, and all finally turns out for the best. But how convincing is the tale?

Not convincing at all according to a number of recent critics. They have found various faults with the Franklin's story, which, they maintain, expose flaws in the Franklin's outlook.[2] Some time ago, I wrote a paper to show that the Franklin's "gentilesse" is not the real thing—at least not the thing we find in the Knight's Tale.[3] However, it is too narrow to find the Franklin's Tale wanting in some particular respect, for example in courtly sentiment or in rhetorical skill or in religious awareness. Its concept of "gentilesse," the central idea of the tale, extends to many things— love, marriage, and literary style. The Franklin's Tale is not really primarily about marriage at all, no more than the Clerk's or the Merchant's; rather it is about an ideal of conduct designed to govern all human relationships, those between lovers, between husband and wife, between debtor and creditor, and even between God and man. The Franklin's solution to all human problems, as will become evident, is the use of reason. If the Merchant's Tale presents a Hobbesian view of man as essentially brutish and selfish, the Franklin presents a Shaftesburian view of man as fundamentally generous and reasonable.

The differences between these two pilgrims are manifest in their introductions, which follow a similar pattern. The Merchant begins with an indignant outburst provoked by the Clerk's Tale and its Envoy, and he is moved to complain in public about his disastrous marriage. The Franklin begins by congratulating the Squire on his tale and goes on to complain about his son. He is rudely cut off by the Host, who, it may be recalled, commiserates, though one suspects somewhat ironically, with the Merchant's plight.

The Franklin's address to the Squire has been interpreted as evidence of social-climbing, a charge that was emphatically denied by Professor Gerould: "Chaucer's Franklin was a member of that class that was already old in the fourteenth century and which has never felt the lack of any higher title than gentleman, though from it have come, first and last, most of the men who have made England great."[4] One might observe that in Chaucer's day that class was some five centuries younger, and its greatest days, as well as England's, were still to come. I agree with Gerould, however, that the Franklin is not a social-climber although I do think he has social aspirations that are clearly evidenced in this scene. The Franklin admires the Squire for his noble heart and not just for his rank. The Squire's Tale is unfinished, but, however it might have ended, its moral is clearly going to be, "That pitee renneth soone in gentil herte," the fourth and final occurrence of Chaucer's "favorite line," voiced in the Squire's Tale by a lady falcon "in hir haukes ledene" (479). The same line could serve as the moral of the Franklin's Tale although the Franklin will give an original interpretation of what it means to be of "gentil herte."

The Franklin knows that material wealth without inner virtue is worthless: "Fy on possessioun,/But if a man be vertuous withal!" (686–687). At the same time he does not despise "possessioun," which is of course what has made him a franklin or freeholder.

His scale of values is suggested by his saying that he would rather "than twenty pound worth lond" that his own son were "a man of swich discrecioun" as the Squire (683–685). Twenty pounds purchased a lot of land in the fourteenth century, but, however symbolic the sum is meant to be, it contains the suggestion that in the Franklin's world moral value can be measured. Aurelius, the squire in the tale, is willing to pay the astronomical sum of a thousand pounds (which he does not have) for Dorigen's favors, and he echoes the Franklin:

> "Fy on a thousand pound!
> This wyde world, which that men seye is round,
> I wolde it yeve, if I were lord of it."   (1227–29)

But, like Dorigen, Aurelius learns that one will be held to account for courtly promises, however extravagant, and that one should not incur debts that one does not mean to or cannot pay. The Franklin believes that wealth without virtue is worthless, but he does not believe in virtue that cannot pay its debts.

His own son, it seems, has neither virtue nor can he pay his debts:

> I have my sone snybbed, and yet shal,
> For he to vertu listeth nat entende;
> But for to pleye at dees, and to despende
> And lese al that he hath, is his usage.
> And he hath levere talken with a page
> Than to comune with any gentil wight
> Where he myghte lerne gentillesse aright.   (688–694)

One can sympathize with the Franklin's disappointment in his son, but it already shows some limitations in the reasoned ideal of "gentillesse" his tale will set forth. He believes that virtue resides in character, not in wealth, and that one should be able to pass on good character to one's heirs not by blood but by teaching and good example. Virtue can be learned. But he has evidently been unsuccessful in impressing his young son with his own teaching and example. No doubt when he "snibs" his son, he lectures him on the subject of "gentillesse." One may also sympathize a little with the boy. It is a classic situation of a father who sees his

family's rise in the world threatened by a son who does not respect
the virtues that have helped the father to be successful. The
Franklin, comparing his son with the Squire, sounds very much
like Shakespeare's Henry IV comparing Prince Hal with Hotspur,
and perhaps Chaucer's Franklin is the more anxious because, like
Henry Bolingbroke, he is a parvenu.

Harry Bailly, an acute barometer of social status and a great
snob, obviously thinks that the Franklin is putting on airs. Professor Lumiansky is certainly right that his abrupt put-down should
be read, "Straw for *youre* gentillesse!"[5] Moreover, the polite
"youre," if that is what Chaucer wrote, is undoubtedly sarcastic,
for with the next line, the Host switches to the familiar form of
address: "What, Frankeleyn! pardee, sire, wel *thou* woost" (696).
The Franklin, for his part, refuses to get down to the Host's level
of discourse and replies with ironic courtesy:

> "Gladly, sire Hoost," quod he, "I wole obeye
> Unto *your* wyl; now herkneth what I seye.
> I wol *yow* nat contrarien in no wyse
> As fer as that my wittes wol suffyse.
> I prey to God that it may plesen *yow;*
> Thanne woot I wel that it is good ynow."   (703–708)[6]

The Host recognizes in the prosperous, fashionably dressed,
well-mannered Franklin a genuine challenge to the feudal caste
system. The old hag in the Wife of Bath's Tale declares: "Crist
wole we clayme of hym oure gentillesse" (1117). Griselda is a
peasant girl whose spiritual nobility places her above her aristocratic husband. But the Franklin is not a character in a fairy tale
or moral allegory. He is living proof that a commoner may pretend, if not to the social rank, to the manners and, yet more important, the morals of the aristocracy and thereby claim the title
of "gentleman." And ultimately, better titles are not out of reach.
After all, Geoffrey Chaucer's granddaughter became a duchess.

The key to the Franklin's idea of "gentillesse" is the word
"freedom." As applied to the Knight, "freedom" means liberality
or generosity, an important component of chivalry. In the Franklin's Tale, however, though the word occurs in this chivalric sense
also, it already means very much what it does to us:

Love is a thyng as any spirit free.
Wommen, of kynde, desiren libertee,
And nat to been constreyned as a thral;
And so doon men, if I sooth seyen shal.   (767–770)

The trouble with both courtly love and medieval marriage, as the Franklin sees it, is that either way one of the partners is subject to the other's will. He is not "free," and without "freedom" neither true love nor true chivalry is possible:

Whan maistrie comth, the God of Love anon
Beteth his wynges, and farewel, he is gon!   (765–766)

In the Knight's Tale and most chivalric literature human relationships are seen in hierarchical terms. Everyone is assigned his place in the great chain of being. Courtly love inverts the natural hierarchy but remains hierarchical in principle. In contrast to this feudal ideal of order, the Franklin holds an ideal that is essentially democratic. He believes that all men are created equal in their capacity for reason and virtue. His view of all relationships is based on law rather than on eternal principles. In society people are bound to one another by contracts (a later age would define the basis of society as a "social contract"), and a contract may be entered into only by free and equal parties. To be noble means, first of all, keeping one's word and one's agreements, whether in love or in a legal transaction.

The Franklin's Tale turns on a series of such agreements,[7] each of which is executed with a formal oath or pledge. Arveragus renounces his title to sovereignty in marriage: "Of his free wyl he swoor hire as a knyght" (745). Dorigen, in return, tells him:

Sire, I wol be youre humble trewe wyf;
Have heer my trouthe, til that myn herte breste.
                    (758–759)

Dorigen does not really mean her promise to Aurelius that she will love him best if he can remove the rocks from the coast of Brittany. What she means is that her love for her husband is as solid and permanent as the rocks themselves. Nevertheless, she makes it a sworn commitment: "Have heer my trouthe, in al that evere

I kan" (998). Aurelius promises to pay the clerk the price of one thousand pounds:

> This bargayn is ful dryve, for we been knyt.
> Ye shal be payed trewely, by my trouthe!   (1230–31)

Obviously the word "trouthe" is crucial in the tale so that we are prepared when Arveragus tells Dorigen that she must keep her promise because "Trouthe is the hyeste thyng that man may kepe" (1479).

But which truth is Dorigen to keep, her rash promise to Aurelius or the marital troth she has sworn to Arveragus? In the Knight's world there is a solution to such conflicting obligations: Palamon and Arcite are sworn brothers and undoubted gentlemen, but their brotherhood lasts only until they have seen Emelye. Is their strife a flagrant violation of their honor? On the contrary, as Arcite says:

> Wostow nat wel the olde clerkes sawe,
> That 'who shal yeve a lovere any lawe?'
> Love is a gretter lawe, by my pan,
> Than may be yeve to any erthely man;
> And therfore positif lawe and swich decree
> Is broken al day for love in ech degree.
> A man moot nedes love, maugree his heed.   (1163–69)

The noble lover accepts a hierarchy even of sworn faith. The laws of reason, of friendship, of self-preservation itself give way to the higher obligation to serve one's lady.

When Dorigen is first confronted by her dilemma, she can see only one way out. Her lugubrious catalogue of maidens and wives who chose death before dishonor serves to emphasize the novelty of the Franklin's solution by suggesting one of the more old-fashioned alternatives to it. Dorigen might kill herself. Or there is another alternative that would surely occur to any gentleman: Arveragus should take his sword and challenge his rival. A sure and realistic solution to any triangle situation is to kill off one member of the triangle. But the Franklin's point is precisely that he will have no such violent solutions. His practical nature and sanguine temperament forbid such irrational and sanguinary methods.

Is it possible to demonstrate nobility in this kind of situation without resorting to bloodshed? Clearly it is entirely in keeping with the Franklin's views and aspirations to argue that reason and a generous heart may accomplish more than feats of arms. There *is* another way out of every contract involving a debt of honor. It may be voluntarily dissolved by the creditor. And that is, of course, what happens in the Franklin's Tale. Arveragus releases Dorigen from her "troth" to him so that she may keep her word of honor to Aurelius, and thus begins a chain reaction. Aurelius, put to shame by the noble example of Arveragus, frees Dorigen from her promise in extremely legalistic language:

> I yow relesse, madame, into youre hond
> Quyt every serement and every bond
> That ye han maad to me as heerbiforn,
> Sith thilke tyme which that ye were born.   (1533–36)

The clerk of Orleans follows suit:

> Sire, I releesse thee thy thousand pound,
> As thou right now were cropen out of the ground.
>   (1613–14)

Thus Arveragus, Aurelius, and the clerk all freely relinquish their rights, and the Franklin concludes his tale by addressing to his audience a courtly *demande d'amour:* "Which was the mooste fre, as thynketh yow?" (1622).

The Franklin's own answer, I suppose, would be that all have been equally "free," but one might object that *none* of them has been "free" because each has given up something that never rightly belonged to him. Arveragus has no right to put Dorigen's "word" to Aurelius above their mutual love, Aurelius has no right to exact a promise that was never from the heart, the clerk has no right to ask a thousand pounds for *seeming* to make the rocks disappear. For the rocks are really always there. The clerk's "natural magic" only tells him when they shall be submerged by the high tide.

This stress on words and appearances recurs throughout the tale. At the beginning Arveragus reserves "the name of soveraynetee" (751) so as not to be ashamed in the eyes of the world. At the end he forbids Dorigen, on pain of death,

That nevere, whil thee lasteth lyf ne breeth,
To no wight telle thou of this aventure,—
As I may best, I wol my wo endure,—
Ne make no contenance of hevynesse,
That folk of yow may demen harm or gesse.   (1482–86)

Arveragus's insistence on keeping up the appearance while willing to suffer the fact diminishes his nobility and raises a serious question about the depth of the Franklin's conception of "gentillesse." Should the mere "words" of a contract be given such overriding importance? The answer can be "yes" only in a world where people will freely give up rights that depend on words alone, as Dorigen and Arveragus relinquish the "rights" in their relationship and as the three men give up their "rights" at the end. But what would have happened if one of the characters had insisted on his "rights," if Aurelius, for example, had said with Arcite "A man moot nedes love, maugree his heed," and had decided to accept Arveragus's sacrifice? That would spoil the story, but the reciprocal acts of generosity that bring the Franklin's Tale to its happy ending are clearly a fantasy. The Franklin's Tale like the Wife of Bath's is a wish fulfillment. In a world inhabited exclusively by calm and reasonable men like Arveragus, Aurelius, and the clerk, all things are possible. But life is not like that, and in his own life the Franklin has not succeeded in teaching "gentillesse" to his own son.

The Knight's Tale is far from realistic, but it recognizes the forces of evil and of the irrational. It, too, has a happy ending, but that ending is paid for by Arcite's death. In the final analysis, the Franklin's idea of living up to one's word of honor, no matter what, is both unrealistic and shallow. Without denying the charm of the ending, one may say that the sacrifices made by the characters at the end are not real sacrifices.

Although the principal emphasis in the tale falls on virtues that are courtly, the Franklin is well aware that the courtly virtues are analogous to the Christian. The characters in this tale, as in the Knight's, live under the dispensation of pagan gods, and the Franklin goes out of his way to emphasize his own orthodoxy; the clerk's illusions are called "a supersticious cursednesse" (1272) such "As hethen folk useden in thilke dayes" (1293). Nevertheless, the tale admits, on another level, a Christian interpretation. The climax of the tale takes place in the winter, as we are informed in the only seasonal passage in Chaucer's poetry that celebrates winter rather than spring:

> And this was, as thise bookes me remembre,
> The colde, frosty seson of Decembre.
>   Phebus wax old, and hewed lyk laton,
> That in his hoote declynacion
> Shoon as the burned gold with stremes brighte;
> But now in Capricorn adoun he lighte,
> Where as he shoon ful pale, I dar wel seyn.
> The bittre frostes, with the sleet and reyn,
> Destroyed hath the grene in every yerd.
> Janus sit by the fyr, with double berd,
> And drynketh of his bugle horn the wyn;
> Biforn hym stant brawen of the tusked swyn,
> And "Nowel" crieth every lusty man.   (1243-55)

The significance of this passage has been profoundly explained by E. T. Donaldson:

> The solution to Dorigen's dilemma is foreshadowed in the memorable passage that precedes the account of the vanishing of the rocks, the passage on "the cold and frosty season of December" when Nature seems most dead and most sterile—yet nonetheless the season of Nowel (from Latin *natalis*, birthday) when Christ came to redeem the dead world and to fulfill the Old Law with the New. For in the poem the Christian virtue of *freedom* (generosity) fulfills the Old Testament contractual law of *trouthe* (the covenant). Both virtues are important, since *trouthe* calls *freedom* into existence as the Old Testament may be said to have called into existence the New. Through generosity the evil that Dorigen has unwittingly brought into being is once more relegated to illusion, and Dorigen, we assume, has learned to distinguish the real from the unreal.[8]

Donaldson is right in calling attention to the legalistic character of Christianity and its two covenants. The various contracts in the Franklin's Tale do remind us of those covenants. Aurelius tells Dorigen that she is free of any promises to him since the time she was born; the clerk tells Aurelius that he releases him as though Aurelius had just crept out of the ground. In each case the language suggests the sinner whose redemption *is* a rebirth.

The Franklin, however, neglects the fact that, while the hope of redemption was born in the dead of winter, the redemption came about through Christ's death in the spring of the year. The "trouthe" of the Old Testament demands a blood sacrifice, and the Savior pays that debt with His own blood. The weakness of the Franklin's "freedom," whether we look at it as a Christian or a courtly virtue, is that no one has to pay. The Franklin's Tale is, like the art of the clerk of Orleans, superficial. The obstacles disappear from sight, but they remain ever-present below the surface.

This is not to minimize or to condemn the generosity of the Franklin's Tale. That would be to read the story in the spirit of Ebenezer Scrooge—before his conversion. However, the conversions at the end of the Franklin's Tale are like the conversion of Scrooge in which we willingly suspend our disbelief. Like *A Christmas Carol*, the Franklin's Tale is filled with the true spirit of Christmas, which, like the spirit of poetry, *can* perform miracles.

CHAPTER XIII

A Moral Thing

SAID ABOVE that the Clerk's was the best of the tales of "moralitee and hoolynesse," yet an excellent case could be made that the Pardoner's Tale deserves that honor. If we look simply at the tale, forgetting about the Pardoner, it is certainly a powerful exemplum of sin and retribution, but of course it is impossible to forget about the Pardoner. Like the Wife of Bath's, the Pardoner's Prologue puts us under the spell of his personality, and his presence is felt throughout his tale. As with the Wife, Chaucer has endowed this pilgrim with an individual style and idiom. In contrast with the Wife's leisurely ramblings, the Pardoner's Prologue moves with a rising pitch of nervous intensity. His manner reminds us of details in the portrait in the General Prologue, the voice, high like a goat's, the eyes, glaring like those of a hare—mad as a March hare's. He draws a picture of himself in the pulpit:

> Thanne peyne I me to strecche forth the nekke,
> And est and west upon the peple I bekke,
> As dooth a dowve sittynge on a berne.
> Myne handes and my tonge goon so yerne
> That it is joye to see my bisynesse.   (395–399)

The image captures his restless birdlike activity; at the same time it mocks the dove of peace whose gift of grace to man he is perverting for his own ends.

The sermon that follows the Prologue is an emotional, theatrical example of the revivalist's art. We are fascinated less by its content than by the posturing of the preacher himself, fulminating, groaning, cajoling, and weeping. In contrast, the tale, once it really begins, unfolds with total objectivity. The Pardoner does not intrude upon our consciousness again until the impassioned preacher's voice breaks in at the end: "What nedeth it to sermone of it moore?" (879) However, the intensity of the tale is that of its teller, and one does not need to understand how the Pardoner has transformed himself into the symbolic figures of his story in order to feel the effect of that transformation.

The tale *is* about the Pardoner. He has told us so himself:

> Thus kan I preche agayn that same vice
> Which that I use, and that is avarice.   (427–428)

Moreover, as will be seen, the sermon and its exemplum apply to the Pardoner, not just in a general way, as they apply to any avaricious man. In the Pardoner's Tale he specifically pronounces judgment upon himself, and in his peroration he asks a question about mankind to which his entire performance—Prologue and Tale—has given a sharply dramatic form:

> Allas! mankynde, how may it bitide
> That to thy creatour, which that the wroghte,
> And with his precious herte-blood thee boghte,
> Thou art so fals and so unkynde, allas?   (900–903)

Why is the Pardoner himself "so fals and so unkynde," and, further, what forgiveness, if any, is there for him? Kittredge called him "the one lost soul among the Canterbury Pilgrims," a judgment few have questioned.[1] His sin, which is against the Holy Spirit, is said to be the only unforgivable sin. Nevertheless, we should suspend judgment, at least until the final word of the Pardoner's fragment. His Prologue and Tale and the brief episode that follows it constitute a morality play in which the stake is not the soul of some ordinary representative sinner but the worst that may be. The Pardoner represents the ultimate challenge to the healing power of St. Thomas. If there is hope of remedy for his sickness, then the store of grace must indeed be infinite.

The drama begins with an unpleasant little scene in which we

see how the Pardoner is regarded as something of a pariah among
the pilgrims even before he tells them about himself. The Physician
has just finished a maudlin tale that has so affected the Host's
heart that he has, in his words, almost "caught a cardynacle"
(313). He requires the remedy of some of the Physician's medicine, or "a draughte of moyste and corny ale," or else "a myrie
tale." Harry Bailly recognizes the therapeutic value of laughter,
and his clowning remarks in praise of the Physician's "urynals,"
"jurdones," "ypocras," and "galiones" (305–306) show him to
be in a high humor. With insolent familiarity, he turns to the
Pardoner:

> "Thou beel amy, thou Pardoner," he sayde,
> "Telle us som myrthe or japes right anon."[2]   (318–319)

The tone implies that he has sized up the Pardoner as an amusing
scoundrel and expects him to tell an unsavory fabliau; however,
the more genteel among the pilgrims, who did not object to the
Miller or the Reeve, draw the line at the Pardoner:

> But right anon thise gentils gonne to crye,
> "Nay, lat hym telle us of no ribaudye!
> Telle us som moral thyng, that we may leere
> Som wit, and thanne wol we gladly heere."   (323–326)

The Pardoner's reply that he needs time to reflect upon "som
honest thyng while that I drynke" is an ironic acknowledgment
of the general opinion the pilgrims have expressed about him.
They expect him to be shocking. What they have not considered
is that he makes his living by telling moral stories, and, therefore,
the Pardoner decides to treat them to a demonstration of his professional skill. He will shock them all right, not, however, with
the immoral story that they expect from him but far more in-
geniously with a "moral thyng." The cynical confession of his
own corruption and the blasphemous spirit in which he preaches
his sermon is more outrageous than any fabliau could be. What
is shocking is the cool indifference the Pardoner affects toward
the possible damnation of the people he deceives and, even more
disturbing, the way he glories in his own deadly state of sin. He
does make a "myrthe" and "jape" out of the hope of redemption,

which is the bond that has brought the company together on the journey to Canterbury.[3]

The motive behind the Pardoner's "confession" has been much puzzled over and debated, but it is one of those debates in which practically everyone is partially right.[4] In a character so full of contradictions, one may look for a double-edged, self-contradictory motivation. On the one hand, he is revenging himself on the pilgrims for their scorn. His shamelessness is an insult to the whole company. In effect, his tone implies: "All you respectable folk are really no better than I am. I have nothing to hide from you, and I don't care what you think of me." Yet, at the same time, the confession is a plea for acceptance, almost a dare to the pilgrims to like him and laugh with him. In a sense, just like the Wife of Bath, the Pardoner's intent is "nat but for to pleye," to amuse the pilgrims by a comically exaggerated account of his trade secrets. But his jokes quickly turn sour, and they are envenomed with the hostility he feels toward his audience. On another level, that audience includes God, for his boast of evil is like a challenge to God to save anyone so wicked. It is at one and the same time angry defiance and a call for help.

He demonstrates the pulpit trick that, he claims, is worth one hundred marks annually:

> Goode men and wommen, o thyng warne I yow:
> If any wight be in this chirche now
> That hath doon synne horrible, that he
> Dar nat, for shame, of it yshryven be,
> Or any womman, be she yong or old,
> That hath ymaad hir housbonde cokewold,
> Swich folk shal have no power ne no grace
> To offren to my relikes in this place.   (377–384)

We are meant to and do laugh at the comic predicament of the people in the Pardoner's congregation, but the Pardoner is aware that he is really like those people who are guilty of "synne horrible" and torn between desire for absolution and fear of public disgrace. Similarly, in this extraordinary Prologue the Pardoner is torn between his longing to be a part of the community of pilgrims and a perverse desire to remain cut off in the proud isolation of his sin.

The Pardoner's sample sermon is a superb mixture of the sacred and the profane.[5] He begins by drawing an epic image of sin beyond the wildest dreams of the poor countryfolk who are his usual auditors. He conjures up a tavern scene with music, dancing, gambling, eating, and drinking that through a twist of language turns into a satanic rite:

> they doon the devel sacrifise
> Withinne that develes temple, in cursed wise,
> By superfluytee abhomynable.   (469–471)

In castigating the sins, the Pardoner personifies and addresses them as though they were standing before our very eyes in all their loathsomeness:

> O dronke man, disfigured is thy face,
> Sour is thy breeth, foul artow to embrace,
> And thurgh thy dronke nose semeth the soun
> As though thou seydest ay "Sampsoun, Sampsoun!"
> And yet, God woot, Sampsoun drank nevere no wyn.
>   (551–555)

The onomatopoeic comparison of the drunken man's heavy breathing to the name of the Nazarite Samson who drank no wine is typical of the free and often incongruous association in this sermon which jumbles together realism and scriptural allusion, the wines of Fishstreet and Cheapside and the blood of Christ. We are perversely reminded of the healing power of that blood in the Pardoner's example of the foulest swearing:

> "By Goddes precious herte," and "By his nayles,"
> And "By the blood of Crist that is in Hayles,
> Sevene is my chaunce, and thyn is cynk and treye!"
> "By Goddes armes, if thou falsly pleye,
> This daggere shal thurghout thyn herte go!"—
>   (651–655)

The sermon draws a picture of sinful human nature, as grotesque in its own way as the Pardoner's self-portrait in his Prologue. In his sermon he is both accuser and accused, one who weeps with the apostle Paul and one of the "enemys of Christes croys,/Of whiche the ende is deeth" (531–533).

The consciousness that the end is death pervades the exemplum of the sermon—the tale of the three rioters who set out to slay death but are slain by him. In contrast to the orgiastic scene of the "devil's temple" with which the Pardoner begins, the actual commencement of the tale is quietly sinister. It is morning, and the clink of a funeral bell—the first *memento mori* of many—penetrates the tavern where the three heroes are drunk before prime. Their alliance—"To lyve and dyen ech of hem for oother"—is of course a blasphemous parody of the Trinity, and their quest to slay Death, a travesty of Christ's redemptive mission. In a fever of haste, they rush out of the tavern to encounter—a strange old man.

Every reader of the tale has experienced the fascination of this muffled figure and has been haunted by his mysterious words:

> "For I ne kan nat fynde
> A man, though that I walked into Ynde,
> Neither in citee ne in no village,
> That wolde chaunge his youthe for myn age;
> And therfore moot I han myn age stille,
> As longe tyme as it is Goddes wille.
> Ne Deeth, allas! ne wol nat han my lyf.
> Thus walke I, lyk a restelees kaityf,
> And on the ground, which is my moodres gate,
> I knokke with my staf, bothe erly and late,
> And seye 'Leeve mooder, leet me in!
> Lo how I vanysshe, flessh, and blood, and skyn!
> Allas! whan shul my bones been at reste?"   (721–733)

Kittredge's identification of the old man is the one that springs most readily to mind: "The aged wayfarer . . . is undoubtedly Death in person."[6] But why should Death be personified as an old man who himself wishes to die? A variety of identifications have been proposed.[7] Of these the most interesting is Robert P. Miller's suggestion that the old man in the tale corresponds to the old man St. Paul speaks of several times (Col. iii, 1–10; Eph. iv, 17–24; Rom. vi, 1 ff.) as a symbol of the flesh or that part of human nature that must die before the spirit may be reborn through the agency of the new man (or the young man) who is Christ.[8] For example, in Fourth Ephesians Paul tells us "to put off . . . the old man, which is corrupt according to the deceitful lusts, . . ." and "to put on the new man, which after God is created in righteousness and true holiness." The old man, or the old Adam, points the way to death, not just to physical death but to the death of the soul, and this is exactly what the old man in the Pardoner's Tale does when he directs the three rioters up the "crooked way." The old man is ancient—he is born with sin and death—and he will roam the fallen world until the end of time.

The most illuminating ramification of Miller's interpretation is that it involves the Pardoner himself, an impotent man who sells sterile pardons and who interacts with the other pilgrims on a journey that is not only realistic but symbolic. There is an implied analogy between the old man and the Pardoner. "He is," Miller argues, "that Old Man as he lives and exerts his influence in the great pilgrimage of life."[9] Like the old man the Pardoner wanders ceaselessly through city and village, sending men up the "croked wey." However, although there is a connection between the Pardoner and the old man in the tale, such an interpretation does not account for the significant differences between them. Miller implies that both the Pardoner and his counterpart, the old man, are inveterately evil, and he concludes: ". . . the Old Man still goes wandering through the world, glaring with sterile lust out of his hare-like eyes."[10] But the wanderer in the tale greets the rioters "ful mekely," begs them to respect his age, and parts from them with the wish that God may save and amend them. Whatever the allegorical significance of his words and actions, his *tone* is that of a humble pious old man and not a bit like the Pardoner's.

The old man does indeed tell us something about the Pardoner, but something more profound than what the Pardoner has already told us about himself: that he is an evil man. The old man tells us about the frustration, the suffering, and the self-destructiveness of evil. For evil may be both like a young man who defies death and like an old man whose only wish is to die.[11] One of Miller's most perceptive insights is the ironic fact that the Pardoner, who corresponds to the old man, affects an appearance of youth.[12] He dresses somewhat flashily "al of the newe jet," rides bareheaded, exposing stringy yellow locks that hang down over his shoulders, proclaims his desire for wine and wenches, and impudently asks the Wife of Bath, in his interruption of her prologue, to "teche us yonge men of youre praktike" (187).

The three villains are among the "yonge folk" who haunt the tavern. Their vices—drunkenness, blasphemy, and avarice—are those that the Pardoner boastfully claims as his own. Their quest to slay Death has an ironic resemblance to the mission the Pardoner abuses, that is to absolve men from the seven deadly sins. Their camaraderie suggests the sort of companionship that we have seen between the Pardoner and the Summoner. A sadistic element dominates the association of these three blood brothers and culminates when one of them is stabbed as he wrestles "in game" with one of the other two. There is a perverse gratification in the violence and the violent deaths of the young men.

But the Pardoner, much as he would like to conceal it by his dress and his forced jollity, is not one of the "yonge folk," nor is the pleasure he professes to find in vice a genuine pleasure. If we listen carefully to his Prologue, I think we may detect the false note of bravado and the sense of strain:

> I wol nat do no labour with myne handes,
> Ne make baskettes, and lyve therby,
> By cause I wol nat beggen ydelly.
> I wol noon of the apostles countrefete;
> I wol have moneie, wolle, chese, and whete,
> Al were it yeven of the povereste page,
> Or of the povereste wydwe in a village,
> Al sholde hir children sterve for famyne.   (444–451)

There is something almost hysterical about the reiteration of "I wol" and "I wol not," like an angry child defying its parents. The Pardoner is, in short, a young-old man, and the confrontation between the three rioters and the old man in the tale brings to the surface a moral and psychological conflict that has been latent all along.

The old man's longing for death, his inability to find anyone who will exchange youth for his age—this expresses the other side of the Pardoner's nature, the terrible weariness of carrying his burden of sin. Thus the three young men and the old man express the conflicting sides of the Pardoner's personality. Their covetousness, their blasphemy, and their boastfulness are the side that the Pardoner has revealed in his Prologue. The old man expresses what the Pardoner has concealed, his despair of release, his isolation from human love, and his deeper alienation from divine love. What is terrifying about the old man is his loneliness. Through him Chaucer reveals the Pardoner's real secret, the joy-lessness of the life he professes to relish so much. Ultimately sin can only make the Pardoner suffer, and he is forced to keep wandering, as he is compelled to go on talking.

Under the ancient oak tree, which like the pear tree in the Merchant's Tale reminds us of the tree of knowledge, the three brothers discover a treasure. They do not realize that they have found Death in the form of the gold and immediately begin to plot each other's deaths, which are acted out swiftly and inexorably beneath the tree. The ironic lesson of the exemplum is obvious enough even to the most ignorant peasant to whom the Pardoner ordinarily preaches this sermon. The logical conclusion to be drawn is that if anyone is carrying Death in his pockets, he should give it to the Pardoner.

With the pilgrims the Pardoner is sharing a further irony. He has told them that he is seeking gold like the man in his story, and by analogy he, too, is seeking death. He feels himself judged to die the death of the three young men. We might say that their deaths psychologically fulfill the death wish of the old man.

The reader may look still further. What really motivates the Pardoner always to preach this sermon about himself, and especially now to the pilgrims from whom, after his confession, he can expect to gain nothing? One of his motives is, as I have suggested, in this as in all of his performances, to blaspheme and to shock. He wants to show the pilgrims how cleverly he can manipulate language for his own corrupt ends, to laugh at his ingenuity, and to express his devil-may-care attitude. If this were all, the tale would be simply diabolical. But through the old man the tale also conveys the Pardoner's subconscious appeal for compassion. The tale not only expresses the terrible lesson of judgment: "The wages of sin is death." It also expresses the corollary message of hope: "But the gift of God is eternal life through Jesus Christ." This is the theme of the Pardoner's eloquent peroration:

> Now, goode men, God foryeve yow youre trespas,
> And ware yow fro the synne of avarice!
> Myn hooly pardoun may yow alle warice,
> So that ye offre nobles or sterlynges,
> Or elles silver broches, spoones, rynges.
> Boweth youre heed under this hooly bulle!
> Cometh up, ye wyves, offreth of youre wolle!
> Youre names I entre heer in my rolle anon;
> Into the blisse of hevene shul ye gon.
> I yow assoille, by myn heigh power,
> Yow that wol offre, as clene and eek as cleer
> As ye were born.—And lo, sires, thus I preche
> And Jhesu Crist, that is oure soules leche,
> So graunte yow his pardoun to receyve,
> For that is best; I wol yow nat deceyve.   (904–918)

The last four lines are the basis of Kittredge's famous interpretation that the Pardoner has here been carried away by his own eloquence to a "paroxysm of agonized sincerity," holding out to his fellow pilgrims the blessing of which he despairs.[13] Kittredge's theory depends on reading too much into the text, but mixed in with the cynical appeal for brooches and rings there is undeniably the magnetism of the idea of grace: to be washed "as clene and eek as cleer/As ye were born." And that idea, as I have tried to argue all along, remains potent in spite of the Pardoner's blasphemies.

As soon as the Pardoner has finished his sermon, he reverts to his jesting manner. Some critics have been baffled by the Pardoner's apparent attempt to sell his relics to the pilgrims after he has confessed that they are fraudulent. But the language shows very clearly that he is joking and that this is just another insult to the company:

> But, sires, o word forgat I in my tale:
> I have relikes and pardoun in my male,

As faire as any man in Engelond,
Whiche were me yeven by the popes hond.
If any of yow wole, of devocion,
Offren, and han myn absolucion,
Com forth anon, and kneleth heere adoun,
And mekely receyveth my pardoun;
Or elles taketh pardoun as ye wende,
Al newe and fressh at every miles ende, . . .   (919–928)

Once again the Pardoner gets carried away. He attempts to take comic revenge on the Host for the latter's "beel amy," but this time the Pardoner overreaches himself. Harry Bailly, who does not shock easily, is genuinely angry and disgusted, and he retaliates viciously. He publicly humiliates the Pardoner with a cruel gibe about another pair of false relics that the Pardoner is doomed to carry with him:

"I wolde I hadde thy coillons in myn hond
In stide of relikes or of seintuarie.
Lat kutte hem of, I wol thee helpe hem carie;
They shul be shryned in an hogges toord!"   (952–955)

The effect is devastating. The busy tongue is suddenly stilled. The Pardoner is so angry that he cannot speak another word. Everyone is laughing at him, an unhealthier laughter than that which followed the quarrel of the Miller and Reeve. It is at this point that the "parfit gentil knyght" takes pity on the Pardoner and intercedes. His action is more truly chivalrous than anything in the Knight's Tale:

"Namoore of this, for it is right ynough!
Sire Pardoner, be glad and myrie of cheere;
And ye, sire Hoost, that been to me so deere,
I prey yow that ye kisse the Pardoner.
And Pardoner, I prey thee, drawe thee neer,
And, as we diden, lat us laughe and pleye."
Anon they kiste, and ryden forth hir weye.   (962–968)

It is a beautifully quiet and understated ending, but it contains the ray of hope that redeems the Pardoner's whole performance and gives it meaning. On a social level, the level of the frame story, the Pardoner has done his very best to cut himself off from the rest of the company. His offering his relics at the end compounds the insult by parodying their quest to seek the holy blissful martyr. They are going for absolution, and he steps forward mockingly as their "suffisant pardoneer." But in spite of everything, through the Knight's intervention, the Pardoner is pardoned and received back into the group. His spitefulness has not been able to destroy the solidarity and the good humor of the company. Without pressing the point too hard, one may read further meaning into the episode. Vice and blasphemy are, in the end, also impotent and have no power over the things they seek to harm. Evil is only the negation of good; sin, only the denial of love. Ultimately only good and love can come of them. The kiss of brotherhood between the Pardoner and the Host is a comic but meaningful reassertion of the brotherhood of man, which the sworn brotherhood of the three rioters has mocked. Just as the Pardoner has failed to isolate himself utterly from his fellow pilgrims, so no man can willfully withdraw from the Christian communion. If the Pardoner can be pitied by the Knight, the *miles Christi*, then perhaps he may be forgiven by Christ himself. It is at least an open question.

CHAPTER XIV

Another Tale
of Innocence

*t*HE PARDONER'S PROLOGUE and Tale indirectly but perhaps more movingly than any of the rest reaffirms the efficacy of the martyr's blood and reassures us that the pilgrims' quest is not in vain. Yet if we ask ourselves whether this fragment of the *Canterbury Tales* is among the "legendes of seintes, and omelies, and moralitee, and devocioun," for which Chaucer in his Retraction thanks God, or whether it belongs with the "translacions of worldly vanitees," which he recants, the answer is probably among the latter even though the epilogue of the tale seems to me to show a more genuine spirit of charity than anything in the Man of Law's Tale or the Clerk's. The Pardoner's Tale is vitiated as "a moral thyng" by the teller's cynical exploitation of naive faith for selfish ends. Even if we read the whole performance as an outright condemnation of the Pardoner and all he stands for, feeling no sympathy whatsoever for him, we are more fascinated by the man himself than by the lesson of sin and corruption.

Indeed, the Pardoner's Tale presents us with a paradox to which the Pardoner himself draws our attention:

> For though myself be a ful vicious man,
> A moral tale yet I yow telle kan.   (459–460)

Bad men may tell good stories. In the Pardoner's Tale we see how the resources of great art can be used by a charlatan to extort money from people through emotional blackmail. And even when, as with the pilgrim audience, money is not the object, the Pardoner exerts his power over us in spite of our knowledge that he is a fraud. He well knows that "lewed peple loven tales olde," and in the case of his own story, no matter what depths of meaning we may perceive in it, on the most basic level we love this tale for the same reasons as the "lewed peple." In the Pardoner's Prologue and Tale, Chaucer demonstrates how poetry in the guise of morality may move men of all kinds. Some artists may in fact be charlatans like the Pardoner, passing off their counterfeits of life in the name of a pretended lesson.

The Prioress's Tale is certainly not told for any selfish motive; it displays the very naive faith that the Pardoner knows how to manipulate so well for his own profit. Yet, in a more subtle way even than the Pardoner's, it raises a question about the morality of exploiting "olde tales" for a religious purpose, because the Prioress truly believes in her miracle. The tale provokes even stronger emotional reactions than the Clerk's story of patient Griselda, arousing deep sympathy and even deeper antipathy. It has long been a favorite among Chaucer's admirers. Wordsworth modernized it. Matthew Arnold chose a line from it—"O martyr sowded to virginitee"—as a touchstone for Chaucer although he found, not surprisingly perhaps, that it lacked high seriousness.[1] Kittredge comments on the moment of eloquent silence with which the pilgrims receive the tale: "The tale's effect upon the Pilgrims is described by Chaucer in two lines of utter simplicity, which touch, so I think, the skirts of Shakespere's garment."[2] Yet the obvious sentimentality of the story and, more significantly, the blind prejudice about the "cursed Jewes" have caused many readers to reject the appeal of the tale. Particularly for readers who have grown up since the Second World War, the attitudes in the tale cannot be overlooked regretfully as the bigotry of a former age but must be rejected with horror. It is not surprising, therefore, that some critics of the present generation have tried to salvage the tale for us by arguing that Madame Eglentyne's sentimentality and her hatred for the Jews reveal the deep flaws in her own character.[3]

I do not think, however, that the reader is obliged to choose between an interpretation that takes the Prioress's Tale on its own terms and one that makes Chaucer seem almost embarrassingly like a modern liberal. The tale does show the limitations of the Prioress although it does not judge her harshly. Moreover, Chaucer's attribution of the story to the Prioress and his adaptation of it does bring out certain ironies in the very popular genre to which the Prioress's Tale belongs.

A question arises whether concerning the Virgin *any* medieval reader would have perceived ironies that are apparent enough to the modern mind. No doubt for many medieval people the question of the probability or the morality of any miracle story about the Mother of God would never even arise, and the Prioress herself is one of those people. Joinville in his *Life of St. Louis,* for example, tells several charming miracles of the Virgin as though they had the same historicity as the rest of his material. Nevertheless, although the miracles of the Virgin testify to medieval faith, they are hardly untouched by medieval skepticism. The authors of the French dramas collected under the title of *Miracles de Nostre Dame* are not unaware of the possibilities for humor and irony in some of the Virgin's miracles. There is, for example, the story of the abbess, who gets in trouble with her clerk.[4] Two jealous nuns, Seur Marie and Seur Isabel, whom the abbess has disciplined for tippling, discover her secret and report her to the bishop. He investigates, but the Virgin has already delivered the baby painlessly and placed it in the care of a holy hermit. The jealous nuns are confounded, but the abbess privately confesses to the bishop who is so deeply impressed at the Virgin's favor to her that he has her transferred to a better convent:

> Puis que Dieu li est tant amis
> Et sa mére vous a si chiére
> Qu'elle a esté vostre ventriére
> Il pert bien qu'estes sainte femme
> Et pour ce vueil que soiez dame
> De l'ostel de Mons et maistresse,
> Ne plus ne serez cy abbesse:
> C'est a vous trop petit estat.[5]

> Since God is such a great friend of yours, and his Mother holds you so dear that she has been your midwife, it is clear

that you are a holy woman, and therefore I want to make you mistress of the House of Mons. You shall not be abbess here any more. It's too small a position for you.

I am not suggesting that this kind of story indicates any irreverence or intentional blasphemy on the part of the authors. However, it demonstrates, I believe, that sophisticated people in the Middle Ages could be as amused by certain miracles of the Virgin, and as skeptical about them, as they would be concerning the Pardoner's relics. To sum up, I do not think that we are obliged to assume that Geoffrey Chaucer's attitude toward any miracle of the Virgin would be one of unquestioning faith. Chaucer *is* charmed and moved by the tale of the little clergeoun. At the same time, his affection for the story does not prevent him from seeing it as the product of the naive imagination, a tale of sincere faith but dubious religious import.

In order to deal fairly with the Prioress and her tale, we must first see it for what it is. No one has seen that more clearly than the Prioress's staunchest modern defender, Sister Maria Madeleva. "No child," writes Sister Madeleva, "ever ventured in wide-eyed awe into a convent corridor but some motherly old Nun broke through the barrier of his shyness with a battery of just such stories."[6] More recent criticism has been less inclined to take the treatment of the Jews in the story for granted. A case has been made that the tale is intended to exhibit the viciousness of legends of ritual murder and the hypocrisy of the Prioress.[7] It has also been said that the Prioress does not grasp the symbolic meaning of her tale. It is really a conflict between the Old Law (the Jews) and the New Law (the little clergeoun). Inasmuch as the Jews in the tale are primarily theological symbols, we should ignore the *litera* for the *sensus* and do not need to feel sorry for them.[8]

However, I do not think that anything can be solved by attempting to account for the treatment of the Jews in terms of historical attitudes, favorable to them or unfavorable, realistic or exegetical. The fact is that the "cursed Jews" represent a psychological rather than a historical reality. They are symbols of pure evil, and they belong to the large class of fairy-tale villains, which includes all kinds of monsters and ogres as well as witches, devils, and wicked stepmothers and stepsisters. The Prioress's Tale is basically a fairy story that has been turned into hagiography, and this fact needs to be taken into consideration in any interpretation. The folkloristic origins of the plot are obvious enough. It is the story of the child who is murdered and brought back to life through some sort of magic. The happy ending required by fairy-tale structure is preserved in some of the analogues where the murdered boy is revived and remains alive. In short, the tale is a fairy story in religious guise, a wonderful story of its kind, but perhaps not the place to look for high seriousness or profound religious feeling. This doesn't mean that I think Chaucer is satirizing childish legends. On the contrary, Chaucer's version is perhaps the supreme example of its genre, brilliantly fulfilling all the requirements of the form, as superior to the rest as the Miller's Tale is to all other fabliaux.[9] If anything, the tale illustrates the power of such legends and the spell they can cast not merely over children but over grownups. Chaucer, I believe, is fully aware of the kind of material he is dealing with and retells the story in such a way as to emphasize its fairy-tale structure. At the same time, however, I think he is also very much aware that fairy-tale justice and Christian mercy are incompatible and that the story moves us for reasons that have nothing to do with religion. The piety is sincere but naive; the tenderness verges on sentimentality; and the morality of the tale is not religious but is a disguised form of the poetic justice of fairy tales.

The tale is certainly appropriate for the Prioress not so much because it brings out her elegance and refinement but because it brings out the childlike qualities that are evident in her portrait and in her Prologue. The basic irony in her portrait is that this rather large woman with her exquisite manners is emotionally still a child. She has grown up in the convent, and she clearly has no conception of the world outside its walls except for the general idea that it is an extremely wicked place. Her deepest affections are for her pets, and she is reduced to tears at the sight of a mouse in a trap.

We are reminded of these characteristics in her Prologue. The Host's extravagant politeness recalls her concern with form and etiquette, but at the same time it has the slightly mock-ceremonial air one might use in asking a special favor of a little girl. The theme of the Prologue is also the theme that the Prioress herself sees in her tale: the praise of God is expressed through the mouths of innocents. And with more truth than she knows the Prioress compares herself to one of these innocents. She invokes the assistance of the mother of God because her human ability is too weak to bear the burden of her praise. In addressing the Virgin she uses some of the standard exegetical symbols for her—the lily and the burning bush through which God spoke to Moses. The reference to Moses, as R. J. Schoeck has pointed out,[10] is perhaps not without significance because the Prioress clearly makes no connection between Moses and his people and the villains of her story. The Prologue shows that the Prioress is able to praise Mary very beautifully, just as she does everything very beautifully. Nevertheless, one may question the depth of her understanding of the symbolism she is using. For her the "white lily flower" and the burning bush are beautiful in themselves. They represent to her the virginity to which she has consecrated her life. But does she grasp what is meant by the fact that through the Holy Spirit, Mary conceived, as the Prioress says, the Father's "Sapience", that is, the incarnation of the logos? For her, virginity is a negative virtue, the innocence of children like those infant martyrs who now walk before the Lamb, "That nevere, fleshly, wommen they ne knewe" (585). The concluding stanza of her Prologue makes these suggestions explicit. Her intelligence, she says, is like that of a twelve-month-old child:

> But as a child of twelf monthe oold, or lesse,
> That kan unnethes any word expresse,
> Right so fare I.   (484–486)

The tale is appropriately a children's story told with a childlike fantasy.

Underlying the figures of the little boy and his widowed mother are those of the Christ child and the *mater dolorosa*. The Prioress characteristically conceives of Christ as the infant Jesus as though he had been one of the innocent victims of Herod's massacre (to which there are several allusions) rather than crucified of his own volition for the sins of mankind. In the tale there is no human or divine father figure, only the widow and the Virgin, the great mother figure of the Middle Ages.

The way in which the Prioress's love for little things emerges has often been pointed out in the repetition of the word "little" in her description of the little clergeoun, his little school, his little book, etc. There are other little ways in which the pathos is heightened. The boy asks his older schoolmate on *bare knees* to teach him the words of the song. He vows to memorize the song even though he should be beaten *thrice in an hour* for neglecting his lessons. The Prioress sees life as full of innocent suffering—the mouse in the trap, her lapdogs beaten with a stick. Even before the little clergeoun is murdered, the tale is full of suggestions that innocence is born to suffer in a cruel, uncomprehending world. It is significant that neither the little clergeoun nor his friend understand the Latin of the *Alma Redemptoris Mater;* all they know is that it is a song in praise of the Virgin. One could say that the tale also is a song in praise of the Virgin based more on sentiment than on a profound grasp of the Virgin's theological role as the Kind Mother of the Redeemer.

The hatred for the Jews and the violence of the murder are in sharp contrast to the school scene but are cut from the same cloth. Both aspects of the story are equally naive and complement one another. Like any good fairy tale, this one succeeds through contrasts between symbols of absolute good and evil. The characters are all black and white stereotypes. The bloodiness is the same as that which many parents and child psychologists condemn in traditional fairy tales. Violence in fairy tales is not real but symbolic, and it is an integral part of the story. There is no moral attached. The story makes its point through images: evil will be destroyed or will destroy itself. The same kind of violence occurs in the legends of the saints with the difference that here it is the innocent who suffer, and it is the strength of their faith that is symbolized by the most imaginative torments. The saints are decapitated, racked, roasted, and flayed alive not so much for good religious as for good aesthetic reasons. In the Prioress's Tale the little boy's throat is cut "to the nekkebon," a gruesome detail that creates not only the desired shudder but makes his singing all the more miraculous. Stories like this are calculated to appeal to the sisters at St. Leonard's. They provide a great deal of *solaas* in the guise of *sentence* so that one has the satisfaction of seeming to be edified when, in fact, one is being entertained.

I don't think it is generally appreciated that Chaucer has probably *heightened* the hatred and violence. In many of the analogues the Jews are converted by the miracle.[11] In others they are punished and called names, but nowhere is the punishment so cruel nor the language so imaginatively abusive as it is in the Prioress's Tale. I do not believe that this indicates any special bigotry on the part of Chaucer or of the Prioress. She has certainly never seen a Jew, and Chaucer could not have known many since the English had long before come up with their final solution. Edward I expelled them from England in 1290.

The heightening does have the effect of increasing the irony that runs throughout the tale: the fact that its poetic justice is at odds with Christian mercy. For that reason a flagrantly *anti-Semitic* miracle of the Virgin is ideal because it lends itself to dramatizing the irony. And that is what I think Chaucer has done, quite consciously, partly by subtle exaggeration—one "little" or one "cursed" too many—but also by the manipulation of Old Testament allusions like that to the burning bush in the Prologue.

I doubt that Chaucer held any special sympathy for the Jews or that he regarded the legends about them as wicked or slanderous. The stories would have interested him as fiction, and he would have recognized that neither the heroes nor the villains in them corresponded to anything real. But Chaucer would have known the Jews not only as legendary monsters but also as the children of the promise. And the contrast between these conceptions of them would have aroused his sense of irony.

The tale is designed, therefore, to remind the more sophisticated reader of both aspects. The pathos of the funeral is heightened by the image of the sorrowing mother:

> His mooder swownynge by his beere lay;
> Unnethe myghte the peple that was theere
> This newe Rachel brynge fro his beere.   (625–627)

The allusion to Rachel refers primarily to Matthew ii:18 on the slaughter of the innocents: "In Rama was there a voice heard, lamentation, and weeping, and great mourning, Rachel weeping for her children." But the gospelist is quoting Jeremiah xxxi:15 because he sees here the fulfillment of a prophecy. The new Rachel is inseparable from the old. She is the archetype of the sorrowing Jewish mother, and Schoeck is surely right that it is deliberate irony to introduce this allusion immediately before the cursed people of Herod are given their deserts:[12]

> With torment and with shameful deeth echon
> This provost dooth thise Jewes for to sterve
> That of this mordre wiste, and that anon.
> He nolde no swich cursednesse observe.
> "Yvele shal have that yvele wol deserve";
> Therfore with wilde hors he dide hem drawe,
> And after that he heng hem by the lawe.   (628–634)

The inhuman murder merits an inhuman death. The justification of the punishment—"Yvele shal have that yvele wol deserve"—is a concise statement of the Old Law: an eye for an eye and a tooth for a tooth. It is also, as I have said, the law of fairy tales. It is this kind of justice that the New Law was supposed to abrogate: "It has been said thou shalt love thy neighbor and hate thy enemies; but I say unto you love your enemies, bless them that curse you, do good to them that hate you, and pray for them that despitefully use you and persecute you." The law of charity is, of course, particularly associated with the Virgin; her kindness is the theme of the *Alma* and of the tale. Since Chaucer has made a point of saying that the Jews were punished "by the lawe," the reader has the right to ask "which law?"

But the Prioress herself should be judged by the New Law, and in this respect I feel that some of her recent critics are less than perfect. I don't think the tale calls into question the genuineness and sincerity of the Prioress's Christian faith any more than the portrait in the General Prologue does. It does, however, reveal the same superficiality that one observes in the portrait, a concern with outward appearance and shallow emotion. Like the portrait, the tale evokes a sense of pity, not only for the little clergeoun and his mother but for its narrator. This is particularly true of the final stanza of the tale, a prayer to the boy martyr Hugh of Lincoln to intercede for us. The key words "cursed" and "mercy" alternate, an epitome of the technique Chaucer has employed throughout the tale:

> O yonge Hugh of Lyncoln, slayn also
> With cursed Jewes, as it is notable,
> For it is but a litel while ago,
> Preye eek for us, we synful folk unstable,
> That, of his mercy, God so merciable
> On us his grete mercy multiplie,
> For reverence of his mooder Marie.   (684–690)

As in her Prologue, so in this short prayer she speaks more truth about herself than she knows. She is revealed in all her humanity as one of the "synful folk unstable," like most of us more susceptible to the emotional appeal of fiction than to the plain doctrine of sermons. Her tale has been justly compared to the brooch that hangs from her rosary and presents the same ambiguity. It is far more worldly than anything we ought to expect from a deeply religious woman, but it also has a childlike innocence and succeeds in offering up its tribute of praise. *Amor vincit omnia.*

CHAPTER XV

Cracks in the Frame
of Illusion

*t*HE CONCLUSION of the Prioress's Tale brings about one of
the most solemn moments of the Canterbury pilgrimage:

> Whan seyd was al this miracle, every man
> As sobre was that wonder was to see.   (691–692)

Whatever doubts one may have about the morality of the Prioress's
Tale, there is no denying its emotional impact on the pilgrims.
The poet himself, as though still under the spell of the rhyme
royal, carries it through the three stanzas that comprise the headlink to the Tale of Sir Thopas, the only link not written in couplets.
However, except for the first two lines, these stanzas are not in
the serious mood that normally attends the use of rhyme royal in
the moral and religious tales—the Man of Law's, the Clerk's, the
Prioress's, and the Second Nun's. After the moment of silence,
the charged atmosphere starts to clear: "Til that oure Hooste japen
tho bigan." Harry Bailly's japing in rhyme royal may be the first
instance of a dissociation of sensibility to which Chaucer is about
to subject the reader.

The Host, after the Miller's Prologue, has been trying all along
to alternate sad tales and merry ones, *sentence* and *solaas*. Now he
looks about for some pilgrim likely to provide a bit of fun, much

as he picked out the Pardoner to provide an antidote to the Physician's Tale:

And thanne at erst he looked upon me,
And seyde thus: "What man artow?" quod he;
"Thou lookest as thou woldest fynde an hare,
For evere upon the ground I se thee stare.

"Approche neer, and looke up murily.
Now war yow, sires, and lat this man have place!
He in the waast is shape as wel as I;
This were a popet in an arm t'enbrace
For any womman, smal and fair of face.
He semeth elvyssh by his contenaunce,
For unto no wight dooth he daliaunce.   (694–704)

Harry Bailly's jokes remind us of the familiar persona of Chaucer, whom we have not heard from since he apologized to us for the painful duty of having to repeat the Miller's Tale. He seems withdrawn and alone, very much like the dreamer in the *House of Fame* or *Parliament of Fowls* who is a spectator in the colorful world of his dream. He is round in the waist, a pudgy doll for a pretty girl to fold in her arms—the best portrait we have of the poet's "unliklynesse." Patronizingly the Host commands this figure to "Telle us a tale of myrthe, and that anon." But this "elvyssh" man makes excuses—he knows just one story, "a rym I lerned longe agoon."

The rhyme is the Tale of Sir Thopas, which Chaucer never gets to finish because after thirty-one and a half stanzas, the Host cannot endure it any longer:

"Namoore of this, for Goddes dignitee,"
Quod oure Hooste, "for thou makest me
So wery of thy verray lewednesse
That, also wisly God my soule blesse,
Myne eres aken of thy drasty speche.   (919–923)

When Chaucer innocently inquires why he may not finish his story like the others, the Host bluntly tells him why: "Thy drasty rymyng is nat worth a toord!"—and asks him to try again. Chaucer obliges, this time with a long moral allegory in prose, the Tale of Melibee.

Sir Thopas is, of course, one of the most delightful and perfect parodies in English literature. In the space of the thirty-one and a half stanzas, Chaucer manages to take off just about every hackneyed convention of the popular romances, medieval horse operas in which the invincible hero battles giants and other monsters in one episode after another. It is one of Chaucer's best jokes, but in the dramatic context of the *Canterbury Tales,* an important question arises: how are we to take the joke, and at whose expense is it? Naturally we laugh at Sir Thopas. However, is the narrator offering it seriously or is he merely playing dumb when he says that this is the only story he knows? Is Chaucer representing himself on the journey incognito and having some fun with the Host and his fellow-pilgrims? Or are we to take him as the quasi-fictional character whom E. T. Donaldson called "Chaucer the Pilgrim" as distinct from "Chaucer the Poet?" If so, then the teller of Sir Thopas is the ultimate fulfillment of that figure. Our faithful reporter really *is* presented as obtuse and unimaginative, and the Tale of Sir Thopas *is* wretched doggerel, the best he knows. In that case, the joke is part of a game between the poet and his audience in which we accept this Chaucer as the one pilgrim whose tale is so insipid and bungling as to be a total failure, just as we pretend that *Troilus* is a translation of Lollius's history or that drunken Robin is the narrator of the Miller's Tale.

All these questions can be reduced to a single question, succinctly phrased by the Host, "What man artow?" It is, indeed, a question for the reader to ask himself, and one that I have been avoiding up to this point. What really is the man who has told us the dream visions, the story of Troilus, and now the tales of the Canterbury pilgrims, and what are we to make of him?

A great deal has been written during the last twenty years about the Chaucerian narrator as a "persona." Nineteenth-century scholars, who took some of the poet's statements about himself literally, sometimes spoke of him as "naive," a notion that Kittredge ridiculed in a famous dictum: "a naif Collector of Customs would be a paradoxical monster."[1] Yet, if the narrator is not truly naive, many of his observations certainly sound that way. In the

Book of the Duchess, Kittredge explained this phenomenon by postulating that the Dreamer in that poem was a "childlike" character not to be mistaken for the poet; however, Kittredge did not extend his theory of a fictitious narrator to Chaucer's later works.

In 1954 E. T. Donaldson's "Chaucer the Pilgrim" introduced the idea of a narrative "persona," long familiar to students of modern fiction, to Chaucer criticism.[2] The idea that the narrator in the *Canterbury Tales* and the earlier poems is a "persona" has won widespread acceptance although it has occasionally been misunderstood even by those who favor it.[3] "Persona" in this instance does not mean an imaginary storyteller like Gulliver or Marlowe. Every author of fiction and every performer (in the latter category we may include most professors of literature) adopts a "persona," and there is a tacit understanding between him and his audience that this public image is related to but not really identical with his private self.

A point that has not been sufficiently stressed is that such a "persona" does not impose the restrictions of dramatic consistency that we would expect from a character in a novel or a play. The author or lecturer who is impersonating himself may at any moment step out of his dramatic part to wink at his audience or to address it seriously. Samuel Clemens as Mark Twain in public readings from his works was a master of the technique. In Chaucer's case, it is not really necessary to conceive of a unified "character" capable of missing the failings of the Prioress but not those of the Summoner, and responding wholeheartedly to the Parson's virtue. If we look closely at some of the lines in the General Prologue, they are certainly not spoken by a naive observer; many are not spoken by an "observer" at all, but by an omniscient narrator. However, except for the beginning and end of the Prologue, we are looking at the pilgrims, not at the narrator, and the overall tone is remarkably uniform. No one is likely to notice slight inconsistencies in point of view until some literary critic calls these to his attention.

In my opening chapter I argued that Chaucer's "persona" resulted from the exigencies of his role as a court poet. Once established, Chaucer used the character of a bemused dreamer and humble clerk of Love with increasing skill as a device for creating irony. Yet, the "narrator" could also be something of an embar-rassment. The fluctuation of tone at the end of *Troilus* may be the best way of expressing the mixed feelings that great work arouses in us, but it also creates a good deal of confusion about the meaning of the poem. Can the naive persona ever make a plain, unambiguous statement? In the *Legend of Good Women* we have the sophisti-cated comedy of Chaucer's persona being held to account for his mistakes by the God of Love and being pardoned by Alceste on grounds of his naiveté. In the General Prologue the narrator's enthusiasm for the pilgrims, his failure or unwillingness to find fault with them, surrounds nearly all of them with an ironic am-biguity. The persona thus becomes the poet's device for avoiding commitments and judgments. There are times when the persona's refusal to take the blame becomes farcical as, for example, when he tells the ladies of the audience in *Troilus* that the real moral of the poem is "Beth war of men." The apologies to the audience at the end of the General Prologue and in the Miller's Prologue, too, read not so much like serious statements the narrator might make as they do like caricatures of such statements.

> Crist spak hymself ful brode in hooly writ,
> And wel ye woot no vileynye is it.   (739–740)

> Blameth nat me if that ye chese amys.   (3181)

At such times, one has the uneasy sense that the poet is not really apologizing to us but is mocking us. After the Miller's Prologue, Chaucer abandoned the voice of the first person narrator. In a sense, the poet retreated even further from our view behind the personae of the various pilgrims.[4] Why does he bring him on stage again now?

It is tempting to see the reemergence of the narrator in the prologue to Sir Thopas as a revival of the old device, and it might be possible to do so, were it not for the Tale of Melibee. Are we to suppose that the Melibee is told by Chaucer the Pilgrim or by Chaucer the Poet, and, either way, does it make any dramatic sense that it should be told by the teller of Sir Thopas? One can hardly imagine two stories more unlike. About the only thing they have in common is that the plot interest is negligible in both. One is almost pure *solaas;* the other pure *sentence.* If we are confronted here by a persona it would seem to be one with a split personality.

The sort of confusion generated by this unlikely combination of tales may be illustrated by the theory of one scholar who argues that Chaucer tells the Melibee in order to punish Harry Bailly for interrupting Sir Thopas. If the Melibee was intended to punish anybody, it must have been Chaucer himself who had to go through the labor of translating it in order to pay himself back for having insulted himself in the frame story. That way madness lies.

Sir Thopas is short enough to be acceptable as a literary joke, but the length of the Melibee defies any theory that it was told for some dramatic purpose. Without doubt it was taken seriously on its own merits by Chaucer and his audience as a moral and didactic story if not primarily as a lively thing of "aventures." It was translated from Latin into French, presumably because the French translator thought it worth the trouble, and Chaucer turned it from French into English for the same reason. Moreover, comparison with its source shows that Chaucer did take some pains to give the Melibee such literary interest as it has.[5]

To look for dramatic consistency here is, I think, to search in vain. If Chaucer had wished to preserve the illusion of a group of pilgrims telling stories, he should have kept discreetly out of sight, as he has since the Miller's Prologue. By now we are so used to the situation that we readily accept each pilgrim as narrator of his own tale. By bringing himself back on stage, whether as Poet or Pilgrim, and thus provoking the question—"What man artow?"—Chaucer breaks the dramatic illusion, much as Shakespeare, through his references to the stage in his plays, reminds the audience that they are in the theater watching actors. At one of the most dramatic moments in the *Canterbury Tales,* as the pilgrims are still misty-eyed after the Prioress's Tale, Chaucer suddenly reminds us that this is a work of fiction. Through the irony that *he* of all the company must choose between a doggerel romance and a prose allegory, Chaucer calls attention to the fact that he is the author of everything—the pilgrims and their tales are all an illusion of which he is the prime mover. In the last analysis, the joke in the Tale of Sir Thopas and the Tale of Melibee is upon the credulity of the audience.

There is a pattern to be observed in this fragment and the two that follow if we read them in the order of the Ellesmere manuscript, which is the order adopted in Robinson's edition. The links are becoming longer and more dramatic. There is more dialogue and action. Chaucer and the Monk have their tales interrupted. Two new characters overtake the pilgrims and are invited to join the company. The Cook gets drunk and falls off his horse. More than ever in these episodes, the group of pilgrims is made to seem actual and alive. Counteracting this impression, however, is the length, artificiality, or stylization of most of the tales. Of course, Chaucer has been playing off the "literary" character of the tales against the realism of the frame all along. The "romances" of the Wife and the Franklin are thus seen as sublimations in which the real-life problems of these pilgrims are magically wished away. The Pardoner's fascination with his own state of sin gets projected into his dreamlike tale of Death; the Prioress's childlike sensibility expresses itself in her legend of child murder. These tales are "dramatic" in Kittredge's sense and help to preserve the illusion of an actual storytelling contest on the road to Canterbury. As we approach the end, the tales seem rather to break that illusion.[6] That is the effect of the Tale of Melibee following hard upon the Tale of Sir Thopas. Whatever literary qualities the Melibee may have if we read through all of its twenty pages of prose, the effect of sustaining our sense of the journey is not among them. The reader may be slightly incredulous as well as amused to discover, when it is over, that, in contrast to his reaction to Sir Thopas, the Host has lent an appreciative ear to this long moral allegory and even applies its lesson directly to his own domestic life. There is an element of the absurd in the Host's contrast between Dame Prudence and "Goodelief, my wyf" because they inhabit such seemingly different planes of reality. It is as though Chaucer had begun playing with our sense of illusion by shuttling us rapidly back and forth between different and divided imaginary worlds.[7]

That is exactly what happens in the Monk's Prologue and Tale and the Nun's Priest's Prologue, which could be more appropriately called an Epilogue to the Monk's Tale. The Host's invitation to the Monk to tell a tale is the most successful of his many attempted displays of wit on the pilgrimage. By complimenting the Monk on his "ful fair skyn" and his virility, Harry Bailly draws again, in dialogue form, the Monk's portrait in the General Prologue. "The world is lorn," laments the Host, mocking that popular medieval topos, not, however, because of man's sinful state but because the Church has recruited all the best men like the Monk and sworn them to celibacy. With broad humor the Host makes explicit the hints in the General Prologue that the lordly "prikasour" is a servant of Venus as well as of Diana, and "this worthy Monk" complacently listens to the Host's pleasantries. For the moment we are back on the road to Canterbury, only to be disoriented once more when this Friar Tuck of a cleric begins a series of tragedies, the common theme of which is contempt for the world and its transient goods.

There is some dramatic irony that this specimen of late medieval pessimism should issue from this monk who basks in the good life, but there is little in the way of dramatic illusion. Had Chaucer wished to characterize the Monk in his tale, he could easily have done so by elaborating one of the tragedies rhetorically as he did with the Prioress's miracle of the little clergeoun. But seventeen tragedies in a row is no more consistent with a dramatic purpose than is the long tale of Melibee.

Those critics are probably correct who think the Monk's Tale goes back to an earlier period (Robinson: "about 1374"), the time of Chaucer's first encounter with works of Dante and Boccaccio (the principal source of the tale is Boccaccio's *De Casibus Virorum Illustrorum*—the Fall of Great Men). The Knight's interruption of the Monk (2767–79) has been rightly interpreted as Chaucer's verdict upon the Monk's inadequate conception of tragedy.[8] That conception, however, might well have been taken quite seriously by a younger Chaucer. In that case, the poet, at the height of his dramatic powers, is exploiting the frame story of the *Canterbury Tales* to pass an amused judgment on an older and excessively monkish work. The Knight's "namoore of this"—the same phrase with which the Host puts a stop to Chaucer the Pilgrim's Tale of Sir Thopas—is then the poet's own sentiment. Chaucer has begun talking to himself within the infinitely malleable frame of his fiction. Within that frame characters like the Monk, the Host, the

Knight, and Chaucer the Pilgrim can be summoned and dismissed at the artist's will.

In writing of the General Prologue, I said that Chaucer had created a world that becomes autonomous. The pilgrims take over and acquire what seems more and more like an independent existence. In this block of tales, however, and in the two fragments that follow it in the Ellesmere order, which I believe to be Chaucer's final order, the poet begins to reassert his "authority," not in his own person, but by manipulating his fiction.

The apex of this art comes in the Nun's Priest's Tale. The continual shifts in point of view throughout that tale have the same effect as the interplay between juxtaposed tales and between tales and links that I have been discussing. Chaucer is constantly building up an illusion only to have it dissolve again, usually in laughter.

The narrator of the tale, the Nun's Priest, is himself something of a phantom. When the Host turns to him after the Monk refuses to tell a different story, we are surprised because we have not been introduced to him before. There is no portrait of him in the General Prologue where the only hint of his existence is a single line that the Prioress is attended by "prestes three." Critics have of course tried to repair Chaucer's omission by constructing a portrait from such circumstantial evidence as the tale and links provide. He generally emerges as a hen-pecked male in Madame Eglentyne's fashionable convent. Such efforts are not entirely without basis in the text, which seems to contain a veiled hit or two at the Prioress, especially the well-known antifeminist passage that concludes with the ingenuous disclaimer:

> Thise been the cokkes wordes, and nat myne;
> I kan noon harm of no womman divyne.   (3265–66)

However, all such attempts to give the Nun's Priest's Tale a firm dramatic setting, as also the attempts to show that it initiates the "Marriage Group," seriously limit a tale that in many ways transcends the narrow frame provided by Priest and Prioress or even by the larger frame of the journey to Canterbury.

If we must have a portrait of the "Nun's Priest," then I would propose that of the poet-preacher in the *Troilus* frontispiece with which this study began. Though the poet portrayed there is nominally Chaucer, he really represents an ideal of what a poet should be. As I have been arguing all along, for a poet like Chaucer to emulate that ideal was no easy task, and he became increasingly conscious of the difficulties involved. The Nun's Priest's Tale seems to me a late, wise, and affectionate reassessment of the poet's task. I have maintained that the various pilgrims are all in one way or another personae of Chaucer the artist. None is closer to the manner at least of the narrator in Chaucer's earlier poetry than the Priest. One may even draw an analogy between the position of the Priest, whose background is obviously humble, as spiritual guide to the ladylike nuns at St. Leonard's and the position of Chaucer as a poet writing for the ladies of the English court. Chaucer, too, has his tongue-in-cheek apologies to the women in his audience:

> Bysechyng every lady bright of hewe,
> And every gentil womman, what she be,
> That al be that Criseyde was untrewe,
> That for that gilt she be nat wroth with me.
>
> (V.1772–75)

In the guise of the Priest, therefore, Chaucer is, I believe, surveying the works of all "makers," especially of course his own. In following the Monk's Tale, the Priest's naturally comments most immediately on the Monk's tragic view of life. Chauntecleer's fall from Fortune's wheel is followed by his rise—he flies into a tree. But the Nun's Priest's Tale also comments on practically everything that has gone before in the Canterbury Tales, in Chaucer's earlier works, and in medieval literature, philosophy, science, and what have you. It is an omnium gatherum of lore and learning that holds up to scrutiny the various means by which man seeks to understand his world.[9]

The tale begins with a description of the austere life of a poor widow and her household. It is a picture in "whit and blak," like the milk and brown bread that deck her table. But appearances can be deceptive. Within the boundaries of this simple household there exists another world. To some eyes it might appear as a farmyard closed in by a ditch and a stick fence, but it depends on one's point of view. The description of the widow's domain sets up a dramatic shift in perspective as we take the point of view of the chickens.

The humor and wisdom of this tale depend on its double perspective. The chicken world of Chauntecleer and Pertelote is at the same time an image of what we like to think of as the "great world." Like the world of the Canterbury pilgrims it is a microcosm and includes elements of the court, the university, the church, and bourgeois domesticity. To describe the Nun's Priest's Tale as a mock-epic is inadequate, for not only epic but many other forms of writing in the Middle Ages are brought to bear on the relationships of Chauntecleer, Pertelote, and the fox. The Nun's Priest's Tale is in some respects the most learned of all the Canterbury tales because it is a satire on human learning.

The tale is cast in the form of a beast fable, one of the simplest types of literature, often used in Chaucer's day, as occasionally still in our own, to teach children their letters. The simple fable, however, has been puffed up with learned digressions and allusions so that it becomes, among other things, a satire on the medieval art of composition as it is taught in the rhetoric books, and particularly on the use of "auctorite" to add weight and significance to a story.[10]

Amid all this wealth of learning, it is essential to keep one's perspective. Our initial view of Chauntecleer is one of dazzling color:

> His coomb was redder than the fyn coral
> And batailled as it were a castel wal;
> His byle was blak, and as the jeet it shoon;
> Lyk asure were his legges and his toon;
> His nayles whitter than the lylye flour,
> And lyk the burned gold was his colour.   (2859–64)

It is a picture to remind us of castles and noble knights dressed in resplendent coats of arms, and it may momentarily cause us to lose sight of the barnyard. Not, however, if we look at that description with the eye of experience. Years ago a paper entitled "Chauntecleer and Partlet Identified" was announced at the annual meeting of the Modern Language Association. Scholars flocked to find out whether the pair might be Richard and Anne, John of Gaunt and Katherine Swynford, or some other noble couple. It turned out that

Chauntecleer and Pertelote are Golden Spangled Hamburgs.[11] The shock of recognition in this case underlines the fact that in the Nun's Priest's Tale the educated are more likely to forget about Chaucer's simple realism than about his romance or intellectual elements.

Roosters are used as game cocks, and Chaucer plays upon this correspondence between Chauntecleer and the epic hero as well as on the fact that a rooster is a breeding fowl, celebrated for its potency. Accordingly, Chauntecleer is not only a mighty warrior but a great lover:

> Real he was, he was namoore aferd.
> He fethered Pertelote twenty tyme,
> And trad hire eke as ofte, er it was pryme.
> He looketh as it were a grym leoun,
> And on his toos he rometh up and doun;
> Hym deigned nat to sette his foot to grounde.
>
> (3176–81)

If one looks a rooster in the eye, he does in fact resemble a "grym leoun," and his gait definitely has a martial swagger. Pertelote combines the character of a courtly lady with that of a hen:

> Curteys she was, discreet, and debonaire,
> And compaignable, and bar hyrself so faire,
> Syn thilke day that she was seven nyght oold . . .
>
> (2871–73)

Most important, however, Chauntecleer and Pertelote also have intellectual pretensions. The argument of the tale turns on their different interpretations of Chauntecleer's dream. He is convinced that the dream is prophetic. Like Hector and Aeneas, like Arcite, like Croesus, Chauntecleer thinks he has been allowed a glimpse of his destiny by some higher power. Pertelote explains the dream matter-of-factly as a case of indigestion. Chauntecleer's dream has been brought on by a dangerous imbalance of humors, an excess of bile that causes him to dream of red and yellow things. In their different interpretations of the dream we see a fundamental difference between men and women. He is the romantic and the fatalist; he sees his personal experience, as Troilus does, linked to the hidden forces that rule our destiny. She tells him to take a laxative and to keep out of the sun. In spite of her pique at his admission of fear, she is genuinely worried about his health and prescribes home remedies:

> A day or two ye shul have digestyves
> Of wormes, er ye take youre laxatyves
> Of lawriol, centaure, and fumetere,
> Or elles of ellebor, that groweth there,
> Of katapuce, or of gaitrys beryis,
> Of herbe yve, growyng in oure yeerd, ther mery is;
> Pekke hem up right as they growe and ete hem yn.
> Be myrie, housbonde, for youre fader kyn!   (2961–68)

Here we have medieval medicine's solution for Chauntecleer's difficulties.[12]

Chauntecleer replies patronizingly to Pertelote's empirical wisdom and her lone authority, Cato, who said "Ne do no fors of dremes." He then proceeds to overwhelm her with his own authorities. It is a typical, albeit one-sided, medieval debate. The fox, too, makes use of "auctorite." He tells the cock that he has more natural feeling for music than Boethius, showing familiarity with that author's *De Musica*. He tells Chauntecleer an anecdote about a clever cock from the *Speculum Stultorum*, a twelfth-century satire, that has a good deal in common with the Nun's Priest's Tale.

But the greatest user of authority in this tale, perhaps in any of Chaucer's tales, is the narrator. He spies a lesson the way Chauntecleer spies a corn in the yard, and he hastens to pick it out for us. He attributes Chauntecleer's fate to a variety of causes. The cock has been blinded by his passion for Pertelote, and this observation leads to the antifeminist position that woman is to blame for all of man's troubles:

> Wommennes conseils been ful ofte colde;
> Wommannes conseil broghte us first to wo,
> And made Adam fro Paradys to go
> Ther as he was ful myrie and wel at ese.   (3256–59)

At least so say the "auctours, where they trete of swich mateere." Elsewhere the narrator blames Chauntecleer's misfortune on the flattery of the fox, and this prompts a warning to lords who are advised: "Redeth Ecclesiaste of flaterye" (3329). Or maybe Chauntecleer's encounter with the fox ought to be attributed to fate. This suggestion leads to a famous digression on predestination with reference to another string of authorities:

> But what that God forwoot moot nedes bee,
> After the opinioun of certein clerkis.
> Witnesse on hym that any parfit clerk is,
> That in scole is greet altercacioun
> In this mateere, and greet disputisoun,
> And hath been of an hundred thousand men.
> But I ne kan nat bulte it to the bren,
> As kan the hooly doctour Augustyn,
> Or Boece, or the Bisshop Bradwardyn, . . .   (3234–42)

The passage should remind us of Troilus's Boethian discourse on free will and predestination. Troilus can not "bulte it to the bren" either, and neither, I think, can Chaucer. But here there is none of Troilus's tortured reasoning. The question is humorously begged.

By means of all this learning and allusion, Chauntecleer's fate is finally linked to the great catastrophes of ancient times. It is at this point, as the cackling of the hens is compared to the lamentations of the Trojan and Roman women, that the widow and her daughters reappear with an effect like that of the carpenter in the Miller's Tale crashing down from the rafters to meet the deluge The chase after the fox, involving the entire village, is built up with all the sound and fury of an epic pursuit in which the participants, however, are

> Colle oure dogge, and Talbot, and Gerland,
> And Malkyn, with a dystaf in hir hand.   (3383–84)

The scene culminates on an apocalyptic image of chaos: "It semed as that hevene sholde falle" (3401). And then the noise and confusion are made to vanish as suddenly as they were conjured up. The narrator once again interposes a sententious comment: "Now, goode men, I prey yow herkneth alle." We return to the simple Aesopian fable with the cock and fox each drawing the lesson of the tale.

The Priest concludes with an admonition to the reader:

> But ye that holden this tale a folye,
> As of a fox, or of a cok and hen,
> Taketh the moralite, goode men.
> For seint Paul seith that al that writen is,
> To oure doctrine it is ywrite, ywis;
> Taketh the fruyt, and lat the chaf be stille.   (3438–43)

This passage has been given great weight in some recent Chaucer criticism. It has been treated as a concise statement of Chaucer's aesthetic, an open invitation to read not only the Nun's Priest's Tale but all of Chaucer's works as allegories in which we must search for the fruit of *sentence* beneath the chaff of fiction.[13] The Nun's Priest's Tale has been interpreted, not surprisingly in view of its references to Genesis and the enclosed yard in which Chauntecleer and Pertelote live, as an allegory of the fall of man.[14]

That interpretation may perhaps serve as an example of the way in which the Nun's Priest's Tale deliberately lays snares for exegetes of all kinds, political or patristic. Every critic who takes up the Priest's invitation to find the "moralite" seems to lose his perspective and his sense of humor and begins to sound as learned and as pompous as Chauntecleer himself.[15]

There is another way of looking at the "moralite" of the tale. The main target of the satire seems to me to be precisely the tendency to look for a moral everywhere, to peck up the kernels of *sentence* "and ete hem yn." This is the weakness of medieval scholasticism and, for that matter, of the scholasticism of any age including our own. Such moralism is a product of man's presumptuous belief that he can explain his condition within his earthly limitations. If the tale is a satire on pride, then it is surely on pride in our human intelligence. This is especially the vanity of authors, and to an even greater degree, the vanity of literary critics.

To a higher intelligence, our world and our efforts to understand it may seem as comic as the debate of Chauntecleer and Pertelote about his dream seems to us. What Chaucer's comedy in the Nun's Priest's Tale enables us to do, if we will only let it, is to detach ourselves from our barnyard. The tale gives us the distance to see epic, tragedy, and philosophy as the products of man's egotism, his vanity of thinking that the universe is centered around him.

But the humor of the tale treats our vanities and pretensions with charity. The barnyard retains, in spite of its fallen state, many of the qualities of the first garden in which Adam "was ful myrie and wel at ese." Life there is a comedy and not a tragedy as it is in the Monk's Tale, although danger may be lurking in the cabbage patch. Chauntecleer and his hens enjoy their little earthly paradise: they bask in the sun, make love, and, above all, they crow and sing. That is to say that they fulfill their animal as well as their rational nature. Paradoxically, Chauntecleer and Pertelote are among the most human of Chaucer's characters, embodying something of many of their predecessors They remind one of course of the birds in the *Parliament of Fowls,* but also of Troilus and Criseyde, and of the worthy Knight and the worthy Wife of Bath. The affection we feel for them is the pleasure that Chaucer takes in all of his creatures, and it is this sense of pleasure in the world and in life that makes the comic view of the Nun's Priest's Tale transcend the tragedies of the Monk and even the tragedy of Troilus. In the Nun's Priest's Tale Chaucer seems to survey his work, and, like the Preacher, he sees that all is vanity. But there is no bitterness in that recognition, for in the end all the arts including the art of fiction are part of an entertaining spectacle that commands our attention only for a time.

After Chauntecleer's impressive catalogue of famous dreamers and interpreters of dreams, a list that spans classical and biblical history, he turns back to the present point in time:

> Now let us speke of myrthe, and stynte al this.
> Madame Pertelote, so have I blis,
> Of o thyng God hath sent me large grace;
> For whan I se the beautee of youre face,
> Ye been so scarlet reed aboute youre yen, . . .
>
> (3157–61)

The last line, unobtrusively slipped in, returns us to the barnyard and reminds us that the talking animals exist only in the fable. Yet the "scarlet reed" around Pertelote's eyes affects us, as it does Chauntecleer, as something more immediate and more real than the rooster's old examples. It helps us and Chauntecleer to forget about Hector and Andromache and all the remembered wisdom of the past that he has so learnedly recited only to ignore it for the beauty of the present moment. For that wisdom and those stories and examples prove as ephemeral and as insubstantial as dreams, and like dreams, they exist only in the mind. Ultimately they, too, will be forgotten, and in the meantime, although they cannot do us much good, neither can they cause us any real harm. An argument about the interpretation of dreams—or the interpretation of poetry—may lead one, like Chauntecleer, to have a minor dispute with one's wife, but all that finally matters is the happy ending.

CHAPTER XVI

Some Last Views of Poetry

*T*HE SECOND NUN'S TALE can be identified as an early work not only because "the lyf . . . of Seynt Cecile" is mentioned in the Prologue to the *Legend of Good Women* but because the nun in the Prologue to the tale refers to herself as an "unworthy sone of Eve" (62). The unworthy son of Eve is undoubtedly Chaucer himself. His failure to change the line is generally attributed to an oversight. I would prefer to think that he allowed it to stand as his signature in the *Canterbury Tales,* as a medieval artist might paint his face somewhere amid the crowd in the background of a picture. Another theory, which I cannot prove, is that the Second Nun's Tale was originally written by Chaucer to atone for the time he spent translating the *Romance of the Rose.* In the opening stanza of the Prologue to the Second Nun's Tale, he tells us:

> The ministre and the norice unto vices,
> Which that men clepe in Englissh ydelnesse,
> That porter of the gate is of delices,
> To eschue, and by hire contrarie hire oppresse,
> That is to seyn, by leveful bisynesse,
> Wel oghten we to doon al oure entente,
> Lest that the feend thurgh ydelnesse us hente.

The first three lines certainly refer to the Lady Idleness who admits the Dreamer to the Garden of Mirth in the *Romance*. Idleness here does not mean inactivity. When Chaucer says that he means "to eschue" her by engaging in her "contrarie," which is "leveful bisynesse," it sounds as though he were opposing his translation of the saint's life specifically with "idle" or "unlawful" business, which I am certain includes what Chaucer in his Retraction calls "my translacions and enditynges of worldly vanitees."

Whether or not Chaucer in this Prologue is reproaching himself for "idleness" of that sort, St. Cecilia's life is presented to the reader as an example of "feithful bisynesse" (24). The Prologue concludes with an interpretation of her name, a convention in saints' lives taken over directly from the Latin source. The virtues of the saint are already prefigured in his name. Cecilia's name can be construed in five different ways. One of these is *caelo et lya* for "heaven" and "Leah," Jacob's first wife who was seen by medieval exegetes as the type of the active life. Cecilia is "hevene" for her holy thoughts "And 'Lia' for hire lastynge bisynesse" (98). The latter phrase implies that there is "bisynesse" that does not last. Another interpretation of her name is *caecis via,* "way to the blind," because she labors to show the true way to those unable to see it. In the tale, of course, this is exactly what she does for her bridegroom and many other pagan Romans. Valerian cannot see Cecilia's guardian angel until he believes and thus attains spiritual sight. Later Cecilia tells the Roman prefect that he is blind because he believes in gods of stone that he can see and touch (498–501). By her "bisynesse" and her spiritual vision, Cecilia multiplies the number of the faithful. Still today, Chaucer says in the final stanza of the tale, men worship Christ and St. Cecilia in the Roman church named for her. Hers has truly been a "lastynge bisynesse."

One could draw an analogy between the work of St. Cecilia and what is supposed to be the work of the medieval poet. It is his business, too, to be *caecis via,* to give vision and to increase the number of the blessed. This is at least one way of looking at the role of the medieval poet, a role from which I feel Chaucer often strayed but to which he always returned. In writing the Second Nun's Tale early in his career, he was emulating his heroine in showing the way to the blind.

Chaucer may have been struck by certain analogies between this work of youthful piety and one of the latest, ripest products of his artistic maturity, the Canon's Yeoman's Prologue and Tale. I do not think he revised the legend to go with the new work or that he wrote the Canon's Yeoman's Prologue and Tale with the idea of linking it to the Life of St. Cecilia. This seems to me to be a spontaneous link of which Chaucer took advantage by the simple act of placing the tales side by side and joining them with a couplet.[1] On the relationship between the legend and the tale of alchemy there is a fascinating article by Joseph Grennen called "St. Cecilia's 'chemical wedding': The Unity of the *Canterbury Tales*, Fragment VIII."[2] The title gives away the principle of unity. St. Cecilia being tortured in a bath of red flames brings to mind what was called the "mortification of metals" in the alchemist's distillatory. The analogy sounds a bit grotesque, but the further one pursues it, the more compelling it becomes. The medieval alchemist called himself a "philosopher"; the prefect Almachius says that he can put up with St. Cecilia's insolence because "I kan suffre it as a philosophre" (490). Almachius worships stone idols; the alchemist is seeking the "philosopher's stone." Cecilia multiplies converts. The alchemist seeks to convert or "multiply" metals. The most persuasive part of Grennen's thesis is his discussion of alchemy itself, based on medieval alchemical treatises. Alchemy was regarded by its practitioners as a mystical science, and the experiments are described in the language also used of religious ritual. Thus alchemists speak of the "wedding" of masculine and feminine elements. When one approaches the crafts of the saint and the alchemist on their common rhetorical level, alchemical science can be seen as a perversion of the true spiritual science that does transform base human metal into gold.

These links between the tales are underlined by what happens in the Canon's Yeoman's Prologue, one of Chaucer's most vivid and dramatic passages. The pilgrims are overtaken by two men riding furiously to catch up with them. They turn out to be a Canon and his servant. The Canon's forehead is dripping sweat "as a stillatorie" (580)—the first hint as to his real profession. He claims that their unnatural haste has been occasioned by their wish to join the company, but the first impression of this pair is that they are driven by an obsession, as indeed they are.[3]

The Canon is a renegade churchman who has abandoned the faith to practice alchemy and to pursue the illusory dream of wealth and power. The alchemist is drawn not simply by the idea of wealth but by the enormous power that will be released by the discovery of the elixir. This is what drives him to keep on with his desperate experiments. We can feel the magnetism of the dream in the Yeoman's boast to Harry Bailly that his master could take the muddy Canterbury road on which they are riding, "turne it up-so-doun,/And pave it al of silver and of gold" (625–626). Pursuit of this dream has driven the Canon to sacrifice everything. He and his Yeoman live in abject poverty, are dressed in rags, and engage in fraud—not really to enrich themselves but to win the means by which to keep on experimenting. Thus the science of alchemy gets turned into a confidence game.

The Yeoman's attitude toward his master is ambivalent. By this time he knows in his heart that the Canon will never succeed, yet he cannot be absolutely sure. And so he continues to act as his master's shill attracting gullible investors and as the laboratory assistant who blows the bellows. He has peered into the fire until his complexion has changed completely. "Why artow so discoloured of thy face?" asks the Host, and the Yeoman replies, "I am so used in the fyr to blowe/That it hath chaunged my colour, I trowe" (664–667). Like Hawthorne's Ethan Brand, the Yeoman has peered at hellfire. The Canon holds him in his grip the way the devil clutches a human soul. Therefore, the Prologue, for all its realism, can also be read as an allegory like the one at the end of the Pardoner's Tale, an allegory that reconfirms the purpose and solidarity of the Canterbury pilgrims. By joining the group travelling to the shrine of St. Thomas, a microcosm of the Christian community, the Yeoman recovers his true direction. He is induced to confess, detaches himself from his evil genius, and is absorbed by the group of pilgrims. The Canon, however, flees like an evil spirit. If we wish, we may see in this episode, too, an exorcism and a morality play.

Naturally this sort of allegory is less obvious than what we find in the simple story of St. Cecilia, and I would not quarrel with anyone who refused to see it at all. For most people the value of the Canon's Yeoman's Prologue resides in its joyous vision of life epitomized in the line: "But it was joye for to seen hym swete!" (579). The energy and delight with which Chaucer draws his reader into scenes such as this is what primarily counts, and it is open and accessible to everyone who takes the trouble to master Middle English. However, in literary criticism, one tends to steer away from the obvious and press harder and harder after some elixir to multiply the meaning of the text. It is a sobering reflection that the most enduring value of what we read lies so plainly before our eyes that we sometimes ignore it.

Nevertheless, I ask the reader to indulge me in one last analogy —between the alchemist and some poets. Most medieval poets are like St. Cecilia. They tell stories with a clear and uncomplicated moral and show us the way to heaven. John Gower is one of these. We do not read him very much now, but his name is probably inscribed on the roll of the saints if not on that of the great poets. Some poets are like the alchemist who falls increasingly under the spell of his art, experiments ceaselessly, and comes close to duplicating the creative process in his imitations of life. Such experiments may also have moral value, but it is much harder to find and to justify this sort of moral than the plain didacticism we find in the Life of St. Cecilia.

The wedding of the tales of the Second Nun and Canon's Yeoman comes near the end of the *Canterbury Tales* and in some ways anticipates the end. Like the Yeoman, Chaucer will give up his alchemy. In the final fragment, Chaucer not only winds up the *Canterbury Tales* but says good-bye to poetry and to his audience. The great work remains unfinished, but even had Chaucer lived to write many more stories, he would still have closed his work with the Parson's Prologue and Tale and the Retraction. It would have been pointless to bring the pilgrims back to the Tabard and to award one of them the prize. Chaucer leaves them still pointed in the direction of Canterbury and renews the basic symbolic idea underlying the pilgrimage: that this is the road we must all travel.[4]

We do not know exactly where we are—only that the pilgrims are entering a little village. It is late afternoon, the sun is rapidly setting, and the shadows are lengthening on the ground. Chaucer's shadow is twice the measure of six feet. The shadow points to the earth that is our common inheritance and also suggests the insubstantiality of the body that casts it. The constellation in the sky is Libra, the scales, which recall the Last Judgment. In view of all this, I do not think it sentimental to speculate that when Chaucer wrote the Parson's Prologue he felt himself close to the end of his own pilgrimage.[5]

The Host respectfully begs the Parson to tell the last tale to "knytte up wel a greet mateere." Like a child at bedtime, he wants to hear one more story: "Telle us a fable anon." But the Parson refuses:

> "Thou getest fable noon ytold for me;
> For Paul, that writeth unto Thymothee,
> Repreveth hem that weyven soothfastnesse,
> And tellen fables and swich wrecchednesse.
> Why sholde I sowen draf out of my fest,
> Whan I may sowen whete, if that me lest?"   (31–36)

I have already discussed this passage in the conclusion of Chapter VIII on the Man of Law's Tale. It is an uncompromising rejection of poetry of *all* kinds. Here there is no apology for "thrifty" poetry, nor is there an attempt to gloss over St. Paul's true position by citing, as the Nun's Priest does (tongue-in-cheek I am sure), Paul's statement that all that is written is written for our doctrine. Paul meant the Old Testament, and Chaucer, when he refers to the statement again in his Retraction (1083), means the Parson's Tale.[6] But fables, whatever moral fruit they may contain, are not primarily for our doctrine. The Parson knows that we really enjoy them for their chaff. The mirth they give he regards as an illusion. With some irony, the Parson offers to tell "a myrie tale in prose" (46).

We can still detect Chaucer's humor. There is something to smile at in the Parson's south-county plainness, his refusal to "rum-ram-ruf" it as they do up North. But I believe he speaks for Chaucer and that this passage is the poetic complement of the prose Retraction. In a solemn moment the pilgrims, as a group, give their assent to the Parson as they gave their assent to the Host at the Tabard. Their worldly guide, Harry Bailly, makes way for their spiritual guide.

The Parson's "Tale" is a two-thousand-line sermon on penitence, and it expresses a truth that, for Chaucer and his audience at least, is higher than the truth of fiction. The text on which it is based is appropriate not only to the sermon but serves as a nostalgic reminder of the plan of the *Canterbury Tales:* "Stand ye in the ways and ask for the old paths, where is the good way, and walk therein, and ye shall find rest for your souls" (Jer., vi.16). But though it reminds us of the pilgrim travelers, the text points to the difference between Chaucer's way in most of the Canterbury tales and his way in the Parson's Tale. The latter is like the legend of St. Cecilia; it sticks to the old path of straightforward teaching, not the bold new paths of fiction Chaucer had devised. In plain prose the Parson's Tale tells us exactly how to find rest for our souls.

The Tale is followed by the Retraction in which Chaucer repents of having written the works for which we primarily read him. He removes the mask of Chaucer the Pilgrim and confesses his sins which consist chiefly of having spent too much time writing the wrong sort of poetry. For many readers, the Retraction is an even bitterer pill than the renunciation of human love at the end of *Troilus.* Various attempts have been made to explain it away. According to one commentator, "One would rejoice if this morbid passage could be shown to be the interpolation of some monk, but as it is, we must suppose that to Chaucer there came an hour of reaction or weakness."[7] Others suggest that the Retraction need not be taken too seriously, that Chaucer simply followed the convention of his day by writing a palinode, the expected thing. The Retraction is of course a problem for those who believe that all of Chaucer's works are allegories promoting Christian charity. If such is the case, the fruit of their doctrine was not sufficiently obvious or accessible to justify them in the poet's eyes.

For myself, the Retraction, especially when taken in conjunction with the Parson's Prologue, is a deeply moving statement of the limitations of art, and one that is very difficult to answer. The justification of poetry is by no means a peculiarly medieval problem although the Christian Middle Ages give it a religious form. Plato had banished poets from his Republic. A legend has it that Virgil wanted the *Aeneid* destroyed. Tolstoy wrote a tract in his later years rejecting his great novels. Kafka asked that his literary remains be burned. The luxury of literature and the study of literature have never been easy to justify in a world torn by harsh necessity, wars, and relentless social struggle.

It is in this broader context that we must place the Retraction. In retracting his works Chaucer does not deny their right to exist, but he wants to warn us about the limitations of poetry lest they be misused, and he wants to be forgiven for the venial sin of having created something of such equivocal worth. He is not really saying anything new but simply asserting once and for all the faith he has always held. As the legend of Cecilia makes clear, Chaucer had from early on in his career written both religious and secular poetry. There was a time—in writing *Troilus and Criseyde*—when Chaucer may have wished to unite religious and aesthetic values. If that is, indeed, what he tried to do, he partly failed in the endeavor, and the artist triumphed over the moralist. In the *Canterbury Tales,* far from bridging the gap between art and morality, Chaucer widens it. He begins to write fabliaux and invents a whole world of people, not for any convincing moral purpose but for the pleasure of imitating life and telling many different kinds of stories. He portrays the sins of the pilgrims faithfully, but in some ways reconciles us to those sins, or at least to the humanity of the sinners. Always he clings tenaciously to life. One reason why the Retraction is so moving is that in it we can still detect Chaucer's love of the poetry he disavows. A student once pointed out to me that the phrase "many a song and many a leccherous lay" reads like a line of Chaucer's poetry.

But this time Chaucer does not equivocate, as I believe he did in composing the end of *Troilus.* The moment has come for Chaucer to abandon his world of illusion for the final reality, which consists of the four last things: Death, Judgment, Heaven, and Hell. Chaucer must detach himself both from the world we call "real," and from the world he has created in his fiction.

He must have been struck at times by his power to make this fictional world, which exists only in the imagination, seem more real than the actual one. The pilgrims, whom Dryden said he could see as distinctly as if he had supped with them at the Tabard, are all imaginary. In spite of Professor Manly, who turned over so many records searching for the historical models of Chaucer's pilgrims, the pilgrims exist only within a work of fiction. Manly's book *New Light on Chaucer,* in which he tries to identify the Man of Law, the Merchant, the Reeve, and many others, pays a great tribute to Chaucer's art in Manly's naive disbelief that Chaucer could have invented so much. The irony that fiction can be made to seem more real than fact, art more permanent than life is already implicit in the comedy of the Nun's Priest's Tale. It is an irony that ultimately raises doubts about the "reality" of the world around us.

Chaucer is not the only poet who is brought by his art to the point where the world itself comes to seem insubstantial, and the people in it such stuff as dreams are made on. The conclusion of the *Canterbury Tales* is like an awakening. One feels that the revels have ended; the holiday of the pilgrims is over. With the Parson's Tale and the Retraction Chaucer dispels his illusion as Prospero dismisses the spirits of the masque; the pilgrims, too, have melted into thin air. Behind Prospero we feel there is Shakespeare, dismissing his actors, taking off his magic robes, and drowning his books. Chaucer concludes the *Canterbury Tales* in a similar mood, and we sense that he is bidding farewell to his stage and his audience. In the Epilogue to the *Tempest,* the actor who has played Prospero begs the audience to set him free. In this last of his epilogues, Chaucer asks his audience to pray for his soul. It comes to much the same thing.

NOTES

The following abbreviations are used in the notes:

AnM	*Annuale Mediaevale*
ChauR	*Chaucer Review*
ELH	*Journal of English Literary History*
JEGP	*Journal of English and Germanic Philology*
MLN	*Modern Language Notes*
MLQ	*Modern Language Quarterly*
MLR	*Modern Language Review*
MP	*Modern Philology*
MS	*Mediæval Studies*
PMLA	*Publications of the Modern Language Association*
PQ	*Philological Quarterly*
RES	*Review of English Studies*
SATF	*Société des Anciens Textes Français*
SP	*Studies in Philology*
Spec	*Speculum*
ST I	*Chaucer Criticism I: The Canterbury Tales,* ed. Richard Schoeck and Jerome Taylor (Notre Dame: Notre Dame University Press, 1960)
ST II	*Chaucer Criticism II: Troilus and Criseyde & the Minor Poems,* ed. Richard Schoeck and Jerome Taylor (Notre Dame: Notre Dame University Press, 1961)
UTQ	*University of Toronto Quarterly*
W	*Chaucer: Modern Essays in Criticism,* ed. Edward Wagenknecht (New York: Oxford University Press, 1959)

All citations from Chaucer and references to Robinson in the text and notes are to *The Works of Geoffrey Chaucer,* 2d ed., F. N. Robinson (Boston: Houghton Mifflin, 1957).

I. Portraits of the Poet and His Early Works

1. Aage Brusendorff, *The Chaucer Tradition* (1925; reprinted Oxford: Clarendon Press, 1967), p.21.

2. Brusendorff's phrase, p.19.

3. See Brusendorff, pp.20, 22; Margaret Galway, "The *Troilus* Frontispiece," *MLR* 44 (1949), 161–177; George Williams, "The *Troilus and Criseyde* Frontispiece Again," *MLR* 57 (1962), 173–178.

4. P. M. Kean, *Chaucer and the Making of English Poetry* (London: Routledge & Kegan Paul, 1972), 2 vols., I, 25. Kean adds that Chaucer "is seen walking among [the audience] in the background scene," but does not point him out. I cannot spot the poet, and Galway, whose conjectures about other figures are expressed with unwarranted confidence, is only tentative in identifying him as one of the two figures standing in the doorway of the castle (pp.167–168).

5. So Brusendorff (p.20) conjectures, but it would be curious if the poet's costume alone had lost its color.

6. Reproduced as Figure 65 in Rosamond Tuve's *Allegorical Imagery* (Princeton: Princeton University Press, 1968), p.205. For a cruder but essentially similar treatment of the same scene, see Figure 28, p.152. Folio 28r of the *Très Riches Heures* of the Duke of Berry shows two apostles, each in a pulpit, preaching to the peoples of the world who are posed in groups beneath the pulpits much like the audience in the Chaucer picture (*The Très Riches Heures of Jean, Duke of Berry* [New York: George Braziller, 1969]). An interesting variation of the composition of two pulpits with their respective audiences is in a fifteenth-century woodcut of the story of Antichrist, reproduced as the frontispiece of Norman Cohn's *The Pursuit of the Millennium,* 2d ed. (New York, Harper & Row, 1961). Enoch is bareheaded and blesses the multitude with his right hand. Antichrist, arrayed as a cardinal, blesses his followers with his left hand. For examples from the *Roman de la Rose,* see note 9.

7. Chaucer's use of a "persona" has become a commonplace among most critics of Chaucer though it has been vigorously contested by a few. The issue seems to me to be something of a red herring. Every storyteller adopts a persona. Chaucer's is determined by *both* social and artistic purposes. The problem will be discussed more fully in Chapter XV on Sir Thopas and the Tale of Melibee.

8. I regard Genius as a forerunner of Rabelais's Friar Jean. His sermon contains comic elements like a parodic *sermon joyeux;* however, I disagree with those critics who maintain that the comedy subverts Genius's authority and deny that he speaks for the author. We don't have to take everything

Genius says as gospel, but neither do we have to regard him as the God of Love's dupe. For different interpretations see Tuve, pp.275–279; John Fleming, *The Roman de la Rose: A Study in Allegory and Iconography* (Princeton: Princeton University Press, 1969), pp.210–226; George Economou, "The Character of Genius in Alan de Lille, Jean de Meun, and John Gower," *ChauR* 4 (1970), 206–208.

9. For an example where Genius sits on a platform supported by wine barrels (in keeping with the character of a *sermon joyeux*) see Tuve, p.257, or Fleming (a clearer reproduction), Plate 39. More commonly Genius preaches from a pulpit as in Bodleian Ms. Douce 195, f. 139v.

10. On structural parallels between the General Prologue and the opening of the *Roman de la Rose* see J. V. Cunningham, "The Literary Form of the Prologue to the *Canterbury Tales*," *MP* 49 (1952), 172–181. The full debt of the *Canterbury Tales* to the *Roman,* especially to Jean de Meun's portion, has not been recognized.

11. *Oeuvres de Froissart, Poésies,* ed. A Scheler, 3 vols. (Brussels, 1870–72), I, 28–29, ll.936–941.

12. For an excellent discussion of these aspects in the *Parliament* and *House,* see Kean, chapter 3, pp.67–111: "New themes in the love vision." The common philosophical concerns, including Boethian ideas, in all three of the early visions are discussed by Daryl R. Davis, "Thematic Continuity in Chaucer's Early Poetry," Ph.D. diss., Indiana University, 1970.

13. The complaint against death can be paralleled in Machaut. See Robinson's note to line 442. However, the forceful contrast with the conventional spring setting is Chaucer's idea.

14. Alfred David, "Literary Satire in the *House of Fame*," *PMLA* 75 (1960), 339.

15. W. W. Skeat, Volume I, *The Complete Works* (Oxford: Clarendon Press, 1894).

16. Robert Payne, *The Key of Remembrance* (New Haven: Yale University Press, 1963), pp.103–104. Laurence K. Shook offers an interpretation of the *House of Fame* as an "Art of Poetry," *Companion to Chaucer Studies,* ed. Beryl Rowland (Toronto: Oxford University Press, 1968), pp.341–353. Father Shook observes, "Many fourteenth-century poets were really writing 'Arts of Poetry' when they were composing the poems we have been too blithely calling works of courtly love" (p.344).

17. Or it may be that the "man of gret auctorite" is about to tell an item of court gossip that Chaucer thought prudent to suppress. See Bertrand H. Bronson, "Chaucer's *Hous of Fame:* Another Hypothesis," *Univ. of Cal. Pubs. in Eng.,* 3 (Berkeley: University of California Press, 1934), 171–192.

18. See Bertrand H. Bronson, *"The Book of the Duchess* Re-opened," *PMLA* 67 (1952), 881, reprinted W, pp.271–294.

19. E. T. Donaldson, "The Ending of Chaucer's 'Troilus,' " in *Speaking of Chaucer* (New York: W. W. Norton, 1970), p.95.

20. Ernst Curtius, *European Literature and the Latin Middle Ages,* trans. Willard Trask (New York: Pantheon, 1953), pp.17–19.

II. The Theme of Love in *Troilus*

1. C. S. Lewis, *The Allegory of Love* (Oxford: Oxford University Press, 1936), p.197.

2. For example, D. W. Robertson, Jr., "Chaucerian Tragedy," *ELH* 19 (1952), 1–37, reprinted ST II, pp.86–121.

3. In this category I place an earlier article of my own, the ending of which I now partially retract. See Alfred David, "The Hero of the *Troilus,"* Spec 37 (1962), 566–581.

4. G. L. Kittredge, *Chaucer and His Poetry* (Cambridge, Mass.: Harvard University Press, 1915), p.151.

5. The classic statement is "The Intentional Fallacy," W. K. Wimsatt, Jr. and Monroe Beardsley, *Sewanee Review* 54, (1946).

6. I am in basic agreement with the "Defense of the Author" made by E. D. Hirsch, Jr. in *Validity in Interpretation* (New Haven: Yale University Press, 1967), pp.1–23 and particularly with his strictures (pp.11–14) about the notion " 'It does not matter what an author means—only what his text says,' " which Hirsch construes as a widespread misunderstanding of the Wimsatt-Beardsley position.

7. Two essays that form an exception to Kittredge's rule by allowing for some ambiguity in the author's intent are Elizabeth Salter, *"Troilus and Criseyde,* A Reconsideration," *Patterns of Love and Courtesy: Essays in Memory of C. S. Lewis,* ed. John Lawlor (Evanston, Ill.: Northwestern University Press, 1966), pp.86–106; and Joseph E. Gallagher, "Theology and Intention in Chaucer's *Troilus,"* ChauR 7 (1972), pp.44–66. Gallagher quotes Salter's essay as "a landmark in its painstaking refusal simply to assume that while writing the *Troilus* Chaucer proceeded with a unity of purpose" (p.56).

8. As Gallagher explains, "according to medieval theology and psychology the will does not of necessity follow reason" (p.66). I do *not* mean to imply that when Chaucer was writing *Troilus* he knowingly went against reason, although I would agree with Gallagher that by the time he wrote the Retraction at the end of the *Canterbury Tales,* Chaucer had come to realize that this is what he had done.

9. The other instances are III.1716, IV.1640, V.763.

10. The word occurs a total of nineteen times in the poetry, including *Troilus,* and an additional five times in Reason's discourse in the *Romaunt of the Rose* which is based on Boethius.

11. T. P. Dunning, "God and Man in *Troilus and Criseyde," English and Medieval Studies Presented to J. R. R. Tolkien,* ed. Norman Davis and C. L. Wrenn (London: Allen & Unwin, 1962), p.174.

12. Ibid., p.181. Gallagher's objection (p.60) that pagan reason is capable of a higher love may be sound theology, but has little bearing, I think, on Chaucer's poem.

13. On the equation of Criseyde with Nature and her changing seasons, see Lonnie J. Durham, "Love and Death in *Troilus and Criseyde," ChauR* 3 (1968), 1–11.

14. E. T. Donaldson, *Chaucer's Poetry* (New York: Ronald, 1958), p.980.

III. The Paradise of Earthly Love

1. The dating of the *Legend* is as certain as anything can be in the chronology of Chaucer's works. See J. S. P. Tatlock, *The Development and Chronology of Chaucer's Works* (1907; reprinted Gloucester, Mass.: Peter Smith, 1963), pp.121–131. The Prologue exists in two versions designated F and G. The revised version, which, for reasons given by Robinson (p.839) and additional ones of my own mentioned below, I believe to be G, was done well into the Canterbury period, 1394–95 according to Tatlock (p.122). I do not exclude, although I think it unlikely, the possibility that some of the legends could have been written before or after 1386–87. What matters essentially to my argument is that the poem was conceived and the F Prologue written during the interval between *Troilus* and the *Canterbury Tales.*

Up to this point chronology has not been a crucial factor to my view of Chaucer's development. With consideration of the *Legend* and the *Canterbury Tales,* the question of order becomes of some importance. I follow Robinson's conclusion that *Troilus* would have been completed no earlier than 1385, "separated by only a short interval from the *Prologue* to the *Legend of Good Women"* (p.811).

2. Since this chapter was written, two excellent studies of the Prologue have appeared that discriminate between the two versions on literary grounds and agree with one another and with a key point in my own argument, namely that the Prologue to the *Legend* is a crucial turning point in Chaucer's poetry. See Robert W. Frank, Jr., *Chaucer and The Legend of Good Women* (Cambridge, Mass.: Harvard University Press, 1972), especially pp.1–10 ("Chaucer in 1386"), and Robert O. Payne, "Making His

Own Myth: The Prologue to Chaucer's *Legend of Good Women,*" *ChauR* 9 (1975), 197–211. Frank bases his interpretation on F; Payne, on G; both agree that G is the revision.

3. Robinson is severe on those who "find unrecognized humor in the *Legend"* (p.482). Since his introduction was written, we have learned much about Chaucer's ironic way with the conventions of "courtly" love, and few would agree with Robinson's position today. What needs to be emphasized is not the presence of irony but the fact that irony does not preclude sympathy or serious consideration for characters and ideas treated humorously.

4. *Sources and Analogues of Chaucer's Canterbury Tales,* ed. W. F. Bryan and Germaine Dempster (1941; reprinted New York: Humanities Press, 1958), p.397. In the G version of the Prologue, the God of Love refers Chaucer to the same source (281–300).

5. It is of course ironic that the most notorious of antifeminist tracts should supply material for a legend of Cupid's saints, but Jerome's arguments against marriage are consistent with his arguments in favor of chastity. His point is that these pagan women valued virtue even though, as the God of Love succinctly puts it in G, "they were hethene, al the pak" (299).

6. Robert Payne, *The Key of Remembrance* (New Haven: Yale University Press, 1963), pp.91–111. Payne develops the idea in "Making His Own Myth" where he describes the Prologue as "a miniature comic myth embodying a poet's search for [an *ars poetica*]" (211).

7. *The Key of Remembrance,* pp.93–96.

8. That is why her myth is retold in Plato's *Symposium,* and Chaucer may well have first learned about it from an allusion to Plato's account in Macrobius's *Commentary on the Dream of Scipio.*

9. For references to English May game observances, including the choosing of May kings and queens, see W. C. Hazlitt, *Faiths and Folklore of the British Isles,* 2 vols. (London, 1905), II, 397–400, and E. K. Chambers, *The Mediaeval Stage,* 2 vols. (London, 1903), I, 143–144, 160–181. Chambers (pp.179–180) points out that the popular festival was taken up by the Tudor court and reminds us of the "Arthurian precedent" in Malory (xix, 1) where Guenevere and her knights, "all rayed in grene for maiynge" are surprised and taken by Sir Mellyagaunce: "[the quene] was oute on mayynge wyth all her knyghtes whych were bedaysshed wyth erbis, mossis and floures in the freysshyste manner." There are a number of references to maying in the Knight's Tale: I.1042–47, 1500–12, 1683–87.

10. For a similar discussion of the meanings of Alceste, see Payne, "Making His Own Myth," pp.207–208.

11. For a more sympathetic view of the legends, see Frank. He is right that the legends deserve a fairer audience than they have received. However,

whether or not Chaucer himself tired of them, the old view that Frank rejects, everyone will agree that "the *Canterbury Tales*, . . . proved to be a more attractive and a more rewarding scheme" (210).

12. D. D. Griffith, "An Interpretation of Chaucer's *Legend of Good Women*," *The Manly Anniversary Studies* (Chicago: University of Chicago Press, 1923), p.40, reprinted W, pp.396–404. Griffith's view is rightly rejected by Robert Estrich, "Chaucer's Maturing Art in the *Legend of Good Women*," *JEGP* 36 (1937), 327–330. I fully agree with Estrich that Chaucer's purpose in the revision was artistic and that G heightens the ironic comedy in the Prologue; I do not, however, share his view of the language and sentiments in F as immature and merely conventional.

13. Concerning the relative seriousness of F and G, my interpretation is almost the reverse of John Gardner's, "The Two Prologues of the *Legend of Good Women*," *JEGP* 67 (1968), 594–611. Gardner feels that the religious imagery in F is mainly satirical and that "[G] presents a new, more serious view of Love" (p.610). Although there is undeniably a comic extravagance in the narrator's daisy-worship in F, the idea behind it seems to me on the whole quite serious. Robinson's refusal to see any humor whatsoever in the *Legend* is one extreme, but I think it equally wrong to see the praise of the daisy as a burlesque, however gentle. Furthermore, I totally disagree that the God of Love escapes with greater dignity in G (cf. Estrich, p.329).

IV. Portrait of the Christian Community

1. See note 10, Chapter I.

2. See Robinson's note to line 1 for a list of passages that have been suggested as possible sources. As the editor observes, "Taken together they show that [Chaucer] was dealing with a conventional theme, in the treatment of which commonplace features inevitably reappeared" (p.651).

3. Arthur Hoffman, "Chaucer's Prologue to Pilgrimage: The Two Voices," *ELH* 21 (1954), 3, reprinted W, pp.30–45.

4. Ibid., p.5.

5. Ernst Curtius, *European Literature and the Latin Middle Ages*, trans. Willard Trask (New York: Pantheon, 1953), pp.94–98.

6. John Fisher, *John Gower* (New York: New York University Press, 1964), p.207.

7. Ruth Nevo, "Chaucer: Motive and Mask in the 'General Prologue,' " *MLR* 58 (1963), 1–9.

8. The word has undergone further degeneration since Chaucer's day. It has acquired an almost exclusively patronizing or satiric sense. A "worthy fellow" is either a social inferior or not "worthy" at all.

9. Three estates is, of course, a convenient simplification; medieval social theory and, for that matter, the General Prologue are by no means so clear-cut. For definitions of "estates" and "estates literature" see Jill Mann, *Chaucer and Medieval Estates Satire* (Cambridge: Cambridge University Press, 1973), pp.3–4. This fine study, which appeared after the completion of the present chapter, demonstrates that the Prologue belongs to a common medieval genre although Chaucer is atypical in the indirectness of his satire, avoiding the more usual fulminations against vices of every kind.

10. Hoffman, p.11.

11. I have given a more detailed discussion of the Franklin's costume in "Sentimental Comedy in the *Franklin's Tale*," *AnM* 6 (1965), p.23.

12. J. L. Lowes, *Convention and Revolt* (Boston, 1919), p.66.

13. On the sexual innuendo, see Edmund Reiss, "The Symbolic Surface of *The Canterbury Tales:* The Monk's Portrait, Part I," *ChauR* 2 (1968), 256–257.

14. Hoffman, pp.12–14, 16.

15. Ibid., p.14.

16. Charles Singleton, "On Meaning in the *Decameron*," *Italica* 21 (1944), 119.

V. The Order of Chivalry

1. I concur with Tatlock's arguments that it was composed between *Troilus* and the *Legend*. J. S. P. Tatlock, *The Development and Chronology of Chaucer's Works* (1907; reprinted Gloucester, Mass.: Peter Smith, 1963), pp.70–83.

2. The theory was effectively put down by Tatlock, pp.45–70; revived on different grounds by Johnstone Parr, "The Date and Revision of Chaucer's Knight's Tale," *PMLA* 60 (1945), 307–324; and once more laid to rest by R. A. Pratt, "Was Chaucer's *Knight's Tale* extensively revised after the Middle of 1390?" *PMLA* 63 (1948), 726–736.

3. Cf. *Tr.* III. 491–504.

4. T. S. Eliot, *Selected Essays* (New York: Harcourt Brace, 1950), p.5.

5. E. D. Hirsch, Jr., *Validity in Interpretation* (New Haven: Yale University Press, 1967), p.8.

6. Charles Muscatine, *Chaucer and the French Tradition* (Berkeley: University of California Press, 1957), p.133.

7. W. C. Curry, *Chaucer and the Mediaeval Sciences*, 2d ed. (New York: Barnes & Noble, 1960), pp.131–137.

8. Muscatine, pp.175–190.

9. See John Halverson, "Aspects of Order in the 'Knight's Tale,'" *SP* 57 (1960), 606–621.

10. Summing up interpretations of the Knight's Tale, J. Burke Severs quotes a 1950 article by E. B. Ham ("Knight's Tale 38") who deplores the critical "clouds of obscurity and latter-day mystifications" and adds, "one can only exclaim now [1968] that these clouds have deepened and darkened," *Companion to Chaucer Studies,* ed. Beryl Rowland (Toronto: Oxford University Press, 1968), p.231. Many continue to take the court-liness and the philosophy of the tale as entirely serious, e.g., Paul Ruggiers, *The Art of the Canterbury Tales* (Madison, Wis.: University of Wisconsin Press, 1968), pp.151–166. But another kind of reading finds humor and irony at the expense of the Knight and chivalry; and Theseus's speech on the Prime Mover has even been taken as shallow political opportunism. See, e.g., Dale Underwood, "The First of *The Canterbury Tales,*" *ELH* 26 (1959), 455–469, and Richard Neuse, "The Knight: The First Mover in Chaucer's Human Comedy," *UTQ* 31 (1962), 299–315.

11. Elizabeth Salter, *Chaucer: The Knight's Tale and The Clerk's Tale* (Great Neck, N.Y.: Barron's, 1962), p.23.

12. The point is well made by Joseph Westlund, "The *Knight's Tale* as an Impetus for Pilgrimage," *PQ* 43 (1964), p.537.

VI. The Comedy of Innocence

1. I am indebted here and elsewhere to Ralph Baldwin's fine study, *The Unity of the Canterbury Tales, Anglistica,* V (Copenhagen: Rosen-kilde and Bagger, 1955), reprinted in part ST I, pp. 14–51. However, I feel that the road to "Jerusalem celestial" contains many detours and that the "unity" of the *Canterbury Tales,* at least in this symbolic sense, can be exaggerated.

2. C. L. Barber, *Shakespeare's Festive Comedy* (1959; reprinted New York: Meridian Books, 1963), p.7.

3. E. K. Chambers, *The Mediaeval Stage,* I (London: 1903), p.287.

4. Mikhail Bakhtin, *Rabelais and His World,* trans. Helene Iswolsky (Cambridge, Mass.: M.I.T. Press, 1965), p.84. Bakhtin's entire discussion of medieval laughter (pp.71–96) bears closely on the thesis of this chapter.

5. Per Nykrog, *Les Fabliaux* (Copenhagen: Munksgaard, 1957), pp. 66–71.

6. See William Frost, "An Interpretation of Chaucer's *Knight's Tale,*" *RES* 25 (1949), pp.303–304, reprinted ST I, pp.98–116.

7. See Knight's Tale, 1376, where Arcite's "celle fantastik" becomes diseased through "humour malencolik," and Robinson's note.

8. Cf. Bakhtin, pp.90–91: "It was the victory of laughter over fear that most impressed medieval man. It was not only a victory over mystic terror of God, but also a victory over the awe inspired by the forces of nature, and most of all over the oppression and guilt related to all that was consecrated and forbidden ("mana" and "taboo"). It was the defeat of divine and human power, of authoritarian commandments and prohibitions, of death and punishment after death, hell and all that is more terrifying than the earth itself. Through this victory laughter clarified man's consciousness and gave him a new outlook on life. This truth was ephemeral; it was followed by the fears and oppressions of everyday life, but from these brief moments another unofficial truth emerged, truth about the world and man which prepared the new Renaissance consciousness."

9. See Paul E. Beichner, "Absolon's Hair," *MS* 12 (1950), 222–233.

10. See R. E. Kaske, "The *Canticum Canticorum* in the *Miller's Tale*," *SP* 59 (1962), 479–500.

11. The phrase "moral edge" is used by Kaske who confronts this problem in "The *Canticum Canticorum*," pp.495–500. Kaske makes it a question finally of "where the greater weight of the comedy created by the allusions is supposed to fall: on the situation, characters, and mores of the *Miller's Tale* or on those of the *Canticum*." He concludes that the allusions are probably not "a parody of the *Canticum*" and that instead they provide a moral perspective from which to judge Absolon and Alisoun who are characterized as the "false" bridegroom and bride. This, argues Kaske, does not detract from the comic effect but enhances it and gives the comedy a "moral edge" without turning it into a "covert sermon." But why must "the greater weight of the comedy" fall *either* on the characters of the tale *or* on those of the Canticle? Why cannot the weight be equally distributed? Kaske does recognize examples where the "burden of laughter is kept neatly divided" (e.g., *The Owl and the Nightingale*), but says that most readers will agree that this is not the case with the Miller's Tale (p.499). This reader, at least, does not agree.

12. Bakhtin, p.90.

13. Ibid.

VII. The Comedy of Experience

1. The difference in atmosphere between the two fabliaux is noted and described by M. Copland, *"The Reeve's Tale:* Harlotrie or Sermonyng?" *Medium Ævum* 31 (1962), 16–17, 30–31.

2. See Paul A. Olson, "The Reeve's Tale: Chaucer's Measure for Measure," *SP* 59 (1962), 1–17.

3. See also Brooks Forehand, "Old Age and Chaucer's Reeve," *PMLA* 69 (1954), 984–989.

4. See R. E. Kaske, "An Aube in the 'Reeve's Tale,' " *ELH* 26 (1959), 295–310.

5. The many delightful *double entendres* on "milling" and "grinding" are discussed by Ian Lancashire, "Sexual Innuendo in *The Reeve's Tale*," *ChauR* 6 (1972), 159–170.

6. For example, "The Miller and the Two Clerics," an analogue of the Reeve's Tale, and "Beranger Longbottom," trans. Robert Hellman and Richard O'Gorman, *Fabliaux* (London: Arthur Barker, 1965), and "The Reeve's Tale and Its Analogues," *The Literary Context of Chaucer's Fabliaux*, ed. Larry D. Benson and Theodore M. Andersson (Indianapolis: Bobbs-Merrill, 1971).

7. On the Reeve's "moral" biases Copland has some excellent observations, pp.25–30, as does Olson, pp.5–8.

8. Per Nykrog, *Les Fabliaux* (Copenhagen: Munksgaard, 1957), pp. 105–139.

9. Quoted also by Olson (pp.8–9) whose fine essay avoids the Reeve's kind of judgment. I fully agree with Olson's conclusion: "By its condemnation of the vindictive man, the *Reeve's Tale* drives men toward a realization of the love to which the Knight and the Parson would draw them" (17).

VIII. The Man of Law vs. Chaucer

1. Twenty-five of the manuscripts fill the gap with the Gamelyn. A few others supply a makeshift "conclusion" to the Cook's Tale. However, the scribe of Hengrwt, who left a space in his manuscript in case the rest of the tale should turn up, states the case honestly and succinctly: "of this Cokes tale maked Chaucer na moore." A few manuscripts are lacking the Man of Law's Introduction, but there is no doubt that it is meant to follow Fragment I. On this and other textual matters I am indebted to John M. Manly and Edith Rickert, *The Text of the Canterbury Tales* (Chicago: University of Chicago Press, 1940).

2. *Works*, p.683.

3. See Carleton Brown, "The Man of Law's Head-Link and the Prologue of the *Canterbury Tales*," *SP* 34 (1934), 8–35, and Charles A. Owen, Jr., "The Development of the *Canterbury Tales*," *JEGP* 57 (1958), 449–476, and "The Earliest Plan of the *Canterbury Tales*," *MS* 21 (1959), 202–210.

4. The remainder of this chapter follows, with some omissions and changes, my article in *PMLA* 82 (1967), 217–225.

5. See Eleanor P. Hammond, *Chaucer: a Bibliographical Manual* (New York, 1908), pp.257–258, 280.

6. For a general discussion of the Man of Law's character with a summary of other views, see R. M. Lumiansky, *Of Sondry Folk* (Austin, Tex.: University of Texas Press, 1955), pp.61–71.

7. The argument is summed up by John H. Fisher, *John Gower* (New York: New York University Press, 1964), pp.285–292. For Fisher's own stimulating interpretation of the evidence see n. 9 below.

8. William L. Sullivan, "Chaucer's Man of Law as a Literary Critic," *MLN* 68 (1953), 1–8.

9. Fisher, pp.286 ff. Fisher proposes a novel and, to me, the most logical reason yet offered as to why the friendship between Chaucer and Gower might have cooled. He suggests that Gower must have felt strongly that in abandoning the *Legend of Good Women* for the *Canterbury Tales,* and especially such scurrilous stories as the Miller's and Reeve's, Chaucer had deserted his high poetic mission and was employing his genius unworthily. Gower may have cancelled Venus's compliment to Chaucer in the Epilogue of the *Confessio Amantis,* not because his feelings had been hurt by the lines in the Man of Law's Introduction but because he thought that the author of stories like the Miller's Tale had ceased to deserve it. In that case, Fisher argues, we may interpret Chaucer's joke about Gower not as the cause of Gower's withdrawing the tribute but as Chaucer's good-humored response to Gower's displeasure at the new direction of Chaucer's poetry.

10. Ibid., pp.287, 290.

11. On Chaucer's use of Innocent, here and elsewhere in the Man of Law's Tale, see Robert E. Lewis, "Chaucer's Artistic Use of Pope Innocent III's *De Miseria Humane Conditionis* in the Man of Law's Prologue and Tale," *PMLA* 81 (1966), 485–492.

12. "Dives autem superfluitate resolvitur et iactantia effrenatur, currit ad libitum et corruit ad illicitum, et fiunt instrumenta penarum que fuerant oblectamenta culparum. Labor in acquirendo, timor in possidendo, dolor in amittendo, mentem eius semper fatigat, sollicitat et affligit: 'Ubi est thesaurus tuus, ibi est et cor tuum'." *De miseria humane conditionis,* ed. Michele Maccarrone (Lugano, 1955), pp.20–21.

13. The appropriateness of the tale to the Man of Law has been argued by Bernard I. Duffey, "The Intention and Art of the Man of Law's Tale," *ELH* 14 (1947), 181–193. See also Paul E. Beichner, "Chaucer's Man of Law and *Disparitas Cultus,*" *Spec* 23 (1948), 70–75, and R. M. Lumiansky, *Of Sondry Folk,* pp.61–71.

14. On the possible humor, see Paull F. Baum, *"The Man of Law's Tale*, ll.1132–33 and 1160–62.

15. Since the appearance of this essay (1967), two critics have argued that Chaucer has slanted the tale itself so as further to satirize the Man of Law; that the Man of Law has distorted and misapplied his sources; that he misunderstands the relation of fortune and providence; that the justice of his tale is obtuse, harsh, and unchristian. See Chauncey Wood, *Chaucer and the Country of the Stars* (Princeton: Princeton University Press, 1970), pp.192–244, and Rodney Delasanta, "And of Great Reverence: Chaucer's Man of Law," *ChauR* 5 (1971), 288–310. Both generously acknowledge my article and have led me to modify my original position though not to change it in any essential way. Chaucer may well have been aware that the morality of the tale has limitations, but these are limitations of a typical kind of medieval story, which appealed to an audience typified by the Man of Law. In writing it, Chaucer, I am still persuaded, was giving his audience what *they* thought they wanted. Wood and Delasanta bring out the specious and unattractive legalism in the tale's preaching, and perhaps the choice of the Man of Law as narrator is more of a comment on this type of tale than the tale itself is a comment on the Man of Law.

16. See Edward A. Block, "Originality, Controlling Purpose, and Craftsmanship in Chaucer's *Man of Law's Tale*," *PMLA* 68 (1953), 572–616.

17. I agree with John A. Yunck that this stanza contains the theme of the tale, "Religious Elements in Chaucer's *Man of Law's Tale*," *ELH* 27 (1960), 256. My reading of the Tale is very close to his.

18. On the thematic importance of Egeus's speech, see Robert A. Pratt, " 'Joye after Wo' in the *Knight's Tale*," *JEGP* 57 (1958), 416–423. Pratt also points out (p.423) the recurrence of the theme in the Man of Law's Tale, ll.1132–33 and 1160–62.

19. Owen, "The Development of the *Canterbury Tales*," pp. 450–452, points out this correspondence but draws the very different inference that the Parson's Prologue must therefore have been written shortly after the Man of Law's headlink. The echoes are no doubt deliberate, but I do not think that this necessarily implies proximity in time of composition.

20. The endlink appears in only 38 manuscripts of which seven identify the jolly pilgrim as the Summoner, four as the Shipman, and twenty-seven as the Squire. Manly and Rickert believed that Chaucer meant to cancel the endlink, but whether or not this is so, he did not abandon the purpose it expresses. A strong case is made by Lee S. Cox that the readings Shipman, Summoner, and Squire are all scribal; that Chaucer actually wrote

the passage for the Wife of Bath when she was the teller of the tale later assigned to the Shipman; but that the leaf with the endlink was misplaced and is therefore missing in some of the oldest and best manuscripts. In this view, it was always Chaucer's intention to follow the Man of Law with the Wife of Bath, a view that, as will be seen, fully accords with my own understanding of the Wife's role in the *Canterbury Tales.* Lee S. Cox, "A Question of Order in *The Canterbury Tales," ChauR* 1 (1967), 228–252.

IX. Experience and Authority in the Wife of Bath's Prologue and Tale

1. The list is abridged from that of Wayne Shumaker, "Alisoun in Wander-Land: A Study in Chaucer's Mind and Literary Method," *ELH* 18 (1951), 87.

2. On the plausible theory that the three parts were composed not necessarily in order and at different times, see R. A. Pratt, "The Development of the Wife of Bath," *Studies in Medieval Literature,* ed. MacEdward Leach (Philadelphia: University of Pennsylvania Press, 1961), 45–79. It makes sense that the Wife's character grew over a period of time, and she seems to have nagged Chaucer until he gave her the longest Prologue assigned to any pilgrim, almost as long as the General Prologue.

3. In the Epilogue to the Man of Law's Tale, the jolly pilgrim attacks the Parson: "He schal no gospel glosen here ne teche" (II.1180); the hypocrite Friar in the Summoner's Tale says that the text of Holy Writ is too difficult for the simple wit of Thomas, "And therfore wol I teche yow al the glose./Glosynge is a glorious thyng, certeyn" (III.1792–93); about the magic properties of the sword in the Squire's Tale, the knight says, "This is a verray sooth, withouten glose" (V.166).

4. D. W. Robertson, Jr., *A Preface to Chaucer* (Princeton: Princeton University Press, 1962), pp.317–331.

5. Ibid., p.330.

6. Johan Huizinga, *The Waning of the Middle Ages* (1924; Garden City, N.Y.: Anchor Books, 1954), p.225.

7. Ibid., p.109.

8. Ibid., pp.109–110.

9. On Solomon: "As wolde God it were leveful to me/To be refresshed half so ofte as he!" (38); "make me fressh and gay" (298); "walke as fressh as is a rose" (448); "But in oure bed he was so fressh and gay" (508); "Housbondes meeke, yonge, and fressh abedde" (1259).

10. The Wife has been given little credit for her generosity by the critics. An exception is Rose A. Zimbardo, "Unity and Duality in *The*

Wife of Bath's Prologue and *Tale*," *Tennessee Studies in Literature* 11 (1966), 11–33.

11. Charles Muscatine, *Chaucer and the French Tradition* (Berkeley: University of California Press, 1957), p.213.

12. On the relation of the question to the issue of sovereignty in Chaucer and the analogues the remarks of Meredith Cary ("Sovereignty and Old Wife," *Papers on Language and Literature* 5 [1969], 384–388) are very much to the point.

X. The Moral Question in the Clerk's Tale

1. *MP* 51 (1953), 77, reprinted W, pp.226–239 and ST I, pp. 160–174.
2. Ibid., p.82.
3. Payne, *The Key of Remembrance* (New Haven: Yale University Press, 1963) sees the Clerk's Tale along with the other rhyme royal tales (Man of Law's, Prioress's, Second Nun's) and the Physician's as a group that he characterizes as the " 'sentimental experiment.' " "It is almost," he writes, "as though [Chaucer] is, in a typically detached and dispassionate manner, working toward a medieval version of *poésie pure*—a moral statement which will be immediately apprehensible emotionally and nearly incomprehensible by any rational or intellectual faculty" (164). If this is the case, then, in my opinion, in the Clerk's Tale as well as in the others, Chaucer is only partly successful because at times reason and emotion tend to pull the reader in opposite directions.
4. For the folkloristic background of the tale see D. D. Griffith, *The Origin of the Griselda Story* (Seattle: University of Washington Press, 1931) and W. A. Cate, "The Problem of the Origin of the Griselda Story," *SP* 29 (1932), 389–405. More recently W. E. Bettridge and F. L. Utley argue that Boccaccio's source was not a version of "The Monster Bridegroom" (Type 425) but some version of a folktale known in Greece and Turkey, which they designate "The Patience of a Princess." See "New Light on the Origin of the Griselda Story," *Texas Studies in Literature and Language* 13 (1971), 153–208. They may well be right; however, my own interpretation and conclusions depend only on the fact that the ultimate source is *a* folktale, not which particular folktale is the source.
5. The Latin text, ed. by J. B. Severs, is printed in W. F. Bryan and Germaine Dempster, *Sources and Analogues of Chaucer's Canterbury Tales* (1941; reprinted New York: Humanities Press, 1958), pp.296–330. A translation is available in R. D. French, *A Chaucer Handbook,* 2d ed. (New York: Appleton-Century-Crofts, 1947), pp.291–311.
6. G. L. Kittredge, "Chaucer's Discussion of Marriage," *MP* 9 (1912), 445–446. Reprinted W, pp.188–215 and ST I, pp.130–159.

7. S. K. Heninger, Jr. argues that the issue is not sovereignty in marriage but the very principle of the divinely ordained hierarchical order, "The Concept of Order in Chaucer's *Clerk's Tale*," *JEGP* 56 (1957), 382–395.

8. See Donald C. Baker, "Chaucer's Clerk and the Wife of Bath on the Subject of Gentilesse," *SP* 59 (1962), 631–640.

9. 459–462, 621–623.

10. Morton W. Bloomfield argues that "a mixture of the superficially tragic and the slightly comic" in the Man of Law's Tale, a combination that tends to put off the modern reader, is a basic element of this and other Canterbury tales among which he includes the Clerk's. See "The Man of Law's Tale: A Tragedy of Victimization and a Christian Comedy," *PMLA* 87 (1972), 384–390. I agree with Bloomfield's analysis, and as I have argued above, the Man of Law's Tale seems to be a straightforward example of this species of "pathetic" tale. However, I feel that in the Clerk's Tale, particularly in the last section, there are moments when Chaucer fails to maintain the distance that keeps the comic element in its place, and thereby upsets the precarious balance required to maintain the seriousness of "Christian Comedy."

11. I am of course aware that not all readers are the same, and that different readers will respond to these same passages in different ways. Some of the elements to which I object are acknowledged and judiciously defended on thematic grounds by John P. McCall: "The *Clerk's Tale* and the Theme of Obedience," *MLQ* 27 (1966), 260–269. However, any interpretation of the tale must reckon with the different levels of style it contains. The most sensitive and balanced reading of the tale in these terms is that of Elizabeth Salter (*Chaucer: The Knight's Tale and the Clerk's Tale* [Great Neck, N.Y.: Barron's, 1962]), whose interpretation of the Knight's Tale has been discussed above (pp.87–88). The two tales present similar difficulties, and total agreement about the effect of either is hardly to be expected.

XI. The Bourgeois Misanthrope

1. Charles Muscatine gives an excellent analysis of what he calls the "mixed style" in the tale in *Chaucer and the French Tradition* (Berkeley: University of California Press, 1957), pp.230–237. As Muscatine says, "it is very much a poem in which the single line and the single image carry enormous weight" (p.230).

2. The interpolation follows "Gan pullen up the smok, and in he throng" (2353):

A great tent / a thrifty and a longe
She said it was the meryest fytte
That euer in her lyfe she was at yet
My lordes tent serueth me nothyng thus
It foldeth twifolde by swete Jesus
He may nat swyue worth a leke
And yet he is ful gentyll and full meke
This is leuer to me than an euynsong

Cited from William Thynne's 1532 edition, *The Works of Geoffrey Chaucer and Others,* Facsimile edition by W. W. Skeat (London and Oxford, 1905), p.97 (folio xxxix). A slightly different version of the same passage is given from Harley MS. 1758 by Martin Stevens, " 'And Venus Laugheth': An Interpretation of the *Merchant's Tale,*" *ChauR* 7 (1972), 128. The passage occurs in all Renaissance editions, and it is interesting to speculate how it influenced Chaucer's reputation from the sixteenth century until the early nineteenth.

3. J. S. P. Tatlock, "Chaucer's *Merchant's Tale,*" *MP* 33 (1935–36), 375. Reprinted in ST I, pp.175–189. Tatlock's pioneer article made the case for "the unrelieved acidity" of the tale, an interpretation of its tone that went unquestioned until Bertrand Bronson's "Afterthoughts on *The Merchant's Tale,*" *SP* 58 (1961), 583–596. Bronson does not think the tale was composed for the Merchant and believes that, if one disregards the Prologue, it becomes "another high card played in the unending Game between the Sexes" (596). The notion that the tale is good-humored and not at all bitter has also been maintained by Robert M. Jordan, "The Non-dramatic Disunity of the *Merchant's Tale,*" *PMLA* 78 (1963), 293–299, and Stevens, op cit., pp.118–131. The traditional view has been upheld by Norman T. Harrington, "Chaucer's Merchant's Tale: Another Swing of the Pendulum," *PMLA* 86 (1971), 25–31, and E. T. Donaldson, "The Effect of the Merchant's Tale," *Speaking of Chaucer* (New York: W. W. Norton, 1970), pp.30–45. My own position in this controversy is sufficiently clear.

4. On the sexual meanings and biblical resonance of this passage see G. B. Pace, "The Scorpion of Chaucer's *Merchant's Tale,*" *MLQ* 26 (1965), 369–374.

5. That such amplification takes the tale far beyond the realm of the simple fabliau is part of the thesis of J. A. Burrow's excellent "Irony in *The Merchant's Tale,*" *Anglia* 75 (1957), 199–208.

6. Donaldson's gloss " 'Such stupid old words he used,' " ("Effect of the Merchant's Tale," p.44), seems absolutely right to me. Stevens (op. cit., p.129) suggests that *lewed* be glossed as "unlearned."

7. For those interested in statistics, the following may be something to ponder over. According to the Tatlock-Kennedy *Concordance* under "God" and "Gods," in total number of entries the Parson's Tale (225) is followed by the Merchant's (57). Next comes the Melibee (43), the Summoner's Tale (42), the Knight's (34), the Clerk's and Man of Law's (31 each), and the Monk's (30). The links have not been counted. If we work this out in percentage per line for the poetic tales the Summoner leads with 7.2%, followed by the Shipman, (5.7%), Merchant (4.8%), Pardoner, Monk, and Nun's Priest (4% each), Second Nun (3.8%), Man of Law (3%).

8. That the women are all in fact deceitful is the point of W. Arthur Turner, "Biblical Women in *The Merchant's Tale* and *The Tale of Melibee*," *English Language Notes* 3 (1965), 92–95; that they are, however, traditionally portrayed as types of Deliverance is demonstrated by Charlotte F. Otten, "Proserpine: *Liberatrix Suae Gentis*," *ChauR* 5 (1971), 277–287.

9. On this passage and on the imagination as a potentially deceptive "mirror," see George D. Economou, "Januarie's Sin Against Nature: The *Merchant's Tale* and the *Roman de la Rose*," *Comparative Literature* 17 (1965), 251–257. For a study of the mirror-image in medieval lyric poetry, see Frederick Goldin, *The Mirror of Narcissus* (Ithaca: Cornell University Press, 1967).

10. I fundamentally agree with Mary C. Schroeder who characterizes the narrator as a would-be "realist" obsessed with hatred for January's blind idealism. The narrator's own "fantasy" ultimately breaks down any such simple distinction between real and ideal. "Fantasy in the 'Merchant's Tale,'" *Criticism* 12 (1970), 167–179.

11. The implications of January's garden as a materialist's sexual Eden are explored by Paul A. Olson, "Chaucer's Merchant and January's 'hevene in erthe heere,'" *ELH* 28 (1961), 203–214.

12. The tale ends appropriately by asking a blessing of the Virgin Mother. The Virgin has not been neglected by the narrator. On the analogy between January and May and Joseph and Mary, see Bruce A. Rosenberg, "The 'Cherry-Tree Carol' and the *Merchant's Tale*," *ChauR* 5 (1971), 264–276.

13. E. T. Donaldson, "Chaucer the Pilgrim," *PMLA* 69 (1954), 934. Reprinted in *Speaking of Chaucer*, pp.1–12, and ST I, pp. 1–13.

XII. The Bourgeois Sentimentalist

1. G. L. Kittredge, "Chaucer's Discussion of Marriage," *MP* 9 (1912), 467, reprinted W, pp.188–215 and ST I, pp.130–159.

2. On literary grounds, R. M. Lumiansky, *Of Sondry Folk* (Austin, Tex.: University of Texas Press, 1955), pp.180–193; on theological grounds, Donald R. Howard, "The Conclusion of the Marriage Group: Chaucer and the Human Condition," *MP* 57 (1960–61), 223–232; on social grounds, R. B. Burlin, "The Art of Chaucer's Franklin," *Neophilologus* 51 (1967), 55–72.

3. Alfred David, "Sentimental Comedy in the *Franklin's Tale,*" *AnM* 6 (1965), 19–27. A few parts of this chapter incorporate points made in this article.

4. G. H. Gerould, "The Social Status of Chaucer's Franklin," *PMLA* 41 (1926), 278–279.

5. Lumiansky, pp.184–185.

6. Italics mine. According to Manly-Rickert, the manuscripts are in agreement about the pronouns of address in this passage. John M. Manly and Edith Rickert, eds., *The Text of the Canterbury Tales*, 6 vols. (Chicago: University of Chicago Press, 1940).

7. My argument about the oaths in the tale was to some extent anticipated by Alan T. Gaylord in an article that appeared while my paper "Sentimental Comedy" was awaiting publication. Gaylord is among the critics who take strong issue with Kittredge, "The Promises in *The Franklin's Tale,*" *ELH* 31 (1964), 331–365.

8. E. T. Donaldson, *Chaucer's Poetry* (New York: Ronald, 1958), pp. 925–926.

XIII. A Moral Thing

1. G. L. Kittredge, *Chaucer and His Poetry* (Cambridge, Mass.: Harvard University Press, 1915), p.180.

2. *Beel amy* may be a form of address (Robinson glosses it as "fair friend"), but the Host undoubtedly insinuates something more than that. John Halverson says it is "Roughly equivalent now to 'Hey, lover!',", "Chaucer's Pardoner and the Progress of Criticism," *ChauR* 4 (1970), 198 n.

3. On this theme there is a beautiful essay by Penelope Curtis, "The Pardoner's 'Jape,'" *Critical Review* 11 (1968), 15–31. The Pardoner's performance is seen as the most important episode in which "the meaning of the journey is tested by the pressures under which the company is placed" (p.15). "He tries . . . to make nonsense of any journey of aspiration to any Canterbury" (p.16).

4. Two articles conveniently summarize much of the controversy about the Pardoner while making valuable contributions to the understanding of Chaucer's character: G. G. Sedgewick, "The Progress of Chaucer's Par-

doner, 1880–1940," *MLQ* I (1940), 431–458, reprinted W, pp.126–158; and Halverson, "Chaucer's Pardoner and the Progress of Criticism," pp.184–202. Halverson's psychological interpretation of the Pardoner admits of complex motivation and accords generally with some of the views expressed below (see especially pp.197–198).

5. Curtis has splendid insights into the sermon, pp.22–28.

6. Kittredge, p.215.

7. Many of these are summarized and discussed in my article "Criticism and the Old Man in Chaucer's *Pardoner's Tale," College English* 27 (1965), 39–44. The discussion of the old man below draws upon that article.

8. Robert P. Miller, "Chaucer's Pardoner, the Scriptural Eunuch, and the Pardoner's Tale," *Spec* 30 (1955), 180–199, reprinted in ST I, pp.221–244.

9. Ibid., p.199.

10. Ibid.

11. This view of the old man and his relation to the Pardoner is indebted to Alfred L. Kellogg's analysis of the Pardoner's Prologue and Tale as a study in the self-punishment of evil, "An Augustinian Interpretation of Chaucer's Pardoner," *Spec* 26 (1951), 465–481.

12. Miller, p.189.

13. Kittredge, p. 217.

XIV. Another Tale of Innocence

1. *The Study of Poetry.*

2. G. L. Kittredge, *Chaucer and His Poetry* (Cambridge, Mass.: Harvard University Press, 1915), p.181.

3. For a judicious survey of opinion *pro* and *con,* see Florence H. Ridley, *The Prioress and Her Critics, University of California English Studies,* 30 (Berkeley and Los Angeles: University of California Press, 1965).

4. "Miracle de l'abbeesse grosse," *Miracles de Nostre Dame,* 8 vols., ed. Gaston Paris and Ulysse Robert, *SATF* (Paris, 1876), I, 57–100.

5. Ibid., p.97.

6. Sister Maria Madeleva, "Chaucer's Nuns," in *A Lost Language* (New York: Sheed and Ward, 1951), pp.57–58.

7. R. J. Schoeck, "Chaucer's Prioress: Mercy and Tender Heart," ST I, pp.245–258. See also Alan T. Gaylord, "The Unconquered Tale of the Prioress," *Papers of the Michigan Academy of Science, Arts, and Letters* 47 (1962), 613–636.

8. Sherman H. Hawkins, "Chaucer's Prioress and the Sacrifice of

Praise," *JEGP* 63 (1964), 599–624. See especially n. 48 in which Hawkins attempts to justify the drawing of the Jews by wild horses (the last straw for most modern readers) with a series of citations, including a sermon by Augustine on the Innocents in which he says that "the saints under the altar can in perfect charity demand the death of their persecutors." I should like to think that neither Augustine nor Hawkins fully mean what they say, and that this "tough doctrine" (Hawkins's phrase for it) is occasioned partly by circumstances. Preachers and critics, as well as Prioresses, may be overzealous at times.

9. Robert O. Payne, *The Key of Remembrance* (New Haven: Yale University Press, 1963), pp. 167–169, analyzes the style. He considers the tale the most successful in Chaucer's " 'sentimental experiment.' " See n.3, chap. X.

10. Schoeck, p.250.

11. It must be remembered that many of the analogues are mere anecdotes. However, an accounting of what happens to the Jews in them is instructive. Carleton Brown in *Sources and Analogues of Chaucer's Canterbury Tales*, ed. W. F. Bryan and Germaine Dempster (1941; reprinted New York: Humanities Press, 1958), pp.447–451, divides the analogues into three groups. In Group C, to which the Prioress's Tale belongs, seven do not mention the fate of the Jews at all; in one any Jew caught in the country after a certain date is condemned to death and the guilty ones are expropriated and driven out; in one the guilty Jew converts to Christianity. In the B Group one does not say what happened; six tell that the Jews were converted; one says that those who did not convert were condemned to wear a special costume; one has the Jew guilty of the crime burned. In Group A, five omit the fate of the Jews; two convert them; one punishes the murderer with death; one executes the murderer and banishes all the rest; one has many slain; one burns them because it has been previously agreed that they would be burned if the boy is found, the widow would be burned if he is not found. The C Group is printed in *Sources and Analogues.* Most of the rest are printed by Carleton Brown, *A Study of the Miracle of Our Lady Told by Chaucer's Prioress, Chaucer Society Publications*, 2nd ser., 45 (London, 1910). In none of the analogues are the Jews drawn by wild horses. This detail does occur in the Anglo-Norman ballad "Hugues de Lincoln," which is not a miracle of the Virgin.

12. Schoeck, p.253.

XV. Cracks in the Frame of Illusion

1. G. L. Kittredge, *Chaucer and His Poetry* (Cambridge, Mass.: Harvard University Press, 1915), p.45.

2. E. T. Donaldson, "Chaucer the Pilgrim," *PMLA* 69 (1954), 928–936, reprinted in *Speaking of Chaucer* (New York: W. W. Norton, 1970), pp.1–12.

3. The notion that the narrator is a "persona" has been criticized by Bertrand H. Bronson, *In Search of Chaucer* (Toronto: University of Toronto Press, 1960), pp.25–32; also by John M. Major, "The Personality of Chaucer the Pilgrim," *PMLA* 75 (1960), 160–162. Donaldson replies to Bronson's criticism in "The Masculine Narrator and Four Women of Style," *Speaking of Chaucer*, pp.46–64. See also, in the same volume, "Criseide and Her Narrator," pp.65–83. The question is admirably discussed by Donald R. Howard, "Chaucer the Man," *PMLA* 80 (1965), 337–343.

4. The point made here, which is implicit in nearly all of the preceding chapters, has been beautifully stated by Howard in "Chaucer the Man." Howard also raises the Host's question—"What man artow?"—and says "no real answer to the question is ever given" (p.342). But Chaucer is, nevertheless, "a real and living presence in his works" (p.337) including the tales of the Canterbury pilgrims.

5. The literary merit of the tale has been ably defended by Paul Strohm, "The Allegory of the *Tale of Melibee*," *ChauR* 2 (1967), 32–42, and Charles A. Owen, Jr., "The *Tale of Melibee*," *ChauR* 7 (1973), 267–280.

6. Morton Bloomfield has shown how the contrast between the frame and tales is used as an "authenticating" device, "Authenticating Realism and the Realism of Chaucer," *Thought* 39 (1964), 335–358. Bloomfield also points out ways, the rubrics for example, in which Chaucer reminds the reader of the fictiveness of the frame (pp.355–358). I am saying here that, beginning with Sir Thopas, Chaucer is using the frame increasingly as an anti-authenticating device. However, I am *not* trying to claim that Chaucer is striving for some kind of "non-organic form." For an attempt to read all of Chaucer's works in such terms, see Robert Jordan, *Chaucer and the Shape of Illusion* (Cambridge, Mass.: Harvard University Press, 1967).

7. On the Host as literary critic and as a unifying force in this group of tales, see Alan T. Gaylord, "*Sentence* and *Solaas* in Fragment VII of the *Canterbury Tales*: Harry Bailly as Horseback Editor," *PMLA* 82 (1967), 226–235. I believe with Gaylord that Chaucer in this group especially is playing with these aspects of the art of storytelling. Gaylord thinks that the Nun's Priest's Tale achieves the perfect combination of *sentence* and *solaas* and has thus been set up as a kind of model of Chaucer's personal aesthetic. On that point I wish to reserve judgment.

8. See R. E. Kaske, "The Knight's Interruption of the *Monk's Tale*,"

ELH 24 (1957), 249–268, and John F. Mahoney, "Chaucerian Tragedy and the Christian Tradition," *AnM* 3 (1962), 81–99. Mahoney makes the excellent point that the important thing for Christians is not Adam's fall but the "reversal of this destiny into joy" (p.88); and he finds that pattern appropriately in the Nun's Priest's Tale.

9. This is a strong reason why I have always felt intuitively that the tale order of Ellesmere is right and that the "Bradshaw-shift," which moves Group VII into third position after the Man of Law's Tale, is wrong. The Nun's Priest's Tale gains a great deal if we read it *after* the disputes and debates of the pilgrims. The notion that it initiates the "debate on marriage" seems to me an entirely specious reason for moving it up.

10. On the meanings and uses of "Fable" in the Middle Ages, see R. T. Lenaghan, "The Nun's Priest's Fable," *PMLA* 78 (1963), 300–307.

11. Lalia P. Boone, "Chauntecleer and Partlet Identified," *MLN* 64 (1949), 78–81.

12. The herbs in this catalogue were regarded as medicinal. M. K. Paffard cites an old remedy using worms to cure colic in horses, "Pertelote's Prescription," *Notes and Queries* N.S., 4 (1957), 370. Corinne E. Kauffman, on evidence of medical treatises, believes, however, that Pertelote, overly solicitous, has prescribed a potentially fatal overdose, "Dame Pertelote's Parlous Parle," *ChauR* 4 (1969), 41–48.

13. The passage provides the epigraph to Bernard Huppé and D. W. Robertson, Jr.'s *Fruyt and Chaf: Studies in Chaucer's Allegories* (Princeton: Princeton University Press, 1963). The first chapter is a good exposition of their method. See also D. W. Robertson, Jr., *A Preface to Chaucer* (Princeton: Princeton University Press, 1962), pp.365–367. Mortimer J. Donovan uses the passage as a point of departure for an allegorical reading of the tale in which "the key to the *moralite* is hidden in the identification of Chauntecleer as any holy man and Daun Russell as heretic and devil" (p.498), "The *Moralite* of the Nun's Priest's Sermon," *JEGP* 52 (1953), 498–508.

14. John Speirs, *Chaucer the Maker* (1951; reprinted London: Faber and Faber, 1964), pp.185–193; also Bernard F. Huppé, *A Reading of the Canterbury Tales* (Albany: State University of New York Press, 1964), pp.174–184. The interpretation is taken the final step by Bernard S. Levy and George R. Adams, "Chauntecleer's Paradise Lost and Regained," *MS* 29 (1967), 178–192.

15. Stephen Manning argues that the Priest's advice to take the "moralite" is ironic, making fun of the notion that every tale must be justified by a moral, "The Nun's Priest's Morality and the Medieval Attitude toward Fables," *JEGP* 59 (1960), 403–416. Judson B. Allen agrees and suggests

that the clues for exegetical interpretations were planted deliberately, "The Ironic Fruyt: Chauntecleer as Figura," *SP* 66 (1969), 25–35. Allen even proposes a plausible single source for Chaucer's ironic exegetical imagery in a 13th century compilation of scriptural glosses directed by Hugh of St. Cher.

XVI. Some Last Views of Poetry

1. As Muscatine observes, "The work is so great as to begin to generate its own relationships." Charles Muscatine, *Chaucer and the French Tradition* (Berkeley: University of California Press, 1957), p.222.

2. Joseph Grennen, "St. Cecilia's 'Chemical Wedding': The Unity of the *Canterbury Tales*, Fragment VIII," *JEGP* 65 (1966), 466–481. See also Grennen's "The Canon's Yeoman's Alchemical Mass," *SP* 62 (1965), 546–560. The connection between the Second Nun's and Canon's Yeoman's Tales was previously suggested by Muscatine, who compares SNT 498–504 and CYT 1412–21 on the theme of blindness, pp.216–217.

3. My interpretation is much indebted to Muscatine, pp.214–221, reprinted ST I, pp.259–267.

4. For details see Ralph Baldwin's splendid discussion, *The Unity of the Canterbury Tales*, pp.83–95. This section is reprinted in ST I, pp.28–37.

5. Suggested by Donaldson who points out the symbolism in these details, E. T. Donaldson, *Chaucer's Poetry* (New York: Ronald, 1958), pp.948–949.

6. I totally disagree with the reading that would apply the Pauline reference and the phrase "this litel tretys" preceding it to the *Canterbury Tales* as a whole. My own views are expressed by John W. Clark, " 'This Litel Tretys' Again," *ChauR* 6 (1971), 152–156.

7. John Wesley Hales, *The Dictionary of National Biography* (London: Oxford University Press, 1892–   ), IV, 166. A few nineteenth-century scholars took seriously the notion that the retraction might be the work of the monks of Westminster from whom Chaucer leased a house during the last year of his life.

INDEX

265

INDEX OF PASSAGES
CITED FROM CHAUCER

Page references for parts of a single line or for lines or passages only alluded to or paraphrased are given in parentheses. The following abbreviations are used: BD = *Book of the Duchess;* HF = *House of Fame;* PF = *Parliament of Fowls;* Bo = *Boece;* Tr = *Troilus and Criseyde* (roman numerals designate books); LGW = *Legend of Good Women* (F and G designate the two Prologues); CT = *Canterbury Tales* (roman numerals designate fragments in Robinson's edition); Buk = Envoy to Bukton.